Seven Steps from Snowdon to Everest

*A hill walker's journey to
the top of the world*

MARK HORRELL

"What is Everest without the eye that sees it? It is the hearts of men that make it big or small."

Tenzing Norgay

Seven Steps from Snowdon to Everest

CONTENTS

PROLOGUE

Imagine the Eiffel Tower were eight times as high, and that it rose not 300, but a dizzying 2,400m above the River Seine.

Instead of standing inside its viewing platform behind a comforting wall of iron latticework, you have to edge out onto a roof of sloping terracotta tiles. Just to make things a little more spicy, the tiles are coated with a light dusting of snow, not enough to sink into, but enough to make the surface a bit slippery. You are wearing crampons on your feet – metal spikes that are useful for digging into snow and ice, but not so handy on a tiled roof – and several strands of old rope threaten to trip you up if you don't concentrate on where you're putting your feet.

Let's just examine some key details here. Imagine the Eiffel Tower rose 2,400m off the ground. That's one and a half miles – or for those of you who prefer to think in metric, nearly two and a half kilometres. Vertically.

If you fall off you will have about twenty-two seconds to think about what it's going to feel like when you splatter, pizza-like, among tourists in the Champ de Mars, instead of a little under eight seconds. You will be travelling at 781 kilometres per hour, instead of 276.

And what must the river and the people look like from those sloping tiles, if you're brave enough to look down? I'm pretty sure I wouldn't know. I'd be too busy edging back inside and heading over to the Louvre, where the viewing experience is a bit less intense.

There's one more thing to consider, and it's not insignificant. Suppose that two years ago a man climbed up, and was so exhausted after shinning up all those metal girders that he collapsed and died of exhaustion, falling flat on his back with the crown of his head pointing towards the Seine. It's a long way down, but there was just enough friction on the tiles to stop him sliding over the edge and making that twenty-two second journey.

You made an early start to avoid the queues when you visited the Eiffel Tower two years later. It was so early that you arrived as dawn was breaking; the dim sunlight cast the horizon in a powder blue, and you realised there was a city down there. As you tiptoed across the roof tiles, you happened to glance down and notice the corpse was STILL THERE, staring up at you and perfectly preserved in a colourful down suit. Well, it would have been staring at you were its eyes not frozen in place.

A bead of cold sweat is crawling down my face as I remember it all.

The Eiffel Tower isn't one and a half miles high – that would be ridiculous – but a few years ago, on the 19th of May 2012, I had a very similar experience to the one I've just described on the North-East Ridge of Everest. It's an experience few people can comprehend when I describe it to them, and the more time passes and memory fades, the more unreal it becomes to me too.

I had been climbing in the dark since 11.30pm, and dawn was approaching as I trod carefully along a narrow rock ledge. Because of the darkness I was relatively unaware of my surroundings and the extraordinary situation I found myself in. I was at an altitude of 8,500m, where the lower air pressure contains only a third as much oxygen as at sea level. This causes the brain to function in unexpected ways, and although I had an oxygen mask strapped to my face to provide vital stimulation, this had a side effect of making life seem even more surreal. I tried to put two and two together, but I didn't even get five. In fact, I think I got a banana.

I reached the end of one of the fixed ropes keeping me secure on that narrow ridge, and clipped in to the next one. To combat the extreme cold I was wearing a pair of down mitts the size of a sea lion's flippers, and I needed to take them off to accomplish the task.

It was after I put them back on and looked up that I saw the corpse.

I had just climbed the First Step, the first of three prominent rock features on Everest's North-East Ridge. It would be described as an easy rock scramble back home in the UK, something hill walkers could accomplish with a few basic handholds. But at that altitude it was an exhausting task. By the time I reached the top I was so tired that I nearly threw up in my oxygen mask, and I wondered how on Earth I would get back down. To say the corpse unnerved me would be like saying sheep are furry.

As the sky became lighter I became more aware of my surroundings, and with it came the realisation of just how much fresh air stretched beneath me. I was creeping along narrow ledges which sloped down towards a yawning abyss. The rock beneath my feet was dusted with snow, not ideal terrain for the spikes of my crampons, and to make it a little more like an army assault course the surface was covered with bits of old rope from previous years. It's fair to say I wasn't entirely happy with the position I found myself in.

Up ahead was the Second Step, Everest's most infamous rock obstacle, rising about forty metres in a series of cliffs and ledges. I clambered up a short ladder tied to the rock, and found myself in a small alcove. To my right a smooth rock the size of a car rose above my head. Somehow I had to get up it.

I stuck my foot in a crack down its left-hand side and tugged on some old ropes that were attached there, trying desperately to heave my right foot onto the top of the rock. It wasn't the most elegant climbing technique, and for anyone watching from below it probably looked like I was trying to mount an elephant seal, but elegance wasn't my primary objective at that moment. I'm no gymnast, but on the plus side at least I wasn't wearing tight trousers.

My foot slid down the rock and I gripped the ropes to keep my balance. I tried a second time without success, and I was conscious of Chongba behind me – my Sherpa companion who had climbed Everest twelve times but never from the north side. I knew he was desperate for me to succeed, and could only imagine what he must have been thinking as he watched me flounder.

I was also acutely aware that 2,400m of fresh air waited for me on the other side of that rock, and my reward for climbing it would be to find myself standing on a tiny ledge staring straight down into the abyss.

My hands were shaking as I gripped the rope and prepared to try again.

We don't know whether the British mountaineers George Mallory and Sandy Irvine managed to climb the Second Step in 1924. If they did then they may have been the first men to reach the summit of Everest, twenty-nine years before Tenzing Norgay and Edmund Hillary accomplished this feat in 1953. We do know they didn't make it down again.

Mallory's body was found not far from there in 1999.

We also know that three Chinese climbers and a Tibetan took at least three hours to climb the Second Step in 1960, during what is now generally accepted as the first ascent of Everest from the north side. Liu Lien-man took four attempts and fell off each time. Chu Yin-hua tried to climb another crack a little above the one I struggled with, and even took his boots off to give himself more grip. They eventually made it up by standing on Liu Lien-man's shoulders, who by good fortune happened to be a fireman. Charlie Chaplin couldn't have choreographed it better, and it lent some respectability to my own slapstick performance, although I was glad only Chongba was watching.

Or so I thought. I looked behind me and saw my two friends Mark and Ian approaching along the slabs with Ang Gelu and Kami Sherpa. I didn't want to hold them up, so I tried a third time. Lifting my right leg as high as I could, I wiggled it around like an overdressed can-can dancer, desperately probing for the top of the rock. It was no use. I couldn't get it high enough; nor could I get any purchase on the rock with my crampon. I turned to Chongba and saw his crestfallen look.

We had come all this way, but it looked like I wouldn't be able to go any further. Was the incident Mark now refers to as *the time I couldn't get my leg over on Everest* to be the final act in my ten-year journey to reach the world's highest point?

I hope you will read on and find out. I also hope you won't get too hung up on the corpse I saw on the North-East Ridge, as many people do when I mention it. Some writers have focused on this theme to cast the modern-day Everest in a negative light without understanding the context.

Despite the slightly macabre opening, this book is not about death. If you picked it up hoping to read a ripping yarn, or a horrifying tale of tragedy and desperation, then read one of the many accounts of the 1996 Everest tragedy, or one of the dozens of mountaineering books on the market that form a sub-genre known unofficially as *disaster porn*.

My story is a bit more uplifting than these. At its heart it's the story of an ordinary guy who did something slightly out of the ordinary.

I don't regard myself as a climber. I am a simple hill walker who had a dream to climb the highest mountain on Earth. In my youth this would have seemed as ridiculous as the mullet haircut I sported as a teenager. I hope that by telling my story I can inspire other ordinary people to look beyond the horizon and follow a dream that might at first seem incredible.

I also have another reason. In recent years Everest's reputation has been tarnished by negative and sensationalised media reporting. The modern-day Everest climber has been caricatured as having no climbing skills, more money than brains, and – somewhat implausibly – is carried to the top on the backs of Sherpas. Although it's true we are no longer elite climbers, we have done a little more to be where we are than this disingenuous caricature suggests. I hope that by the end of this book I will have dispelled some of the misconceptions and helped to restore the reputation of Everest and those who climb it.

This is my story.

The start of a journey: the Pyg Track on Snowdon

1 HILL WALKING

I never showed much athletic prowess as a child. One of my earliest memories is of a primary school sports day when I was required to run two laps of the playing field. Halfway round I developed a stitch and had to run the rest of the way bending forward with my stomach clenched. Counter-intuitively this may have improved my finishing position; when my friend Crofty saw me running like that he thought I needed to relieve myself, and he burst out laughing, enabling me to overtake.

My success continued into secondary school, where my crowning achievement was coming fifty-fourth out of 108 people in the school "fun run" and being delighted to finish in the top half (I've put the phrase *fun run* in inverted commas for a good reason, although it was long before I learned the meaning of the word *oxymoron*).

On one occasion I came last in the high jump after failing to clear a metre, a height I can now step over.

So much for athletics; at climbing I was even worse. In his book *Psychovertical*, the big-wall rock climber Andy Kirkpatrick describes first learning to climb on the cliffs of a disused quarry called Little Switzerland on the outskirts of his home town, Hull. Like Andy I also came from Hull, but our similarities ended there. When I visited Little

Switzerland at the age of twelve to learn how to abseil with
the Boy Scouts, my descent lasted all of three metres before I
felt the safety rope slip over my shoulder and climbed back
up again in a fit of panic. When my Scout leader saw my
head reappear at the top, he roared with laughter.

'Oh, Mark, you are wet!' he said.

Andy Kirkpatrick has described himself as *Hull's second-
best climber*. Needless to say, I'm not the best one.

As for ball games, I went to school during an era of
teachers' strikes when sport outside the school curriculum
ground to a halt. Throughout primary school, and for much
of my five years of secondary school, I was never taught
skills. I played only two cricket matches. In the first one I
swished at a few balls with the bat before getting clean
bowled for nought, and I dropped a catch when the ball
bounced off my chest. In my second and final match I was
told to bat last, and when I took a catch the congratulations I
received from my teammates belied the magnitude of my
achievement.

'That was better than last time, Horrell – I was sure you
was going to drop it,' they cried. So was I.

In one of my football matches for the school second team
I remember heading the ball backwards into the path of an
advancing striker. After he picked the ball out of his net our
goalkeeper was more encouraging than my cricketing
teammates.

'Have they signed you for Liverpool yet, Horrell?'

Confronted with profound mediocrity at competitive
sports, I was lucky to discover hill walking – an activity
which required nothing more than the ability to put one foot
in front of the other. Or so I thought.

My first proper hill was Helvellyn in the English Lake
District, which I climbed with my brother Perran when we
were teenagers. He was more adventurous than me, and

insisted the only way to climb it was along a route known as Striding Edge. I didn't know much about hill walking, but I knew from GCSE geography that Striding Edge was one of Britain's best-known examples of an arête, a ridge formed when two glaciers carve out U-shaped valleys in parallel, leaving a narrow crest of rock between. As geography was one of my favourite lessons, I was keen to get a look at this geological phenomenon first hand.

Unfortunately I had inherited my father's poor head for heights (something you might think would be a drawback in my later career as a mountaineer – and you would be right). My geography teacher had described how the ice age carved out one of England's most picturesque landscapes, but he hadn't mentioned how effective glaciers are at sharpening rocks into the geological equivalent of meat cleavers. I discovered early on that I didn't enjoy scrambling along a meat cleaver, particularly when falling off it meant being dashed to smithereens on rocks a few hundred metres below me.

I suggested to Perran it may be easier if we found a route a little below the ridgeline. He agreed, and soon we were tiptoeing along the edge of a cliff, wishing we were back on the ridge.

The east side of Helvellyn is an excellent example of what is known in geography as a *combe*: a steep-sided hollow on a mountainside formed by glacial erosion. In this example the hollow contains a small lake called Red Tarn, and the three steep sides enclosing it are Striding Edge to the south, Helvellyn itself to the west, and a slightly wider (and easier) ridge to the north called Swirral Edge. Another combe, or to give it its Welsh spelling *cwm*, will play a prominent role later in the story, but I digress.

As we pondered sploshing into Red Tarn over a hundred metres below, it was clear even to our inexperienced eyes the route we had chosen beneath Striding Edge wasn't a wise one, and we retraced our steps. Back at the start we passed a man with a map who looked like he knew what he was doing, so we asked him for advice.

'Go up Swirral Edge,' he replied. 'Swirral Edge is easy.'

For a short while this remark proved true and we made good progress, but just short of the summit we reached a steep snow slope which we had to climb using footsteps made by previous hikers. Easy as it may sound, this was effectively my first experience of winter mountaineering, and coming so soon after my introduction to ridge scrambling, I felt as awkward as a sausage in a salad.

The film *Four Weddings and a Funeral* was yet to be released in cinemas, but I pre-empted Hugh Grant's opening lines. As Perran skipped up to the summit without a care, I nervously followed behind, trying not to look at the dizzying drop into Red Tarn.

'Fuck, fuck, fuck, fuck,' I cried.

'Come on you big girl's blouse, it's a piece of piss,' Perran said.

'Fuck, fuck, fuck, fuck,' I replied.

Aided by my brother's kind words of encouragement I gritted my teeth and made it to the summit of my first proper hill. It was cold and windy, and we were deep in cloud. I could see about as much as a myopic mole holding his binoculars the wrong way round, and I was covered in a light film of drizzle.

But in a strange sort of way I quite enjoyed it, and I wanted more.

A short while after this I was with my father, walking a coastal footpath along a cliff edge in Sutherland, north-west Scotland. We looked across the sea and saw a sixty-metre pillar of rock emerging from the surf. It was called the Old Man of Stoer, and it was one of Scotland's best-known sea stacks.

What amazed me was not how nature had fashioned such a remarkable geological phenomenon, but that two figures appeared to be climbing it as violent waves dashed against the rocks beneath them. It amazed me because the top of the pillar looked as welcoming as Osama bin Laden's cave, consisting of a tiny platform of rock and a giant drop to the ocean far below. The view was better where we were, standing on a cliff high above them, and they were only going to have to climb back down again and swim across to the shore. Their immediate futures held the prospect of falling from a great height and dashing themselves on the shallow seabed, or the strong possibility of being swept onto razor-sharp rocks by a giant wave. What they were doing seemed as pointless as lying in a Turkish bath, sweating profusely, while a man with a moustache flays you with a wet towel. And far more dangerous.

'What are those two nutters doing, Dad?' I said.

'Don't ask me. They're mad,' he replied.

It was only later that I discovered sea-stack climbing is a popular activity among British rock climbers. Mountaineers usually come from one of two backgrounds: hikers or climbers. I'm very much the former, and in my early development as a novice hill walker, the concept of deliberately seeking out difficult routes up a mountain when there's an easier alternative felt a bit like eating ice cream with a knife and fork. Surely it's the taste of rum and raisin you're after, not the thrill of slicing?

But when I reflected on my journey at Everest Base Camp many years later, it was neither the psychopaths shinning up a sea stack nor my nervous introduction to hill walking that I was reminded of, but another mountain – one that has a special place in the hearts and minds of hill walkers, and whose name is inextricably linked with the history of

Everest.

Picture me a few years after my experience on Striding Edge, scrambling along another, narrower ridge. In hill walking, the word *scramble* is used to indicate an ascent somewhere between a walk and a climb. A scramble requires the hiker to use their hands, but isn't dangerous enough for safety equipment, or tricky enough for any of the more quirky technical moves rock climbers use, such as jamming their hand into a narrow crack in order to gain purchase (a technique I once tried using in a car door).

I was a much more experienced hill walker by then, and while I still didn't find heights any more comfortable than Gore-Tex underwear, I was a confident scrambler, happy to keep to the crest of the ridgeline while hiking alone. Nevertheless I was grateful for the thick cloud hiding the 300m drop to the combe below me, in much the same way a man facing the firing squad is grateful for a blindfold.

'Is the bar open?' said a figure emerging from the mist ahead of me.

The ridge was Crib Goch, one of the more interesting routes up Snowdon. At 1,085m, Snowdon is the highest mountain in Britain outside Scotland. Although Crib Goch is a relatively easy scramble for a sure-footed person, there's no margin for error, and a minor slip or stumble can quite easily result in a fall to your death. Getting down from it without killing myself was definitely my principal objective at that moment, and I expected it to feature quite highly on the priority list of the man coming the other way, but apparently not. He seemed more concerned with getting his next beer.

It was a bit surreal, but it was turning into a funny sort of day. An hour earlier I staggered up the rocky steps of the Pyg Track to a col just a few short strides from the summit of Snowdon, when I heard a chug-chugging sound to my right, and looked round to see a train steaming past.

Yes, that's right, a train.

You might wonder what I was thinking when I saw it. Was it a sense of achievement that I was just a few metres away from the top of the highest mountain I had ever climbed, tempered by disappointment that it was cloudy and I couldn't see a thing from up there? Or a slight feeling of annoyance that I could have caught a train instead of slogging it up on foot? Or maybe it was: *what the hell is a train doing up here on top of a mountain*, and *when are the men in white lab coats going to come and take me away?*

No, it was none of that. I looked back down the trail and shouted to my father as he stumbled up the slopes behind me.

'Good news, Dad – I've just seen a train come past.'

His eyes lit up. 'Great,' he replied. 'That means the bar must be open and we can have a pint.'

And this is how Snowdon – one of Britain's most iconic mountains – is best known to many of the people who climb it. It's the only hill in Britain where you can get a drink at the top.

If you're not a hill walker, you may be wondering why people bother to slog their way to the summit in the rain when they can just take the train up. But then why do people queue at the bottom and take a train up into the clouds to have a drink in a fairly ordinary bar, when there are plenty of pubs down at sea level?

Where's the fun in chugging along in a train when you can walk up, smell the fresh outdoor air, shed a few pounds, and have a sense of achievement thrown in? For hiking enthusiasts who have often become hopelessly wet and muddy climbing a hill when they've no hope of seeing a view from the summit, I don't need to answer this question. And for those of you who have never experienced this, all you need to know is that I was loving it.

It was my first time in North Wales, and my father had the idea of climbing the Welsh 3,000ers, the fourteen peaks in Wales over 3,000ft in height. All of them are located in Snowdonia National Park, a compact region of 2,000 square kilometres containing some of Britain's highest hills. We climbed Foel Fras, an outlying peak in the far north of the park, and the following day moved onto the Carnedds, where we sheltered in thick mist behind a stone wall on the summit of Carnedd Llewellyn, sharing a bottle of red wine as a pair of forlorn sheep looked on.

By the time we reached Snowdon my father was beginning to have doubts about one of the 3,000ers we hoped to climb, Crib Goch. There are many routes up Snowdon from every direction, but the classic one every hill walker aspires to do is the Snowdon Horseshoe. Starting at the Pen-y-Pass car park, where the main road crosses a high pass on Snowdon's northern side, walkers hike up to a saddle overlooking Llyn Llydaw, which is a lake lying in a natural bowl called Cwm Dyli. From the saddle walkers divert off the main trail to scramble up a steep rocky hillside and reach the knife edge of Crib Goch, not so much a summit as a long ridge.

While it's possible to walk along the top of the ridge, many people take the safer, if less elegant, option of straddling it *à cheval* (that is, like a horse). This isn't great for the trouser fabric – some of those rocks are quite sharp – but wiser men prefer to risk a light breeze to the crotch and a few sniggers in the summit bar than a terrifying tumble ending in certain death. There are also a couple of sections, known as the Pinnacles, where a spot of easy rock climbing is required.

Beyond Crib Goch the ridge drops a little, broadens out, then rises again to the top of Garnedd Ugain, another of the 3,000ers. From there the path curls to the left, up and over Snowdon, along another ridge and over a peak called Y Lliwedd, before dropping down to Llyn Llydaw and completing the horseshoe.

In fine weather the Snowdon Horseshoe is a grand – if exhilarating – day out, as long as you have a good head for heights. In poor weather, which it is on most days, there are parts of it that aren't much fun, and unless you're a good navigator it's easy to wander off along one of the many footpaths that converge on Snowdon's summit from all directions, and end up on the wrong side of the mountain entirely. It's a sprawling, intricate massif of individual summits joined by ridges broad and narrow. Towering cliff faces overlook secluded combes that are speckled with colourful lakes.

While the Snowdon Horseshoe is the classic walk, the jumble of ridges and combes offers a great many routes with views of the mountain from all angles. Not everybody fancies the trouser-splitting exhilaration of scrambling along Crib Goch, and there are easier options. For example, the most northerly of Snowdon's main routes is the Llanberis Path. This is the route most likely to make the more irresolute hill walker say to themselves *why am I bothering?* It lies on the same stretch of hillside as the railway line, but if your confidence is undermined by passengers leaning out of the carriage making obscene gestures, it's more likely these are aimed at the rock climbers making their way up the sheer 200m rock face of Clogwyn Du'r Arddu, across which the Llanberis Path enjoys a dramatic grandstand view. Between these two extremes of propulsion, the simple hill walker is made to feel they've chosen a pastime that treads the middle ground of common sense. The Llanberis Path is also the one by which 49-year-old Stuart Kettell climbed Snowdon for charity, pushing a brussels sprout with his nose. It took him four days and twenty-two sprouts.

On my first ascent of Snowdon with my father, we chose the splendidly named Pyg Track on the eastern side of the mountain. Some people believe the route gets its name because it crosses Bwlch y Moch, or the Pass of Pigs, on its ascent from Pen-y-Pass (if you're wondering how to pronounce the Welsh word *bwlch*, which means *pass*, then record yourself next time you stifle a vomit). Others believe *Pyg* is simply an acronym of Pen-y-Gwryd, the name of a hotel on the eastern side where many of Snowdon's early climbers used to meet. But frankly, who cares. The weather was cold, wet and miserable as we climbed through the dramatic amphitheatre of Cwm Dyli. In his younger days my father was a talented sportsman, but his head for heights made me look like Blondin. He was as likely to scramble along Crib Goch as I was to tightrope across the Niagara Falls, but he had no problem with the Pyg Track, which rose steeply to the col between Garnedd Ugain and Snowdon.

It was at the col that I saw the train chug past. The Snowdon Mountain Railway opened in 1896 in inauspicious circumstances. On its maiden voyage the engine started accelerating uncontrollably above Clogwyn Station, high up on the Llanberis Path, before hurtling off the line and over cliffs into Cwm Glas. Luckily an alert railway manager, who happened to be on the train, uncoupled the carriages and applied the emergency brake, saving the lives of his passengers. Climbers have to endure many hazards, including rockfall and avalanche; it's not known whether any climbers in Cwm Glas that day had to duck when they saw a train come flying over. Although the engine didn't survive its first outing, the railway reopened the following year and has operated continuously ever since. By the end of 1897, 12,000 people had travelled on the Snowdon railway. In 2005 the figure was 140,000,[1] and that's why I wasn't especially surprised when I saw it steam past me.

We took photographs on top of Snowdon's raised summit platform, had a beer in the bar at Summit Station, and made our way back past the col and up to Garnedd Ugain. Here my father ticked off another 3,000er and made the sensible decision to descend back down the Pyg Track, but I decided to press on along Crib Goch in a direction most people would describe as the wrong way. Very few hikers come back down the ridge from Snowdon's summit for reasons I was about to discover.

The ridge was straightforward to begin with, but then it began to narrow. Nobody told me about the Pinnacles, and I was surprised when I found myself confronted with proper hardcore rock climbing. OK, it wasn't what a proper hardcore rock climber would describe as a rock climb – technically Crib Goch is classed as a Grade 1 scramble, the easiest level, meaning ropes should only be required by the exceedingly nervous. On the Beaufort Scale it would be described as a breeze. Rock climbers would grade it little more than a 1b, which for most ordinary people is a type of pencil.

But I sense I may be losing some of you with these grading systems, so I'll conclude this digression with some sage advice: never talk to a rock climber about climbing grades, or you may end up wishing you were at a Star Trek convention.

To put it in terms you may be more familiar with, I'll just say the Pinnacles gave me the same discomfort a man feels when the person in the next cubicle asks him to pass through some toilet paper. I wasn't entirely happy, but I couldn't turn back; chasing my father down the Pyg Track would have been mortifying.

A light film of mist dampened the rock and caused my gloves to slide off the surface. I had to take them off to give my hands more grip, but at least I couldn't see the stomach-churning drop beneath me. I eased my way over the rock tower and lowered myself down the other side. I was very slow and careful, but I managed the moves without difficulty and felt my confidence surge.

Scrambling along the knife-edge ridge of Crib Goch, with Snowdon's summit in cloud beyond the crest

Not long after, I saw figures emerge from the mist ahead of me. They were very happy when I told them the bar was open as I stopped to let them squeeze past. The knife edge turned out to be the easy bit. With the dizzying heights shrouded by cloud I didn't need to resort to straddling the rock, and I couldn't believe my good fortune when I reached the end of the ridge. There were a few hair-raising moments, but I had dealt with the obstacles admirably. Or so I told myself.

But I had forgotten something very important.

There aren't many hill walkers with a story to tell about falling off a rock and plummeting hundreds of metres, but there are plenty with tales about becoming lost in thick mist, descending into the wrong valley and having to walk for miles to get back to their car. Some of the less experienced ones end up hopelessly lost and even have to phone for help. Some have no choice but to call the Mountain Rescue Service after falling short distances and breaking an ankle.

I was pleased with myself for reaching the end of the ridge, but following a ridge requires few navigational skills. The real danger was yet to come.

The rough trail up to Crib Goch from Llyn Llydaw is much easier to follow from below. From above it's less clear, and when I inevitably lost it I found myself scrambling across exposed slabs and staring down five-metre drops, with no sight of a track below me. It took a painfully long time to descend in the mist, and I frequently had to double back when I found my route ending abruptly at a cliff. It was the scariest thing I had ever done, and I longed for it to end. I was lucky not to break my ankle jumping down a two-metre crag, and I agreed with my brother that Swirral Edge was a 'piece of piss'.

I wasn't feeling quite as smug when the slope of the rock eased and I found my way back onto the trail. I was panting with relief and I knew I had been lucky to make it down without injury. But I was better for the experience, and I didn't need to tell anyone how frightened I had been.

When I arrived back at the Pen-y-Pass car park, my father was already waiting.

'How was that?' he asked.

'It was great fun, I really enjoyed it. You should have come,' I said, learning to lie like every good mountaineer before and since, who has experienced selective recall after an exhilarating ascent.

Maybe it hadn't been such fun, but it was a learning curve, and I would soon feel comfortable completing ridge scrambles like Crib Goch on my own. But had you told that early version of me that a few years later he would be completing the same moves on the North-East Ridge of Everest, he would probably have asked you whether he'd be sharing a rope with Santa as well. If that person appearing out of the mist on Crib Goch had not said *is the bar open?* but *excuse me, mate, is this the way to Everest?* then the early me would have laughed so hard that he ruptured his spleen and plummeted off the ridge.

So much for me. In 1953 a group of climbers on Snowdon weren't far from the summit of Everest at all. John Hunt, leader of the 1953 British expedition, had chosen the climbers' hut at nearby Helyg as the base for some of their preparations, and Tom Bourdillon had been chosen to look after the oxygen apparatus. Bourdillon was a physicist who developed rocket motors, and had been on two Everest reconnaissance expeditions led by Eric Shipton in 1951 and 1952, where he experimented with oxygen. He was a talented rock climber, highly regarded after leading the Great Slab route on Clogwyn Du'r Arddu, the giant cliff face overlooking Snowdon's railway line (I won't attempt to explain the pronunciation this time, but most people just call it *Cloggy*).

Tom Bourdillon's position as a rock climbing specialist is best illustrated by Shipton, who was sitting with him above the village of Namche Bazaar near Everest, and gazing across a deep valley to a vast rock wall. Shipton asked him if he would like to spend the next month exploring the mountains south of Everest, or climb the rock.

'I'm sorry, Eric, I'd choose the rocks,'[2] Bourdillon replied in a gentle, apologetic manner.

In other words, he was another one of those people who prefer to shin up a sea stack than walk along a picturesque coastal path.

Bourdillon was developing a *closed-circuit* system, which recycled the oxygen that the climber exhaled. The alternative *open-circuit* system was more trusted; while it didn't recycle, it did allow climbers to breathe air from outside, and was therefore less dangerous in the event of the apparatus failing. Bourdillon was convinced the closed-circuit apparatus could be better, and he chose the meeting of the Everest team at Helyg in January 1953 to try out the carrying frames during an ascent of Snowdon. The mountain is busy with walkers all year round, and it's not recorded how any of them reacted upon seeing a group of men walking up and down it in gas masks.

We do know how another Everest hero was greeted by a fellow hiker on Snowdon a few months later. The newly knighted Sir Edmund Hillary, fresh from becoming the first man to climb Everest with Tenzing Norgay, was a couple of hours late for a celebration event organised by the Alpine Club at the Pen-y-Gwyrd Hotel, the pub at the bottom of Pen-y-Pass where the Everest team had spent many an evening boozing prior to their expedition. When he heard the rest of the team had set off up Snowdon, he went after them, ill-equipped in casual clothing and a pair of sneakers. Halfway up he passed a distinguished-looking gentleman who noticed his inappropriate attire and subjected him to what in those days was called a *thorough dressing-down* and what we now call a *severe bollocking*. Ill-equipped and inexperienced people like Hillary gave the mountains a bad name, the gentleman explained.

Later that evening Hillary was introduced to the president of the Alpine Club back at the Pen-y-Gwryd, and found himself shaking hands with a familiar character. In his autobiography Hillary described the handshake as a little limp-wristed.

The 1953 expedition team used Snowdon and its surroundings for much of their preparation, but the mountain's association with Everest goes back further than that. George Mallory was an obscure 35-year-old schoolmaster with no experience of climbing in the Himalayas when he was chosen for the 1921 Everest reconnaissance expedition, the start of a journey that in just three years would make him part of Everest folklore.

He arrived at Cambridge University in 1905 and quickly became very popular with his peers, not always for his climbing ability. 'He had a strikingly beautiful face,' Mallory's school tutor Graham Irving once said of him, 'especially the rather large, heavily lashed, thoughtful eyes ... extraordinarily suggestive of a Botticelli Madonna.'[3] The writer Lytton Strachey said, 'George Mallory! ... My hand trembles, my heart palpitates ... oh heavens! Heavens!'[4] The artist Duncan Grant painted him *au naturel,* and his tutor Arthur Benson said, 'I had noticed in King's in the morning a fine-looking boy ... He is to be under me, and I rejoice at the thought.'[5]

Mallory had already climbed in the Alps during his school days, and at Cambridge he joined the Climbers' Club, which ran regular meet-ups at the Pen-y-Pass Inn beneath Snowdon's Pyg Track. There he met Geoffrey Winthrop Young, a mountaineer of some standing who was one of Britain's top alpine climbers until an injury during the First World War left him with an amputated leg. Winthrop Young also saw something to admire in Mallory, including his climbing ability: 'He swung up rock with a long thigh, lifted knee, and a ripple of irresistible movement.'[6]

At least, I think he was admiring his climbing ability.

If only Mallory could have conquered mountains as easily as he conquered these enthusiastic admirers, then the history of Everest might have been different. In 1921, while still a disillusioned schoolteacher looking to do something more meaningful with his life, he unexpectedly received a letter from the Mount Everest Committee, a body formed by the Alpine Club and the Royal Geographical Society with the aim of organising a national expedition to Everest. The letter was signed by Percy Farrar, Secretary of the Alpine Club, whom Mallory had met several years earlier during one of the Climbers' Club gatherings on Snowdon. It was terse and to the point: 'Party would leave early April and get back in October. Any aspirations?'[7] Mallory accepted.

As principal climber on the 1921 expedition, he ended up having a key role in exploring Everest's upper reaches and discovering a route to the summit. He was invited to join the 1922 expedition as climbing leader, and reached an altitude of 8,225m on slabs beneath the North-East Ridge. By the time a third expedition was organised in 1924, Mallory's name was inextricably linked with Everest in the public imagination. He had been on lecture tours across America, where a newspaper reported him as replying to the question *why climb Everest?* with the answer *because it's there.*

On the 8th of June 1924 he set out from Camp 6 beneath the North-East Ridge with climbing partner Sandy Irvine. They were seen briefly climbing a rock step just below the summit before cloud swept over, concealing them from view. They were never seen again, and people still debate whether Mallory and Irvine reached the summit twenty-nine years before Edmund Hillary and Tenzing Norgay.

And so it was that a few college chums meeting at a pub

beneath the flanks of Snowdon helped to sow the seeds of Everest history.

In fact, a lot of climbing history took place on Snowdon. In 1798 a pair of vicars, the Reverend William Bingley and the Reverend Peter Williams, made one of the world's first recorded rock climbs when they ascended the Eastern Terrace on Clogwyn Du'r Arddu looking for the Snowdon lily. Modern climbers might describe what they did as a scramble rather than a climb, but they've had 200 years of advances in climbing technique and equipment to help them, and were the two gentlemen of the cloth alive today they might justifiably say to one of these whippersnappers, *rock shoes? Try climbing it in a cassock!* These days the two vicars could have stopped mounting a pulpit to give sermons, and become what modern-day Everest climbers call a *motivational speaker*.

In the 1920s Clogwyn Du'r Arddu started to become one of Britain's most popular rock-climbing faces. In 1928 two men who were to play a prominent part in the many hapless British attempts on Everest in the 1930s, Frank Smythe and Jack Longland, made the first ascent of the West Buttress using techniques some modern climbers would regard as cheating. These included placing chockstones (pebbles jammed into cracks to secure a loop of rope), banging in pitons, and *gardening* (removing sods of earth and grass from the rock in order to find firmer holds). Indeed, Smythe himself even remarked that anyone who can drive a piton into a rock is 'capable of pulling a trigger upon a fox',[8] which is perhaps a little harsh. Issues of *climbing purity* – the mechanical aids a climber is permitted to use for their ascent to be regarded as by *fair means* – would become a familiar topic to me during my journey to Everest. They are as old as climbing itself.

A quarter of a century later, Smythe's climbing aids

would seem crude. In 1952 the rock climber John Streetly described the first ascent of Red Slab on Cloggy's West Buttress.

> *At this point the first real handhold of the climb was manufactured by extensive gardening in the crack immediately below the overhang. Here the general dampness and moss made rubbers both useless and dangerous, so they had to be removed quickly and tucked away in case they were necessary later on.*[9]

But before you wonder which part of his anatomy he was using to climb, I should explain that in those days *rubbers* meant rubber-soled climbing shoes rather than condoms, and he ended up completing the rest of the ascent in his socks.

Eventually I concluded arguments about climbing purity were a bit silly and that another Everest climber, Wilfrid Noyce, summed it up best in the book *Snowdon Biography* when he said, 'In the great sport of mountaineering there are, thank heaven, no rules, and only one absolutely general principle, that of "getting up"'[10] (Noyce would himself help Hillary and Tenzing *get up* Everest by carrying oxygen apparatus to the South Col during the successful 1953 expedition).

At that stage in my life I still seemed as likely to climb up rock as to attend a public execution. I was keen to do more walking though, and I supplemented my hill walks with some long-distance footpaths. My first multi-day hike was the South Downs Way, along a chalk escarpment beside Britain's south coast. As it was the first time I had walked thirty kilometres a day for six days, I cheated: I booked into bed-and-breakfast accommodation every night instead of camping, and managed to arrange my itinerary so that I always stopped at a convenient pub for lunch (hill walkers don't seem to be quite as concerned about issues of *walking purity*). While walking the Ridgeway in Wiltshire the following year, I was dismayed when I reached my lunchtime pub in a rainstorm only to find it closed. Luckily there was a cricket pitch opposite, and I was able to shelter in the porch of the pavilion for an hour while I took a rest.

These conveniences weren't possible back on the hills, though. I bought a set of Cicerone guidebooks called *Backpacker's Britain* which introduced me to the delights of wild camping. Every so often I spent a weekend off the beaten track carrying my tent, sleeping bag and stove across a rugged hillside, and sleeping beside a clear mountain stream in the middle of nowhere, listening to the sounds of nature as they lulled me to sleep. I enjoyed every minute of these trips, and was discovering I could walk for England. But there was little to suggest I would ever do anything more extreme than this.

What happened next was a total surprise, and it was one that required a gentle kick up the backside from the foot of fate.

2 HIGH-ALTITUDE TREKKING

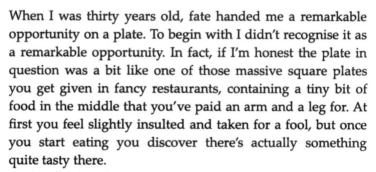

When I was thirty years old, fate handed me a remarkable opportunity on a plate. To begin with I didn't recognise it as a remarkable opportunity. In fact, if I'm honest the plate in question was a bit like one of those massive square plates you get given in fancy restaurants, containing a tiny bit of food in the middle that you've paid an arm and a leg for. At first you feel slightly insulted and taken for a fool, but once you start eating you discover there's actually something quite tasty there.

For the first few years of my working life I worked for a dot-com startup, a fledgling internet company that produced websites for heavy engineering industries. A handful of us helped to build the company until it could be sold to a larger corporation for a small fortune. That was the theory and it worked to a degree. Our managing director became a millionaire, and those of us lucky enough to be considered valuable were given a small percentage as a thank you.

I was grateful for my modest windfall, but my holiday allowance throughout that time was as generous as a streaker's wardrobe. Although I loved getting into the country for short hill walking trips, they were over much too quickly. I lived in London and could manage weekend breaks to Snowdonia or the Lake District, or a week in

Scotland, but anything further afield I could only read about.

I was an avid reader of mountaineering disaster books like *Into Thin Air*, which recounts a terrible day in 1996 when eight mountaineers died in a storm on Everest's South-East Ridge. Those who survived were so badly frostbitten they had to have their arms cut off. I also read *Touching the Void*, the story of a man who crawled for three days with a broken leg after falling into a crevasse and being left for dead. I read about George Mallory's disappearance into the mist on Everest in 1924, and Captain Scott's team collapsing one by one from starvation after losing their race to the South Pole. I read *Annapurna*, about the first ascent of an 8,000m peak – when the author Maurice Herzog had to leave his frostbitten fingers and toes at a railway station in India after some makeshift amputation – and other classics of climbing literature such as *The White Spider*, recounting a series of gruesome deaths on the North Face of the Eiger.

Of course, it would be ridiculous to repeat any of these dangerous exploits myself, but it never occurred to me that one day opportunities might arise for me to visit many of these places in relative safety. At the time I wasn't even thinking of doing anything adventurous.

When our internet company was sold to a larger publisher, I assumed I would stay and work my way up the ladder. But working for a small company didn't prepare me for corporate politics. When a shark swallows a sardine, it's usually the shark who gets more out of the relationship, and I discovered that it's the same with mergers and acquisitions. I was suddenly on the corporate ladder, but I was standing on other people's toes – people who knew much better than I did how to climb to the next rung. This may be a familiar story for some of you, but this isn't a book about floundering in a sea of corporate hogwash. It's about escaping all that and finding something much more fulfilling.

My job became as satisfying as a game of *Truth or Dare* with chartered accountants, but it did lead to a great discovery I may never have made without it. Sometimes it's impossible to stop yourself from falling, but you can always get back up again. Often the best things in life are born out of adversity, which in my case meant a career brick wall. I had a nice five-figure windfall from the sale of the internet company, and this gave me the confidence to quit my job and go travelling.

So in January 2002 I handed in my notice, and a month later I was free to go anywhere I liked.

But where to go and what to do? I wanted to go walking somewhere, but I wasn't the boldest of people. That Christmas my brother bought me a camping stove and a guidebook to trekking in Patagonia, but if he thought I was just going to book a flight, pitch up in Argentina with a stove and a guidebook and head off to the mountains, he had to be joking. During his gap year he hitch-hiked around South America, and before he went he spent the summer listening to *Teach Yourself Spanish* tapes and sewing wire cable into the straps of his backpack because he'd heard thieves in Peru operated by cutting through them with a knife while they were still on your shoulders. The idea of going anywhere this might happen sounded absolutely terrifying.

Then a friend introduced me to group travel. This involved joining a guided trip with an itinerary that had been arranged in advance by a tour operator. OK, it was hardly Robinson Crusoe, but let's face it, a guided holiday in the Himalayas had to be more interesting than scrambling along Crib Goch on my own for a pint at the highest bar in Britain. My friend sent me a few links to the websites of trekking companies.

The trips on offer were graded with adjectives like *easy*,

moderate, tough, challenging, and the hardest one, *bear-gryllsian,* a term I'd not heard before that conjured up vivid images of using survival skills like grilling a bear.

Each grade included a description of the conditions that might be expected on the trek. An easy trek might have the following description:

Must be prepared to amble slowly like a window shopper on Oxford Street. Extreme patience is required and there is a modest risk of falling asleep while walking. Anyone able to drive to a McDonald's and stuff their face with burgers would be suitable for this trip.

Meanwhile at the other end of the scale, the description for a bear-gryllsian trip would be something like this:

Walking days can be twenty-five hours long, often without water. Food on trek can sometimes be ropey. Must be prepared to spend three hours each day on the toilet and walk with a cork rammed up your anus. Frostbite a risk. Expect to lose three stone in weight and at least one appendage.

Although I had completed a couple of long-distance walks, the leafy villages of southern England seemed unlikely to prepare me for savage mountain passes in the Himalayas. My pack had been about as heavy as Cliff Richard singing Van Halen numbers during a rain break at Wimbledon. I wasn't sure I would be able to cope with two weeks of hiking at high altitude, and I worried I might hold everyone up. Snowdon was still the highest mountain I had ever climbed and I was concerned about the effects of altitude sickness.

My trekking guidebook hadn't been very helpful on this last point, and made it sound like I was almost certain to die.

High-altitude cerebral edema [it helpfully explained] *is a swelling of the brain tissue caused by the build-up of fluid in the brain. Symptoms include severe headaches* [well yes, I expect they would if your brain is being slowly inflated like a sack of water], *persistent vomiting, loss of coordination, staggering, falling, blurred or double vision, confusion, hallucinations, and loss of mental faculties such as memory.*

On the whole this didn't sound so very different from a boozy night in Soho, but the consequences seemed much more severe.

A severely inflated brain can prevent the blood from flowing to it. This means oxygen cannot reach the brain and it will cease to function.

Bloody hell, and if this wasn't enough there was a torso equivalent:

The first sign of high-altitude pulmonary edema [continued my guidebook with an evil cackle] *might be a gurgling sound in the lungs caused by a build-up of fluid* [here we go again]. *In the advanced stages, essentially the victim will be drowning in a shallow lake of frothy sputum.*

OK, so I may not have recalled the words of my guidebook perfectly, but it was definitely something along those lines. I decided to exercise caution and opted for a trek graded *moderate*. The possibility of my head expanding like a giant beach ball while my stomach rumbled like a pair of toddlers sucking milkshake through a pig's intestine made me shy away from trekking grades which began by stating that training might be required.

On the whole, though, researching my first big high-altitude trek hadn't put me off. On the contrary – the apparent dangers simply made me feel like it was going to be even more of an adventure. I picked out a holiday to Nepal which would take me to two separate mountain areas, Annapurna and Everest, with a couple of days' jungle safari on elephant back in a place called Chitwan. It was all very exciting: not only would I get to see the highest mountain in the world, as well as the one where Maurice Herzog lost his fingers, but I would get to ride an elephant. Who wouldn't swap a dull office job for this, given the chance?

※ ※ ※

I was a little apprehensive about the other trekkers I would be sharing my holiday with. I expected them to be fitter and more intrepid than me, the sort of people who might wrestle a crocodile in Chitwan, or run up Poon Hill in the Annapurnas carrying a bag of rocks. I wondered whether I would be able to fit in, but wouldn't it be exciting once I got to know them! My friends were going to be really impressed with me after this one.

The tour company had provided us with blue branded duffle bags to pack all our kit for the holiday. The luggage carousel at Kathmandu Airport was an early opportunity for me to spot the would-be commandos bound for the Annapurnas with me, but this failed when I discovered they were running several trips concurrently. Over a hundred identical blue bags circulated round and round the baggage carousel, with people of all shapes and sizes picking them up. I assumed many of them were bound for luxury excursions involving foot massages and little slices of cucumber stuck to their eyelids. They certainly couldn't be trekkers, judging by the look of them.

The airport was chaotic and something of a culture shock for someone who had never travelled in the developing world before. I was forced to sprinkle a few dollars liberally among some helpful locals who generously insisted on unburdening me of my bags and carrying them three metres across a road. Luckily the tour company had arranged for someone to come and meet me, or I might have arrived at my hotel with an empty wallet.

I have been to Nepal many times now and the drive from the airport to Thamel, Kathmandu's tourist heart, feels like coming home. There is no direct route. Taxis and buses have to squeeze up narrow potholed alleyways, dodging cyclists, scooters, and kids playing football. Kathmandu is predominantly Hindu and the cow is sacred, so scrawny bovines wander the streets freely without a care in the world. It's compulsory for motorists to beep their horns every few seconds, and stopping at a light often results in a beggar dodging through the traffic to scratch on the window of your vehicle. Dirty concrete multi-storey buildings look unfinished, with steel reinforcing bars sticking out of the top suggesting another level is going to be built – though in many cases they are pretty much a permanent feature of the building. At any time of day you can see people brushing their teeth in a gutter while somebody else urinates beside them. Chaos reigns, and the traffic police who stand at junctions appear about as useful as free booze at a tea-drinking festival. Sometimes I enjoy watching the bedlam, and at other times I sit in the back of the taxi ignoring it completely. On my first visit, having been robbed by hustlers outside the airport terminal building, it shocked me. I had never seen such poverty before, and I didn't know where to look.

By contrast our characterless three-star hotel just outside Thamel was an oasis of calm. The marbled foyer was clean and the staff were neatly dressed. The blue duffle bags were piled high and we divided into our various tour groups. It was only then I realised I had been somewhat conservative in my choice of holiday. Ours was the gentlest trek by some distance, and far from being teamed up with Sylvester Stallone impersonators playing Rambo, with oiled biceps and a sash of bullets slung over their shoulders, I found myself matched with a group of old ladies from Ludlow Women's Institute. I was the youngest by nearly twenty years. This meant we had no chance of outrunning rhinos in Chitwan, but at least we could set up a stall and offer them mince pies.

I was crestfallen, but I need not have worried. Although they were all much older than me they turned out to be an active bunch, and relaxing and friendly company for the next few weeks. And they weren't all old ladies. There were also two retired police officers, and after a week or two of travelling with them I discovered that another gentle giant of a man in his sixties had quite an extensive library of dirty jokes. And we did have one crocodile-wrestling tough guy in Pemba, our trek leader.

We also had one very important thing in common. For all of us it was our first time in Nepal and we were about to travel through some of the grandest mountain scenery on Earth. Although I didn't know it then, this small country just 800km long and 200km wide, wedged between China and India, the two most populous countries in the world, would become something like my second home.

Nepal is a relatively small country, but the diversity of its landscape is vast. The lowland plains of the Terai in the south are barely a hundred metres above sea level, and contain several jungle and wetland national parks, including Chitwan. The area is malarial, but home to many species of birds and large mammals, including rhinos, tigers and elephants. The band of hills across the middle of the country is heavily populated and denuded of forests after centuries of intensive cultivation. Most of it is farmland, but of a type I had never seen before. Lush green precipitous hillsides were cut into row upon row of terraced fields, rising up over hundreds of metres. Villages sprawled across hillsides in the unlikeliest of places, and every other square inch of land was cultivated.

The north of the country is the heart of the Himalayas. The large variation in altitude here means there are many different climate zones in close proximity. Bamboo forests rise up into forests of giant rhododendron trees. Above this, alpine conifer forests give way to areas of scrubby juniper and dwarf rhododendron. The highest parts of the country are crowned by mighty glaciers and snow-capped peaks, culminating in the summit of Everest at 8,848m. Eight of the world's ten highest mountains either rise entirely within Nepal or straddle its borders. And if this isn't enough there is a bonus landscape of high desert plateau in some parts of the far north, where the northern border with Tibet stretches beyond the Himalayan divide.

Our trip took us through most of these landscapes, starting with the cultivated midlands as we drove for a day from Kathmandu to the start of our trek in the Annapurnas. By cultivated I don't mean there were art galleries or string quartets playing by the side of the road – on the contrary, the traffic on the narrow winding road which weaved its way around steep hillsides was far from cultivated. The technique of overtaking round blind corners while furiously beeping horns to alert drivers coming the other way was one I'd not seen before.

Much of the journey from Kathmandu to Pokhara, Nepal's second city and the gateway to the Annapurnas, runs alongside the Trisuli River, a popular destination for white-water rafting. While it was a pleasant distraction to watch rafters whiz past on rapids, on the whole I preferred not to look out of the window on that side for fear of seeing the many abandoned buses that had tumbled down the bank. We were lucky in one respect, though. We had a nice comfortable tourist bus just for our group, with ample space for seats and luggage. While some of our bags were on the roof, at least they were tied down and not likely to go flying off when emergency braking was called for – which was often. Public buses were so crowded that dozens of people squeezed onto the roof, often with live chickens.

Although the driving was scary, it wasn't my abiding memory of the journey. In Nepal the landscape screams at you like a madman in a yodelling contest. The road passed through lush hillsides crammed with terraced fields and farmers' cottages spread over wide intervals. Some houses were perched hundreds of metres above the road, at the end of narrow dirt pathways crawling all the way up from the roadside. I remember thinking it must be a bugger if you lived there and needed to pop out for a pint of milk.

The view opened out as the road approached Pokhara, and we were given our first close sight of snow-capped Himalayan mountains. Looking back, I think my first impression of the Annapurnas probably owed as much to my imagination as reality. At 1,085m Snowdon was still the highest peak I had ever climbed, while Annapurna was 8,091m and the tenth-highest mountain in the world. I couldn't imagine what it would be like to look at a mountain that high; it was mind-boggling. Pokhara lies on a broad plain 800m above sea level. I knew I needed to look nearly five miles up into the air, and I can't be sure I didn't crane my neck up at the odd cloud imagining it to be a Himalayan snowcap.

But I was sure two days later when I stood on top of a modest hillside (by Nepali standards) called Poon Hill. The phrase *took my breath away* is overused, but if it's actually possible for amazing views to suck the oxygen out of you then watching the sunrise from Poon Hill would be like having a vacuum cleaner rammed down your throat and switched onto full blast until it sucked your lungs inside out and left them dangling from your mouth. Poon Hill rises to the comparatively meagre height of 3,210m, and from its summit you can see not just one, but two of the world's fourteen 8,000m peaks. As well as Annapurna to the north, 8,167m Dhaulagiri rises prominently across the Kali Gandaki valley to the west.

To get there we had to hike for two days out of farmland and up through rhododendron forest on a trail famous for its 3,000 steps. I had always thought of rhododendrons as ornamental flowers in public gardens, and I had no idea they grow into thirty-metre trees in their native Himalayan habitat. It was early spring, the trees were starting to flower, and we could look up and see colourful reds and whites blooming in the canopy above us.

The morning after we arrived in Ghorepani, a little tourist village on a ridge, we were dragged from our beds in the small hours of the morning. We climbed for an hour by torchlight along a muddy path to the summit of Poon Hill to watch the dawn. The silhouette of the mountains which emerged from the darkness is very familiar to me now. I bought a panoramic print of it in one of the teahouses in Ghorepani, and it still hangs in a frame above my bed. Four years later I returned to Poon Hill after hiking the

Annapurna Circuit and watched it emerge again. It's one of Nepal's best-known viewpoints because it's accessible to any reasonably fit hiker, only two days from the road and at a relatively low altitude.

Dhaulagiri is the more impressive of the two 8,000ers, though it's further away across the valley. It dwarfs its neighbours Dhaulagiri II and Tukuche on either side, and appears as a sheer tent-shaped wall of ice. By contrast Annapurna is a crumpled bundle of snow and rock, partially obscured by the more prominent triangle of Annapurna South, which dominates the view from Poon Hill and looks much more like a mountain is supposed to.

To the right of Annapurna is Machapuchare (or *The Fishtail*) – a much lower peak than its neighbours at just 6,993m, but by far the most striking in appearance. From Poon Hill it appears as a steep pinnacle, but it's actually a twin-summited trapezium which gives it its name. In 1957 the British climbers Wilfrid Noyce and David Cox got to within fifty metres of its summit before they came across columns of blue ice barring their way 'like the claws of some great dragon'.[11]

Their expedition was led by Colonel Jimmy Roberts, an officer in the Gurkha regiment of the British Army who spoke fluent Nepali. After the expedition he persuaded the locals that Machapuchare should be designated a holy mountain, and that its summit must not be defiled by human feet. Since Roberts's 1957 expedition, no climbing permits have ever been issued for Machapuchare. It remains unclimbed.

Those first few days of trekking in the Annapurna foothills introduced me to teahouse trekking, a concept that sets Nepal apart from other high-altitude trekking destinations. The foothills were remote by western standards, and in places days from the nearest road, but its people were rapidly adapting to tourism. We rarely walked for more than an hour without coming across an old shack or stone hut with a hand-painted sign advertising the *Super View Guest House*, the *Annapurna View Hotel*, or the *Lovely Himalaya Resort*.

Mark at Poon Hill in the Annapurnas, as Annapurna South and Machapuchare rise with the dawn

Despite their grand if slightly quaint-sounding names, these teahouses were far from luxurious – but they offered everything a rough-and-ready trekker needed. For one or two hundred rupees a night (or a couple of dollars) accommodation consisted of no more than a wooden cell containing two narrow beds, each with a foam mat. If we were lucky there were a few nails banged into roof beams to hang our kit to dry. Down the corridor was a squat-style toilet with a bucket for toilet paper and a tap above a concrete floor for washing hands. Each teahouse had a dining room offering a surprisingly varied menu of *dal bhat* (a traditional Nepali dish of rice and lentils), noodles, macaroni, and even pizza. Entertainment was provided in the form of comical spelling mistakes like *cheese noddles*, *string roll*, *chocolate cak* and, my favourite, *chicken bugger*. Some even had hot showers, which involved standing naked under a bucket of lukewarm water in an outhouse across the yard, singing loudly because the door had no lock.

One of the features of teahouses which took some getting used to was the thin plywood walls which enabled anyone to eavesdrop on the conversation in the room next door.

After our dawn spectacle on Poon Hill we followed an icy trail along a ridge of rhododendron forest to the village of Tadapani in a magnificent setting high up in the forest. From there we could look across a cushion of cloud in the valley beneath us to a wispy silhouette of mountains on the far horizon. We were relaxing around a large central table in our teahouse when one of the older ladies stood up and announced it was International Women's Prayer Day, and they were going to conduct a prayer service on behalf of all women.

We fell silent, and as they began chanting by candlelight I looked around the room to exchange a sympathetic glance with my male companions, but to my dismay they were all glancing down at the table in respectful silence. As a non-practising agnostic, I felt as awkward as a nun at a hen party just as a fireman enters the room. I stood up quietly and headed for the door, but my exit didn't go unnoticed. I was sure I had seen one or two disapproving glares, and back in my room I wondered if I had upset the ladies of Ludlow by appearing disrespectful. I was sure I would need to apologise the following day to maintain group cohesion, but luckily my room-mate John, a 50-year-old yoga enthusiast, came to the rescue. Later in the evening he returned to the room, sat down on his bed, and said in a voice of surprise so loud it must have penetrated three sets of partition walls and reached everyone in the teahouse:

'Bloody hell, I had no idea we had so many God-botherers in the group.'

I went to sleep sure that my own little *faux pas* would be forgotten, but it wasn't turning out to be the intrepid adventure I had envisaged. What would my friends think of me when I told them about this incident? I was supposed to be an explorer on a great expedition, drinking bog water from the inside lining of a baboon's scrotum then digging a hole to crap in with my bare hands and wiping my backside with tree bark, and here I was sitting in a dining room with a nice warm cup of hot lemon while I selected items off a neatly laminated menu. Instead of thrashing through dense jungle with a machete then fighting my way over windswept passes on a remote Himalayan peak, where I would wrestle a yeti to the ground and scream 'hands off my sister', I found myself chanting prayers with old ladies around a comfortable table in a teahouse, yearning for the next time I would be able to speak a rude word in conversation.

I flicked through my trip itinerary and reminded myself of the definition for a trek graded *moderate*.

Suitable for most hill walkers, a good level of fitness is required as the trek will involve a considerable amount of ascent and descent and the occasional difficult day.

I was finding it hard to reconcile this description with my experience of actually walking. Evidently the difficult days were still to come.

I was in the process of learning that everything is done in slow motion at high altitude. I assumed the reason our guides were leading us slowly up hills was so that older people in the group could keep up. I didn't realise they were doing it as much for my own good as anyone else's. There are two golden rules of walking at high altitude: to avoid over-exertion, and to drink more than you would at sea level to avoid dehydration. Neglecting the first often leads to the second, and the trekkers who overdo it and become dehydrated are the ones who suffer from altitude sickness.

It's commonly believed that fitness has nothing to do with your ability to cope at altitude. While this is partially true – theoretically the fitter you are, the greater your ability to climb a hill without getting tired – fit people are no less likely to push themselves than unfit people. In fact, people who exercise a lot are often competitive, and determined to show others in the group how strong they are by travelling at the front. It would be a few years before I became relaxed enough to amble at the back and perfect the art of the high-altitude slow plod. What I didn't realise during my very first high-altitude trek was that if I whizzed up the trail and worked up a sweat like I did when I was out in the Welsh hills, then I would definitely get altitude sickness.

On the day after our prayer evening, we had a short walk through jungle to the next village, Ghandruk. Pemba said it would take just three hours, but John and I were the strongest in the group by some margin, and we were becoming frustrated ambling along every day like a three-legged tortoise. We noticed that one of our guides, Krishna, led at a slightly quicker pace than the others, so we offered him a bottle of Tuborg beer to get us to Ghandruk in under two hours. He expressed doubts, but agreed to give it a go. Then he shot off down the hill like Usain Bolt being chased by a tiger.

It may have been on this journey I first learned the meaning of the word *hubris*.

The Everest Marathon, held every two years in – wait for it – the Everest region of Nepal, isn't usually won by a non-

Nepali, and sometimes all of the top-ten finishers are Nepalese athletes. This isn't just because their bodies are better adapted to coping with the lower levels of oxygen at high altitude, but because they're much better at completing the race without falling over. Most of us aren't very good at running down steep hills on rough trails without looking at our feet. What we are very good at is falling flat on our faces if we try. But Nepali mountain boys are so sure-footed they are able to adjust their balance with every step without having to look at the ground.

What followed was a bit like challenging Roger Federer to a game of tennis, but making him play with a frying pan instead of a tennis racket. Krishna ran down the trail for about a hundred metres, then turned around to watch me and John chase after him. He saw two buffoons tiptoeing across rocks as if they were hot coals. Every now and again one of us stumbled and stopped for a moment to regain our composure. We managed to reach Ghandruk in an hour and a half, and Krishna got his Tuborg, but we could have been walking along the seafront at Brighton for all we saw of the country we passed through, so busy were we looking at the ground. The others arrived two hours later enthusing about their lovely walk. The forest had been alive with pheasants, cuckoos and barbets, and they had even seen some monkeys.

Ghandruk is one of the most photogenic villages in Nepal. It perches on a hillside high above the deep valley of the Modi Khola River, which crashes down from the Annapurna Sanctuary, a famous natural amphitheatre surrounded by the highest peaks of the Annapurna region. Many of the houses in Ghandruk are mediaeval in character, built from rough stone with slate roofs, and the hillside below is carved into neat terraced rice fields. Annapurna South and its satellite peak Hiunchuli rise above the village, and the two-pronged profile of Machapuchare can be seen across the valley.

I surveyed it all as I sat in the sun with a pot of black tea, at a table in the neatly paved courtyard in front of our teahouse. I realised that this was what I had come here for. It didn't matter that I was sitting in a comfortable plastic chair sipping tea. Nobody back home could possibly comprehend the beauty of the scene before me, unless they came to see it for themselves. If I wanted to demonstrate my fitness or athleticism (or madness) I could sign up to do an Iron Man. I came here to see the mountains, and to really appreciate them I had to savour them at a slow pace.

It was one of the happiest holidays of my life, though it would be the first of many to the world's great mountain ranges. I was so busy relishing the new sights that I didn't even mind that for the first time since I was a child I'd gone three weeks without swearing.

The Annapurnas were a revelation, but we still had to explore the Everest region – a very different experience. It began with an infamous flight to the village of Lukla in a tiny Twin Otter aircraft. To get some idea of what it's like, imagine you're in a metal tube of human sardines flying through the air. Sixteen people are crammed alongside you with their thighs pressed against their chests, and great big rucksacks resting on their knees. You're sucking on a boiled sweet that a stooping air stewardess hands you as she squeezes her way down the aisle. Up ahead the door to the cockpit is open and you can clearly see the pilot is reading a newspaper, which he puts down when a large gust of wind buffets the tube and throws everyone sideways. This happens quite regularly, but after a while you stop noticing, because out of the window the scenery is dramatic. The highest mountains in the world tower above the clouds in front of you, and you try to work out which one is Everest. Even the forested lower foothills rise high above you. Come to think of it, the foothills look alarmingly close.

What makes the Lukla flight so hair raising, though, is not the flight itself, but the landing. There aren't many places in the mountainous Solu-Khumbu region of Nepal that are suitable for an airstrip. In 1964 Sir Edmund Hillary was busy building schools and hospitals for the local Sherpa people with funds from the Himalayan Trust, the charity he set up after his ascent of Everest. He was struggling to supply the building materials he needed, most of which had to be carried on the backs of porters for many days, up and over valleys and passes. He began looking for a good location to build an airport. The best he could find was this narrow shelf, perched on a ledge of terraced fields high above the steep-sided Dudh Khosi valley. The runway is so short it has to be canted at a steep angle to bring planes to a stop before hitting the mountain wall at the back. Legend describes them taking off by simply dropping off the end of the runway into the yawning chasm below, though I have watched them many times now and I can confirm they do indeed rise into the air first.

For first-timers, landing in Lukla can be alarming, even when they're unaware pilots have to land by line of sight and in quick succession. In 2008 three planes arrived at Lukla minutes apart. The first two landed without difficulty, but as the third approached the runway, a cloud swept in front of the pilot's view out of the cockpit window, and he landed fractionally too far to the left. One of the wings became caught in a wire fence and the plane burst into flames as it continued its journey up the runway. Eighteen people were killed, mostly tourists. The pilot was the only survivor.

In 2002 I was unaware of the precise nature of Lukla Airport, only that it was supposed to be a bit of an eye-opener to land in. I was surprised when, as if by magic, what looked to be the shortest runway in the world appeared out of nowhere. By now the pilot had put down his copy of *The Himalayan Times* and let the plane fall gently onto the tarmac before ramming on the brakes. We came to something resembling an emergency stop in front of a high wall with lots of sightseers standing on top taking photographs. It was quite an experience.

The Solu-Khumbu region of Nepal, popularly know as the Everest region, is the spiritual home of the Sherpas. Originally Tibetans, the Sherpas migrated into Nepal over the Nangpa La pass beneath Cho Oyu, the world's sixth-highest mountain, probably in the 16th century. The name *Sherpa* means *easterner* because they originally came from the Tibetan region of Kham to the east. They were mostly traders who made a secondary living by farming. Unlike Nepalis from the south, they were used to the high desert climate of Tibet and easily settled in the mountain region of Solu-Khumbu. To them it was a green paradise. Prevailing weather systems come from the Bay of Bengal in the south-east, depositing rain and snow on the south side of the Himalayan divide, leaving the north Tibetan side dry. The Sherpas made their home in the Khumbu, growing crops on its fertile slopes, and trading salt, wool, grain and cotton with their kinsmen across the Nangpa La in Tibet.

By the early 20th century their migratory trading lifestyle had taken many of them across the high passes to Darjeeling in North-East India. It was around this time the British were becoming interested in exploring the Himalayas on the northern fringes of their Indian empire. Many expeditions were launched from Darjeeling, and the British found the Sherpas, with their background of living in the high mountains and travelling across them, ideally suited to employment as porters and mountain guides. Nowadays the name *Sherpa* has become synonymous with a particular type of mountain guide specialising in all the hard work required to get western mountaineers to the summits of the world's highest mountains, but its true meaning is a particular ethnic group originally from the Solu-Khumbu.

We found trekking in the Khumbu a different experience to the Annapurnas. In the latter we were on a ridge, trekking beside a wall of mountains, but in the Khumbu we were right in among them, following a trail up a steep-sided valley. Lukla is at 2,800m, so we were nearly as high as we had been on Poon Hill, in the alpine zone of sparse pine forest. However fertile the Sherpas may have found this land, it was more barren than the Annapurnas. The lush rhododendron forest was much less abundant.

There may have been fewer rhododendron flowers lighting the forests, but in another respect it was a more colourful place than the Annapurna foothills. This was because of the profusion of prayer flags decorating every building. I would become very familiar with these symbols of Tibetan Buddhism swinging from any high point or windy place across the Himalayas. Their five colours represent nature's elements: sky (blue), air (white), fire (red), water (green) and earth (yellow). When we looked closely we saw that each flag was inscribed repeatedly with the Buddhist mantra *om mani padme hum*. As the wind strikes the flag, the belief is that prayers are sent into the air to appease the spirits of the earth.

Sherpa families were adapting to the steady increase in tourism, and most earned some sort of income as guides, porters or teahouse owners. While the standard of teahouses was improving rapidly, not all aspects of the trekking experience had been treated with an equal degree of attention. One area where the Annapurnas fared better was the toilets. Pemba spoke very good English and warned us that in the Khumbu toilets could be 'a bit grim'. He was right. Nothing illustrates this better than a place we stayed in a village called Kjanjuma, up the hill from Namche Bazaar, the Sherpa capital. I was directed to an old shed across the yard with a hole in the floorboards for disposing of my home-made chocolate cake. I was in the process of taking my trousers down when I heard a little voice below me.

'Hello, sir, hello!' it cried.

I peered through the hole and saw a man with a spade shovelling out the pit. I don't know which of us was most frightened.

But what this particular teahouse lacked in the toilet department, it made up for by having the most scenic shower cubicle I've ever had the pleasure of washing in. It wasn't the most sophisticated shower, and certainly wasn't the most powerful, but it had everything you needed and more. Essentially a greenhouse in the garden, its nearside was painted black to preserve the dignity of the occupant from anyone walking past on the trail or peering out of a window on the top floor of the teahouse. Its far side was made entirely from glass, and looked out across a valley of pine forest to Ama Dablam, perhaps the most striking mountain in the Khumbu. It was shaped like an armchair, with a triangular summit spilling down to elevated ridges that spread out on each side like a welcoming pair of arms held out to embrace the pilgrim traveller. Ama Dablam looks like it's been hewn into a throne by the mountain gods to look out across their domain. And who's to say it hasn't? Its name translates as *mother's jewel*, and it's so named because of a steep glacier (the *dablam*) spilling down from the summit, which is supposed to look like a giant sapphire hanging around the mother's neck. I don't know about that, but it was breathtaking enough to take my mind off any wildlife in the forest that might be looking up at *my* crown jewels as I took my shower.

The Sherpa capital of Namche Bazaar is one of the most spectacularly situated villages in the world, standing at 3,440m in a combe high above the deep Bhote Khosi gorge. The sloping ridge of 6,187m Kongde Ri rises over the village on the opposite side of the valley. When I returned in 2009 I was astonished by the number of multi-storey hotels which had sprung up around the combe, and the ring of hammers on rock saluting the many more being built. Back in 2002 it still had the feel of a village, with a couple of tiers of traditional Sherpa cottages encircling the basin. As an indication of how long ago this was, I remember climbing a hill to a post office in order to send a postcard with an Everest stamp. Just think – a postcard. Can you remember those? By 2009 the post office had been replaced by a profusion of internet cafés, which are now giving way to bakeries with free Wi-Fi.

Namche Bazaar marked my first experience of altitude sickness, not in myself but in one of my companions. John had acquired the nickname *The Human Dustbin* on account of his remarkable appetite for dal bhat. In the teahouse at Namche this famous appetite was hiding somewhere under the table and we were all very worried. Watching John struggle over an untouched plate of food was as surprising as watching a pig play the accordion, but happily by the following morning he had recovered enough to finish everyone's leftovers at breakfast as usual. Mild headaches and appetite loss are two of the most common ailments in people who are still acclimatising. I've experienced them many times now, and learned they are nothing to worry about. You spend a little longer acclimatising and they go away.

Altitude sickness is the main reason views of Everest need to be earned. Not everyone understands this, but we had been walking for several days and were about to receive our reward when we climbed the hillside above Namche on our way up the trail. I'm glad I had someone with me to point it out, though, for Everest wasn't the most prominent mountain from that angle – a bashful black pyramid peering above the towering wall of the Nuptse-Lhotse ridge that crossed in front of it. To its right Ama Dablam was the mountain screaming for attention.

We stopped for a pot of tea at the Everest View Hotel. Built by a Japanese company and opened in 1973, it once had its own airstrip at the top of the hill. Its purpose was to provide luxury accommodation for rich tourists flying in for the weekend to see Everest; but flying to 3,800m for a day trip isn't a great idea, and many guests were sick as soon as they arrived. Visitors soon learned it's better to walk. We were happy to sit on the comfortable veranda sipping tea as we looked out at Everest.

Had any of my companions told me that some day I would be a tiny speck on Everest's slopes, they would have had more tea than they bargained for when I spat mine all over them, roaring with laughter.

My first visit to Nepal ended at a place called Tengboche, the site of the most important Buddhist monastery in the Khumbu, on a high ridge projecting into a fork in the valley. When the great Himalayan explorer Bill Tilman became the first westerner to visit Tengboche in 1950, he remarked that, 'lamas [monks] may laugh at our love for climbing mountains, but undoubtedly they themselves take great delight in looking at them.'[12] The Dudh Khosi River we had followed most of the way from Lukla climbed north up to the Gokyo Valley, where a series of picturesque lakes nestle beneath Cho Oyu's enormous South Face. To the north-east the Imja Khola Valley continued towards Everest.

We had a spare afternoon and I fancied a bit more of a leg stretch, so I decided to go for a short walk up a hillside behind the teahouse. This slope stretched all the way from the relatively balmy climate of Tengboche at 3,800m to the dramatic silver-saddled snow peak of Kangtega. At 6,685m it would have taken me a bit more than an afternoon to reach its summit, so I contented myself with aiming for a little shoulder about 400m above me.

But as it happened I couldn't even reach that. As I climbed, the patches of snow around me became thicker and thicker and merged into one, until it became clear that to reach the shoulder I would need to climb through them. Imagine that – climbing through snow! This was supposed to be an easy walk. I looked below me and realised with alarm that a slip would not mean sliding on my backside down to Tengboche, which would have been rather fun, but off to the side, down a precipice hundreds of metres high to the pine forests far below. I lacked an ice axe to arrest my fall because in those days an ice axe was as familiar to me as the cockpit of a Twin Otter aircraft. All I carried was a rough stick hewn from a rhododendron tree, which an enterprising teahouse owner had sold me in the Annapurnas. My little afternoon pootle was feeling more like a mountaineering expedition, so I turned round, not even sure whether I'd cleared the magic 4,000m mark.

I was determined not to be defeated. Back at the teahouse I managed to interest John in my expedition, and the following morning two of our Sherpa guides, Shyam and Nima, agreed to escort us up to the rocky shoulder. I was astonished when, upon reaching the modest snowfield which had turned me back the previous day, they continued not upwards through the snow, but sideways on a short traverse to an area where the snow thinned. All the while they used their ice axes to cut footsteps for me and John to follow, and as we looked down we could see the Ludlow ladies and our other companions watching our progress from the teahouse. We felt like real mountaineers.

In the end, we didn't reach the shoulder. Shyam and Nima decided there was too much snow, and it would be too dangerous for the two unskilled idiots they were escorting to proceed. But as we sat on a smaller outcrop surrounded by snow, with Tengboche far below and Everest, Lhotse and Ama Dablam towering above the deep valley, we were satisfied enough with our adventure.

'This is the best thing I've ever done in my life,' John said. 'I tell you what, I've definitely got to try and climb Kilimanjaro some day!'

I tried not to show quite as much enthusiasm, but secretly I was as thrilled as he was.

They say familiarity breeds contempt, but I don't know whether this is true with the Himalayas. Many times since then I've sat on a lofty perch beneath mountains far less grand than Everest and Ama Dablam after only a modest scramble, but I've always experienced the same sense of peace, contentment and exhilaration that I felt on that occasion – the feeling of being a true explorer even when you're merely following in the footsteps of others. Something similar draws travellers back to the Himalayas again and again.

Nepal's first genuine trekking tourist was Bill Tilman. Born near Liverpool in 1898, Tilman's introduction to high mountains, like mine, came relatively late in life, but he certainly made up for lost time. He was in his early thirties and working as a plantation owner in Kenya when he read about the climbing exploits of another plantation owner, Eric Shipton. Tilman wrote to Shipton to ask if he could accompany him on some of his climbs. Shipton agreed, and they climbed Kilimanjaro, Mount Kenya, and several peaks in Uganda's Rwenzori Mountains together. Despite Tilman's inexperience, Shipton found him the ideal climbing partner: taciturn, strong, fearless, and able to endure any form of hardship. The pair went on to form one of the great partnerships in mountain exploration, travelling widely through the Himalayas and figuring prominently in the British Everest expeditions of the 1930s.

For most of its history, Nepal remained in isolation behind the natural defences of the Himalayas. While the British were exploring the high peaks throughout their Indian empire, Nepal's borders, containing some of the jewels of the Himalayas, remained firmly closed. But with India gaining independence from the British, and China on the verge of a Communist revolution, the situation changed in the 1940s. Nepal was sandwiched between powerful neighbours and started to make tentative steps to end its isolation. From 1947 several scientists were granted permits to carry out work, and in 1949 Nepal's ruling family, the Ranas, allowed mountaineers in to explore.

Tilman made three treks in Nepal in 1949 and 1950, to each of what are now the country's three main trekking regions. In the first of these he explored the Langtang region north of Kathmandu with a team of climbers and scientists. He hoped to reach the summit of a major unclimbed peak, but after dismissing 7,422m Ganesh Himal as too difficult, he turned back on 6,387m Ganchenpo because the summit snowfield required too many steps to be cut in the snow.

Tilman's sirdar (Sherpa leader) for the trek was Tenzing Norgay, who was by then a veteran of four Everest expeditions. Four years later he would become the first man to reach its summit with Edmund Hillary. Despite his climbing record, he was extremely humble. He doubled up as both sirdar and cook, and Tilman lavished him with praise for having 'a deft hand for omelettes which he turns out nicely sloppy but firm.'[13] Which is useful, because there's nothing you need more on a mountain than a sloppy but firm omelette.

The following year Tilman went to the Annapurna region and explored much of the area that would later become familiar to thousands of trekkers as part of the popular Annapurna Circuit. In what was becoming a familiar theme, his party tried and failed to climb another unclimbed mountain. This time it was 8,163m Manaslu that looked too difficult. While they made a valiant effort on 7,525m Annapurna IV, their attempt on 6,981m Kang Guru seemed set for success after establishing a camp at 6,500m, but after taking four hours to climb a hundred metres because of yet more step cutting, they were forced to admit defeat.

Step cutting (literally, cutting steps in the snow) is a technique I used on my very first mountain climb up Swirral Edge on Helvellyn, and you may be wondering if there was a slightly less tiring method of climbing mountains Tilman could have used instead. To give you an idea what's involved, imagine your staircase was simply a mound of dry earth which required twenty blows with a spade for every step. You would be pretty tired by the time you reached the first floor landing, and that's just three metres above you. Hacking your way up a hundred-metre snow slope at high altitude is an entirely different kettle of fishy dal bhat, likely to leave you gasping like a chain-smoking scuba diver. You would end up wishing there was an easier way, surely?

There was, but for some inexplicable reason, Tilman repeatedly avoided using it.

When Austrian climber Heinrich Harrer made the first

ascent of the North Face of the Eiger in 1938, he needed to cut steps with his ice axe every time he reached a section of steep snow. He had already spent a long day climbing the face and had spent a night up there with his climbing partner Fritz Kasparek, when halfway through the second day he was astonished to look behind them and see 'two men running – and I mean running, not climbing – up it.'[14] The German climbers Ludwig Vörg and Anderl Heckmair had set off up the face the same morning and caught the Austrians up. They had found the easier way up steep snow slopes and were wearing ultra-modern twelve-point crampons.

The ten-point crampon, a grid of metal spikes that can be strapped to the sole of a boot, was invented in its modern form in 1908. Had Tilman worn a pair on his boots in 1950 instead of cutting steps with his ice axe he could simply have walked up. The first personal computer was introduced in 1975, and had I shown a similar lack of willingness to adapt to new technologies I would still be writing these words on a typewriter.

Yet despite their failure to climb a new peak, Tilman's expedition explored a lot of new territory in a region that would become a mountain lover's paradise. By the end of it all Tilman admitted they would 'depart for home, poor in achievement but rich … in memories and in experience',[15] a motto every mountaineer can relate to, and I certainly did.

But Tilman wasn't finished with Nepal. Back in Kathmandu he bumped into two old American friends, Oscar Houston and his son Charles. Charles Houston had climbed Nanda Devi in India with Tilman in 1936, and was one of America's leading Himalayan mountaineers. The Houstons had been granted permission to explore the Khumbu region, which meant they would become the first westerners to view Everest from the south side, and they invited Tilman to join them. Tilman accepted, observing there was 'fun to be expected from seeing Sherpas, as it were, in their natural state'.[16] By this he didn't mean he wanted to see them naked, but that it would be interesting to visit them in their ancestral home of the Solu-Khumbu.

In Tengboche, where John and I had impressed the Ludlow ladies with our epic climb, Tilman was pleased to discover the monks 'had the pleasant custom of fortifying their guests with a snorter for breakfast'[17] (I think he meant alcohol and not cocaine). But for Tilman and Charles Houston the real purpose of the trip was to reconnoitre a route up Everest. They had only two days to do so, and their reconnaissance proved inconclusive.

In 1921, George Mallory looked from the north side down into the narrow valley which approaches Everest from the south-west and named it the Western Cwm. He gave it the Welsh spelling *cwm* rather than the English *combe* because it reminded him of the Welsh valleys he explored during his trips to Snowdonia as a student (though in truth it bears about as much resemblance as the Niagara Falls does to a flushing toilet). The keys to climbing Everest from the south lay in climbing into the Western Cwm, climbing from the Western Cwm up to the South Col – the pass between Everest and its neighbour Lhotse – and finding a route from the South Col to the summit. Although Tilman and Houston discovered a route into the Western Cwm up the Khumbu Icefall, they couldn't say whether the South Col could be reached from the Western Cwm or the summit could be reached from the South Col, and Tilman's friend Eric Shipton would help to answer these questions the following year.

His Everest reconnaissance was to be Tilman's last visit to the Himalayas, the place that made his name as an explorer and left him with many fond memories. But the history of trekking in Nepal was only just beginning.

Now the figure of Colonel Jimmy Roberts enters the story. We have already encountered him leading an expedition to Machapuchare in the Annapurnas. As a Gurkha officer in the British Army who could speak fluent Nepali, he was employed as transport officer for many western expeditions exploring the Himalayas, including Tilman's to Annapurna, and the famous American expedition of 1963 which put the first American Jim Whittaker on the summit of Everest. These experiences led him to believe the mountains of Nepal should be accessible not just to elite climbers, but all lovers of mountains. In 1964 he set up a guiding agency called Mountain Travel Nepal, and advertised in the American travel magazine *Holiday* for a guided trip to the Everest region in the spring of 1965, costing $15 a day with all expenses included.

Whether it was accident or design that caused him to advertise the trip as a guided *trek* rather than the more commonly used *walk* (in the UK) or *hike* (in the US) is not known, but it certainly made the trip sound more exotic. The word *trekking* has been used by the adventure travel industry ever since to describe long-distance walking holidays in remote locations.

Roberts's first clients would have been no surprise to me after my first visit to Nepal: three elderly American ladies. The trip was a success. He proved that you don't need to be a superman to travel in the Himalayas, and I for one am eternally grateful to him for recognising this. Between 1964 and 1974 the number of visitors to Nepal leapt from 10,000 to 90,000, and by 1977 there were at least 70 registered trekking agencies operating in the country. In 2011 there were 730,000 visitors and the Trekking Agencies' Association of Nepal (TAAN), set up in 1979, now has around 800 members.[18]

Some people will probably tell you a three-week trekking holiday in the Himalayas with a group of old ladies from Ludlow isn't much of an adventure, but believe me, it is for some people. It certainly was for me, and when I sat on that rocky outcrop above Tengboche with my new friend John and contemplated Everest's rock pyramid sitting grandly above the Nuptse wall, I knew this was no jam-making holiday in the Cotswolds to raise funds to repair the church roof. This was a real adventure, and I wanted more of it.

I realised it might be my one and only chance to experience the wider world before I was sucked back into a desperate existence of nine-to-five corporate drudgery, squeezing the soul out of me and flushing my sense of wonder down the toilet bowl of corporate sewage.

To put it another way, I didn't want to go back to work just yet.

No sooner was I back home in London than I was rummaging through trekking brochures and browsing websites for my next trip. John's words as we sat on that rocky outcrop had ignited a spark of ambition in me, but at that stage Kilimanjaro, the highest mountain in Africa, still sounded incredibly difficult. It seemed a big step up from teahouse trekking with grandmothers. I looked up trekking grades on the websites of adventure travel companies, and discovered that Kilimanjaro (or 'Kili', as I was learning to call it) wasn't quite in the *bear-gryllsian* grade, but it was easily *brian-blessedonian* – another new adjective that, among other things, meant behaving in a larger-than-life way. I needed to progress from my *moderate* trip, which had been rather more moderate than I anticipated.

I chose the Huayhuash Circuit around a small remote

mountain range in the Peruvian Andes called the Cordillera Huayhuash (pronounced *why-wash*, which coincidentally, is many a trekker's motto). It was a two-week guided camping trek with full logistics provided by a local Peruvian company, including food and kitchen crew, mules and muleteers to carry our kit, English-speaking guides and a western leader provided by our UK tour operator. It promised to be a little tougher than my teahouse trek in Nepal, crossing seven high passes over 4,500m as it completed a full circuit of a range which included six snow-capped mountains over 6,000m.

For me it offered another attraction. It was the place where Joe Simpson's book *Touching the Void* was set – a story which made my teahouse trek in the Himalayas look like a stroll through a shopping arcade wheeling a pram with polka-dot balloons tied to the back. I didn't mind, though; I didn't need to have an experience reminiscent of *Touching the Void* to feel like I had been on an adventure, any more than I needed to record all the episodes of *Strictly Come Dancing* to watch when I got back.

In 1985 Joe Simpson made the first ascent of the West Face of 6,344m Siula Grande, the second-highest peak in the Cordillera Huayhuash, with his climbing partner Simon Yates, but got into a spot of difficulty on the way down. A short way below the summit he fell and broke his leg while descending the North Ridge. He slid down the mountain head first on his back, and only came to a stop when his good leg became tangled in the rope above him. He was at an altitude of 5,800m, and still had a long descent down a steep snow face and across a glacier to his base camp at 4,500m.

Yates lowered him down the face rope length by rope length, but their descent came to an abrupt halt when Simpson slid down an overhang and found himself dangling in mid-air. In a precarious position, and a few seconds away from being pulled off the mountain, Yates was only able to save himself by snatching a knife out of his rucksack and cutting the rope, freeing himself of the dangling burden beneath him.

It might have ended there for Simpson, but it didn't. When Yates cut the rope, Simpson had only about fifteen metres to fall to the glacier below, but unluckily for him there was a yawning crevasse directly beneath him. He landed on a ledge a short distance inside, but he was unable to climb back out with his broken leg. When Yates reached the bottom of the headwall he took one look into the dark abyss and realised Simpson must be dead, so he continued on his way.

With no hope of rescue, Simpson abseiled deeper into the crevasse until he saw a narrow shaft of daylight and realised there was a passageway back to the outside world. He crawled up a short ice ramp and found himself on the surface of the glacier. Frostbitten, exhausted and badly dehydrated, he crawled for three days back to base camp, not knowing whether Yates would still be there when he arrived. On his hands and knees, covered in blood, shorn of all dignity and needing a pee, he found it easier to wet himself than go to the trouble of unzipping his trousers. He knew he was back in base camp when he noticed an unpleasant smell and realised he was lying down in the place they used as a latrine. Luckily Yates was still there, and Simpson survived to write one of the great survival stories of mountaineering literature.

I was hoping my trek wouldn't be anything like that. Just in case I was in any doubt, the map I bought in Huaraz, the nearest town to the start of the trail, carried the following warning message:

*Climbing and hiking in remote mountainous regions such
as the Cordillera Huayhuash is dangerous; if you are not
convinced read* Touching the Void *by Joe Simpson.*[19]

On the first day of the trek I learned a little more about
the *swelling of the brain tissue* at high altitude my trekking
guidebook had promised me before I went to Nepal. In fact,
I was given an unusual practical demonstration. We learned
that our first campsite at the village of Llamac would be
sited on the school football pitch, so we bought a ball in
Huaraz in case anyone was feeling energetic enough for a
kick-around. We pumped it up and stored it in my blue
duffle bag to be carried by one of the mules, but as things
transpired I was lucky that particular mule managed to
make it to Llamac without shitting itself in terror and
galloping over a cliff. When I opened my duffle bag in
Llamac I discovered the football had exploded due to the
pressure differential between the air inside the ball and the
thin air of the high-altitude Cordillera.

And at that stage we were at only 3,000m. If that kind of
thing was also happening to my brain tissue, by the time we
reached the highest pass of the trek at just over 5,000m I
would be needing some sort of close-fitting helmet to stop
my head exploding. Or perhaps I should make a small
incision in my skull to release the pressure gradually; I was
starting to feel the health advice section in my guidebook
was wholly inadequate.

But in many ways I was pleasantly surprised. It was my
first experience of a long-distance high-altitude camping
trek, and I had a lot to learn. We started to settle in to a
routine which made the whole camping experience feel like
luxury. Every morning at six o'clock we were woken up with
bed tea brought to the porch of our tents. My tent-mate
Brian, a soft-spoken Shetlander, was always up before me,

and I would wake each morning and peer out of my sleeping bag to see him reaching over with a steaming mug of tea. We packed our things before breakfast to give to the muleteers, then headed to the dining tent for more tea, coffee, cereal and eggs. By the time we finished breakfast, the muleteers had packed away our tents and were already on the trail. We generally left at 7.30 and finished our day's walk at about three in the afternoon, settling into our tents which had invariably been erected by the muleteers by the time we arrived. We assembled in the dining tent at four o'clock for tea and biscuits. I was pleasantly surprised to find there were tables and chairs. After tea, some stayed in the dining tent playing cards or Scrabble, while others returned to their tents to read, write up diaries or snooze. We ate at seven o'clock and were mostly settling down to sleep again by nine.

We had a toilet tent about two metres square, in which a small pit had been dug in the grass. After we finished we sprinkled a couple of handfuls from a pile of earth to hide our deposits – the equivalent of a flush. It would be a few more treks before I became comfortable with squat toilets. With practice, a hole in the ground becomes as straightforward to use as an ordinary sit-down western toilet, but at that stage I was still having to hold on to one of the metal tent supports in order to avoid falling over. I was afraid that a particularly nasty fall would result in me pulling the whole tent over and giving my companions an early morning surprise when they woke up and saw me sprawled in a heap on the edge of camp, with my underpants round my ankles.

With all these comforts at my disposal I was free to walk at a leisurely pace and appreciate the scenery, which proved to be very different from the mountains I had experienced in the Himalayas. Rather than passing through many different climate zones as the altitude changed, as I had in Nepal, the majority of the Huayhuash Circuit kept at a constant 4,000m or above, on some days rising as high as 5,000m to cross a high pass before descending again.

The Cordillera Huayhuash sits on the main South American continental divide. While everything to the west drains into the Pacific Ocean only a hundred kilometres away, everything on the eastern side drains into the Marañón River, a principal tributary of the Amazon, and ultimately reaches the Atlantic Ocean 5,000km away. This leads to contrasting climates on each side. The east is a good deal wetter and comprises treeless high-altitude grasslands known as *puna*. Much of this scenery reminded me of the Highlands of Scotland, with rolling grassy hillsides peppered with rocky outcrops, frequent mist and rain and the occasional snow shower. There were even a few damp bogs to cross, though these were quite unlike Scottish bogs due to the profusion of *tsampa* cushion plants. These tiny plants grow only about a millimetre a year, and bond firmly into rocky green carpets which could be crossed like stepping stones. The scenery on the western side was similar but the climate much drier, with bogs replaced by the occasional quenual (or *polylepsis*) tree, supposedly the highest-growing tree in the world, sometimes perching on steep rocky slopes at 4,800m.

What made the Huayhuash truly beautiful were the turquoise glacial lakes nestling in every valley at the feet of dramatic towering ice peaks. It's a comparatively young mountain range, formed by plate collision about sixty million years ago. In geological terms this means the mountains have not had long to erode, and are characterised by knife-edge ridges and fluted walls of ice. Because the trek completed a circuit of the whole range, we were able to see these striking peaks from all angles – when the clouds lifted, at least.

The Cordillera Huayhuash was first explored by the German geologist Wilhelm Sievers in 1909 while he was looking for the source of the Marañón, and the peaks were first climbed in 1936 during a combined scientific and mountaineering expedition by the Austrian Alpine Society. Climbing wasn't on my radar in those days, and even after I became a mountaineer, difficult technical peaks like these were well beyond my capabilities. It was the trekking and the scenery I came for, and my first taste of expedition life. Most of my companions were more experienced trekkers than I was. Nearly all of them had trekked the Annapurna Circuit and had come to the Huayhuash because it offered a more remote trekking experience. While the Annapurna Circuit contains villages all along the route, with teahouses rarely more than an hour apart, the Huayhuash is for the most part a wilderness, with only four villages on its fringes, two of which were bypassed by the trekking circuit.

Seasonal herder's huts, or *chozas,* peppered the landscape, where families move for several months of the year to tend livestock and catch fish in the mountain streams. Most of these were deserted when we passed by, and the ones that were inhabited could be spotted long before we reached them by herds of alpacas grazing on the grasslands nearby. From a distance these woolly llama-like creatures resembled giant long-necked sheep.

Not all of the group were high-altitude trekkers. We had a pair of retired Scottish hill walkers called Rob and Johnny who had climbed all 283 Munros (peaks in Scotland 3,000ft or more in height). We called them the *Munroistas,* and Rob explained it had taken him 'fooourrrty fooourrrr yearrrs' to complete them.

Johnny was by far the most memorable character in the group for the simple reason that he kept falling over. Not that he was ever hurt. Each time he just got back up, dusted himself down and continued as though it were the most normal thing in the world – which for a 67-year-old man it certainly wasn't. The first couple of times it happened I was quite shocked, and offered a hand to help him up and check he was all right. Eventually I became used to it happening and just ignored it, but some of his falls were so comical it was a struggle to keep myself from laughing.

The first of these occurred as we were descending from Punta Cuyoc, the highest pass of the trek, down a steep and tricky scree slope with many loose stones underfoot. When the worst of it was over, I heard a rumble behind me and turned round to see him rolling down the slope in a nasty fashion. It was worrying for those of us watching, but Johnny seemed unconcerned. Later on I was walking behind him along a gentle traverse when I saw him slip. He tried to arrest his fall but finished up sitting in a bush beside the trail. This would have been fine had there been anything behind the bush to stop him falling through it, but unfortunately there wasn't, and his posture became gradually more reclined until he ended up executing a backward roll, flying out of the bush and down the mountainside. All this happened in slow motion – rather like Wile E Coyote pursuing Roadrunner off a cliff – and I could do nothing to prevent it as I met his gaze and observed the helpless expression on his face.

On another occasion I was stepping over some awkward rocks when I heard an almighty crash behind me and turned to see him sprawling around on the ground between boulders. He arose, sporting some impressive cuts and bruises, but insisted he was absolutely fine.

He saved his very best until the end. We spent the last night of the trek back on the football pitch in Llamac, and we'd managed to obtain some beer. I was carrying a bottle in each hand when I followed him out of the dining tent, so again I could do nothing to help when he slipped and grabbed the two flaps of the tent door as he started to fall backwards. He tried to pull himself forwards using the flaps, but was leaning so far back that all he succeeded in doing was lift the tent up bit by bit. As I watched these two forces struggle with one another I thought he would tip the whole thing onto its side, along with all the tables and chairs inside it, but eventually he accepted the inevitable, let go of the flaps and allowed himself to sink gently onto his backside. I'm ashamed to say I had drunk a lot of beer by that stage in the evening, and I was quite unable to suppress my roar of laughter.

Some of us had picked up bottles of rum in Lima for the princely sum of eight Peruvian Soles, or about $2.50, but we were having to ration it to last the trip. When a young couple called Roy and Helen announced they would be hosting a quiz night on our rest day in the Quebrada Sarapococha (otherwise known as *Joe Simpson Valley*), we realised we were going to need a couple more bottles. Luckily our Peruvian guide Pepe had a plan. The village of Huayllapa lay just twenty minutes off the trail, and as he and I were slightly quicker walkers he suggested the two of us could slip away and do a booze run.

But the mention of alcohol aroused interest. When the day came, six of us dropped down the steep track to Huayllapa – which anyone who has seen the TV show *The League of Gentlemen* will recognise as the Royston Vasey of the Cordillera Huayhuash. The very first building we came to had a blue-painted door with an anatomically exaggerated naked woman scribbled in chalk. We were convinced it must be the local brothel and moved quickly on. The village square contained a satellite dish so large it would function effectively as Peru's early-warning system in the event of a nuclear attack from Ecuador. Two drunk trumpeters were playing badly to a line of twenty schoolchildren, who immediately stopped what they were doing to cry 'caramelo, caramelo' as we passed (apparently most *gringo* tourists hand out sweeties).

Shops weren't very evident, but Pepe found one. It didn't advertise itself as a shop, and it felt like we were entering somebody's front room, but it clearly was one: shelves were jam-packed with stationery, batteries, groceries, soft drinks and, bizarrely, a harp. When Pepe asked for rum, an old lady pulled out a dusty old bottle of home brew from underneath the counter and started unscrewing the cap. Not wishing to be poisoned with much of the trek still to complete, we politely declined and turned to leave. But the entrance was now blocked by, it seemed, every child in Northern Peru, and it took some time to extricate ourselves.

We eventually found what we were looking for in another shop, but as we were leaving the narrow main street we encountered a man driving a bull. He was gesticulating frantically, and most of us ran a short distance down the road to hide round a corner, but a young medical student called Andy decided to stand nonchalantly in the gutter. This would have looked as cool as Marlon Brando smoking a cigarette at the South Pole had the bull not stopped beside him and shaken its horns as it pawed the ground. He was stricken with terror, and we thought his eyes were going to pop out of their sockets. Fortunately the bull thought better of it and moved on, but not without a peal of evil laughter from its owner.

It was an interesting morning. When we were back on the picturesque and peaceful trail I wondered if I had dreamed it all. A closely contested quiz took place that evening in Joe Simpson Valley, with *The Alpacaholics* eventually conceding a narrow defeat to *Touching the Vodka*.

The following day we walked up the Quebrada Sarapococha, a long glacial valley extending into the heart of the Cordillera Huayhuash, clutching our copies of *Touching the Void*. We were going to see the West Face of Siula Grande and the glacier Joe Simpson crawled along for three days with a broken leg. It was the ultimate mountaineering disaster tour, and could only have been improved had we lowered ourselves down his crevasse and felt its yawning chasm echo around us like a black hole of death.

We climbed steeply from our camp then gradually ascended the gently sloping western side of the valley on a bank of dry grass strewn with sharp and irregular boulders. It was a hot day, and we stopped for a break near the foot of the moraine at the snout of the glacier. While we sat and nibbled at our mid-morning snacks, our trek leader, Carey – who had been carefully studying the photos in *Touching the Void* – suddenly cried out.

'Look, we're at Siula Base Camp!' she said, pointing at a giant shoe-shaped rock not fifty metres away from where we were sitting.

In *Touching the Void* there is an iconic photograph of Joe Simpson's crumpled body lying in a heap at Simon Yates's feet as a quartet of muleteers pack away their camp beneath a large overhanging boulder. The boulder was so distinctive there could be no doubt we were sitting right beside it – and this was the moment when disaster tourism started to become tacky. After taking turns to pose for photographs beside the boulder, I suggested to Roy and Helen they recreate the original for their family album. Helen drew the short straw and lay down in a patch of donkey droppings while Roy stood over her like a playground bully gloating at his victim (years later, and unabashed, Roy contacted me to ask for a copy of the photo to show at their wedding).

We continued up the valley, and ahead of us the

staggering ice-fluted faces of Yerupaja and Siula Grande floated into view. A glacier, streaked and dark from rocks strewn on the surface, spilled down before them. We were on a grassy shelf above the glacier, and now that we knew the precise location of his base camp we had a real impression of the distance Joe Simpson must have crawled. There's a strange contradiction between the risks he and Yates must have taken to complete this impressive first ascent, and the tremendous will to live Simpson possessed to get back to safety. Lesser men would simply have curled up and died, yet most of us would never have chosen to be there in the first place. It's a great story though, and if mountaineering-disaster tourism ever catches on Joe Simpson deserves some credit.

Mark at the distinctive rock that was Joe Simpson's base camp,
appropriately attired in a cotton T-shirt advertising his local beer

The crowning glory of the Huayhuash Circuit, Laguna Jahuacocha, was saved till last. We descended a narrow dale to emerge above a beautiful east-facing garden valley, with the serenest emerald lake embracing its top end. A wall of ice crowned by two soaring mountains rose above it all: on the left the tapering 5,870m wedge of Rondoy, and to the right the dramatic twin towers of Jirishanca at 6,094m. The view was spectacular enough, but the valley also contained an abundance of bird and plant life. Gnarled and ancient quenual trees climbed up the valley sides, and the shores of the lake were a tangle of reed beds. While puna ibises probed the shallows with their long curved beaks, Andean geese swooped across the water. We had passed through some remarkable scenery over the previous few days but this was the jewel in the crown of the Cordillera Huayhuash, and if it weren't paradise enough a young family in a herder's cottage on the shores of the lake was selling bottles of Cristal lager.

We were supposed to have a rest day at Laguna Jahuacocha, but not all of us were quite as able to relax as others. Rob and Johnny had precisely the right idea. They heard the pools of the clear mountain streams spilling into the lake were a good place to catch trout, and decided to spend the day fishing. Andy took it a stage further, and decided a day spent watching them fish would be even more relaxing, though with hindsight I suspect he may only have done so because he was hoping Johnny might fall in.

Brian and I opted for a short walk, but made the mistake of following behind our two guides Carey and Pepe in the misguided belief they knew where they were going. We walked along the shores of Laguna Jahuacocha and beyond, where the trail rose to a higher glacial lake behind a steep bank of broken grey moraine. This lake was called Laguna Solteracocha, and it was as bleak as Laguna Jahuacocha had been idyllic. It would have been a good place to stop, and a pleasant stroll back to the campsite would have made for a satisfactory spot of exercise on our rest day. But Carey and Pepe were already high above the northern side of the lake, making their way up to a pass at the top of a large scree-laden hillside. We couldn't help ourselves and continued after them, but the path wasn't clearly defined, and they were going so quickly that we had to run to keep up. Running up a steep scree slope is rather like going the wrong way up an escalator – only the faster you go the more rapidly the terrain gives way beneath you. I was starting to understand what the contestants felt like running up the travelator at the end of the TV show *Gladiators*.

But then, as now, I discovered that a tiring climb is nearly always worth the effort. At the top of the pass we looked down into the valley we had walked through on the second day of our trek, and with it came the realisation that we had circled the entire mountain range. To our south we now had a new angle on Yerupaja. It was no longer a sheer face of fluted ice but a tented triangle, almost climbable – almost, but not quite. One of the joys of a trek which circumnavigates a mountain range is that, like a Hindu god, every mountain can have a dozen different guises depending on where you stand to gaze.

Back at our campsite we were treated to the traditional Peruvian cookery technique of *pachamanca,* or *pot-of-the-earth,* otherwise known as underground baking. It looked like an easy way to cook: heating a pile of rocks over a fire, chucking all the food onto the rocks and covering everything with soil.

'Johnny, why don't you pop the fish on now?' Andy said as they started to throw on the soil.

There were a few loud guffaws and Johnny looked hurt. Apparently their day of fishing had been a bit more restful than they'd hoped.

It was an interesting meal, and everything was cooked in

about half an hour. I would try it at home, but it would make a hell of a mess of my kitchen.

It was with a tinge of regret and a great deal of satisfaction that we left Laguna Jahuacocha the following morning, knowing that our trek was nearly at an end. It was certainly one of the most beautiful locations any of us had ever been to, and most of us knew we would never clap eyes on it again. But over the years I have returned to many of these beautiful places, and perhaps one day I will visit the idyllic lakes and mountains of the Cordillera Huayhuash once more.

Beauty is reason enough, but the Huayhuash Circuit also served another purpose for me. My teahouse trek in Nepal had been far too moderate. This had been a good step up: we had camped for fourteen days in a remote landscape, crossed seven high passes and climbed above 5,000m, and it hadn't been too difficult at all.

I was ready for the next step: a high-altitude summit.

3 A HIGH-ALTITUDE SUMMIT

In Ernest Hemingway's short story *The Snows of Kilimanjaro*, about a man who lies in a cot moaning at his wife as he dies from an infected scratch picked up on safari in East Africa, the frozen carcass of a leopard found near the summit of Kilimanjaro is used to symbolise immortality by rising above the mundane.

Kilimanjaro was to be the first of several *trophy hunters'* mountains I ended up climbing. Until then, everyone I met on treks actually enjoyed trekking. Not that surprising, you're probably thinking: why would anybody spend several weeks trekking in remote mountains if they didn't enjoy it? But for many people, climbing Kilimanjaro is all about enduring splitting headaches and appetite loss for a week, forcing down ropey food, struggling to squat over a smelly hole in the ground while experiencing acute diarrhoea, monotonously putting one foot in front of the other for hours on end, and vomiting into a volcanic crater. Many of them don't even like walking and can't abide camping. They're so exhausted by the time they reach the top they can't even remember what it was like up there; they have no intention of doing anything like it ever again, and yet they have no regrets about putting themselves through the ordeal.

For heaven's sake, why?

We can do worse than look to Hemingway for the answer. He begins his short story with a reference to the carcass of a leopard that was found close to the summit. He points out that no one has explained what the leopard was doing up there.

Don't bother reading the story if you're expecting him to give the answer, but I think we can take it as read the leopard wasn't up there to enjoy the scenery. The main character of the story is a writer, and the plot alternates between the writer's wistful reminiscences about the interesting events he never immortalised in his writing, and his unpleasant behaviour toward his kind and loving wife, whom he blames for his decadent and wasted life.

The leopard Hemingway mentions in the opening paragraph is not a figment of his imagination, but was actually found in 1926 by an English doctor called Donald Latham on the crater rim at a place now called Leopard Point (you don't say!) The following year a German missionary called Pastor Richard Reusch found it again and cut off a piece of its ear to keep as a souvenir, but by the early 1930s it had disappeared. Leopard Point is at an altitude of around 5,700m, well above the height you might expect to find any living creatures, and it's natural to wonder why the leopard was there. For Hemingway, this question wasn't important, but the very fact of its presence gave the leopard a certain immortality. To put it more bluntly, by climbing Kilimanjaro it had become the most famous leopard in Africa.

There have been many silly ascents of Kilimanjaro. In 2014 a Swiss mountain guide ran to the summit and back in 6 hours 42 minutes. An 87-year-old once climbed it, as did a 7-year-old boy. The broadcaster and travel writer Nicholas Crane cycled up it, and there is a story of a man who walked all the way to the summit backwards only to discover somebody else had done exactly the same thing a few days earlier. Following the example of many charity marathon runners, perhaps the bravest ascent was by Douglas Adams, author of *The Hitchhiker's Guide to the Galaxy*, who once climbed Kilimanjaro dressed in a rhino outfit to raise money for the charity *Save the Rhino*. Now call me a coward, but if there's one thing worse than being gored to death by a rhino then it's probably being humped to death by a rhino – an eventuality which I would say is considerably more likely climbing Kilimanjaro than, say, running the London Marathon.

Perhaps some of these people enjoyed climbing the mountain, but it's also likely some of them hated it. It doesn't matter. They all had their reasons, whether it's being the first, the fastest, the oldest, the youngest, to get material for a book, to fundraise for charity or raise awareness. The one thing all of these ascents had in common was the participants weren't primarily doing it because it sounded like a nice place to go for a holiday. It's certainly true a great many people, and probably most of us, climb Kilimanjaro for the enjoyment, but there are an awful lot who don't.

This is a theme I would encounter often on my journey to Everest, and one that I would end up having to defend myself against. At its most innocent the accusation is that you are climbing the mountain for the sense of achievement alone; it makes you feel good about yourself. At its more cynical the accusation is that you are climbing it for the *bragging rights*. On a mountain like Kilimanjaro this might manifest itself in the many charity trekkers who hope to raise more money for their charity by climbing Kilimanjaro than they would by, for example, walking 200km along their local canal towpath. On a mountain like Everest it manifests itself in the professional mountaineers who raise money from corporate sponsorship, and the motivational speakers who acquire a certain kudos from climbing Everest that they don't by climbing a mountain nobody has heard of. In the case of Everest it has become a much more emotive issue, but more about that later.

I was near the beginning of my journey when I arrived on Kilimanjaro, and unaware of many of these undercurrents. I may have had a bit of it myself; I really wanted to get to the top and didn't want to come home saying I hadn't made it. I was yet to learn the lesson that failing to reach the summit is part and parcel of mountaineering, and sometimes there's nothing you can do about it. But it was also true I was really enjoying my trekking, and quite capable of doing something more strenuous. I was expecting Kili to be tough, but I expected to enjoy it as well.

Kilimanjaro is one of the most prominent mountains in the world, a gigantic solitary volcanic cone rising above the plains of Tanzania just south of its border with Kenya. It has three main summits, including the jagged rock crown of Mawenzi and the gentle hillside of Shira, but it's the giant cone of its middle summit, Kibo, that is the goal of all trekkers. The highest point on its crater rim, 5,895m Uhuru Peak, is the highest point in Africa. The mountain is 80km long and 60km wide; 4,565m Mount Meru, 60km away, is the only nearby mountain that comes close to it in size.

You would think a mountain this distinctive would be obvious for miles around, and sure enough on a clear day it can be seen from Mount Kenya 350km away, possibly the longest line of sight between two places anywhere on Earth. But for much of the time Kilimanjaro is wreathed in cloud and can't be seen at all, even by people standing right underneath it. My father once went on a wildlife safari in Amboseli National Park in Kenya, right on its northern slopes, and said he didn't see Kilimanjaro at all the whole time he was there.

Although the Greek astronomer Ptolemy made reference to a great snow mountain in the region of the Equator as early as the 2nd century AD, for a long time its character seemed so unlikely travellers doubted whether it existed. By the 19th century explorers and missionaries were beginning to penetrate Africa's interior, and the first European to see Kilimanjaro was a German missionary called Johannes Rebmann. In 1848 he was leading a caravan to spread the word to the Chagga people of East Africa when he saw 'something remarkably white on top of a high mountain'.[20] He asked his guide, who said the white he could see was *coldness*. The Chagga word *kibo* means *snow*, and it's now the name of Kilimanjaro's main summit. When Rebmann reported the discovery of snow near the Equator in that well-known scientific journal the *Church Missionary Intelligencer*, many people didn't believe him.

We now know the reason there's snow on Kilimanjaro has nothing to do with its latitude but because of its altitude. Gases are warmer at high pressure; and conversely air is much colder at the lower pressure of extreme altitude.

My concern wasn't the cold temperature, because I knew I could address this by dressing up more (by which I mean warm down clothing rather than a bow tie and dinner jacket). I was uneasy about the lower air pressure which can lead to altitude sickness. Kilimanjaro was a natural step up from the Huayhuash Circuit, but I still wanted to make it as easy for myself as I could. Although I thought I would be fit enough, the altitude was an unknown. Punta Cuyoc, the highest pass on the Huayhuash Circuit, was 5,030m, and I had been fine; but Uhuru Peak, the top of Kilimanjaro, was

5,895m and represented a large gain in altitude.

The best defence was to get pre-acclimatised by climbing another mountain first – then by the time I reached Kili the altitude would be less of a problem. So in October 2002 I signed up to climb Mount Kenya.

Mount Kenya in – wait for it – Kenya, is the second highest mountain in Africa. Like Kilimanjaro, it's a giant isolated volcano that rises thousands of metres above the East African plains, but in many ways it's a very different mountain to its taller neighbour. Where Kilimanjaro is dominated by the huge cone of Kibo rising above a large plateau, and can be walked up easily, Mount Kenya is a much more intricate mountain with many peaks, valleys and lakes. Its two main summits, 5,199m Batian and 5,188m Nelion, are both serious rock climbs, only for the most able technical climbers. While its third summit, 4,985m Point Lenana, can be walked up, many of its other summits are rocky scrambles. As well as having many peaks clustered towards its middle, Mount Kenya has a number of U-shaped valleys spreading out from the centre like spokes of a wheel, and some of the trekking routes involve crossing from one to another over broad ridges. If 19th-century readers of ecclesiastical magazines were sceptical about snow on Kilimanjaro, Mount Kenya may have caused them to question their faith. The Equator passes right through it.

Another missionary, Ludwig Krapf, was the first European to see Mount Kenya in 1849. The marvellously named Sir Halford Mackinder was the first to climb Batian in 1899, and our old friend Eric Shipton was the first to climb Nelion in 1929.

Mackinder had a bit more to contend with than the modern traveller. In one respect he was lucky: the section of the Uganda Railway from Mombasa to Nairobi had just been completed the previous year, cutting down his journey time significantly, but otherwise it wasn't so easy. His caravan had to flee Nairobi earlier than anticipated after an outbreak of smallpox, and was charged by a rhino a few days north. His two European guides, Cesar Ollier and Josef Brocherel, had cause to use their ice axes sooner than expected cutting down vegetation to pass through the Kikuyu forest to the south.

But his biggest problem was with the local guides. To say he didn't entirely trust them would be like saying Lance Armstrong's urine sample was somewhat misleading. Mbuthia was a 'wizened Kikuyu chief with avarice and cunning written in every line of his face', while Mudui of Katumba was 'a man of singularly deceitful and repellant countenance'.[21] Magonia was 'a notorious drunkard', while Kamanga was 'a pleasant man, but of no strength of character'. His most reliable guide, Kereri was 'pleasant and intelligent, but of slippery character', which meant it was necessary 'to verify everything by the cross-examination of more stupid persons'.[22]

Mackinder's suspicions weren't entirely without foundation. An early porter strike had to be checked by a display of firearms, and Kereri not unreasonably vanished when the time came to meet a chief who had kidnapped several members of his family. Two Swahili members of their caravan were later killed during an ambush by rival tribesmen and one of their camps was looted during the night.

Other problems were of their own making. After climbing above the jungle and ascending into the boggy grassland on Mount Kenya's lower slopes, they were enchanted by the weird plant life of phallic giant lobelia spikes growing up to six feet in height, and the green-tousled tree groundsels, with their twelve-foot hollow trunks that fell over if you leaned on them. While they were surveying the grassland, one of them carelessly discarded a match, thinking no harm would be done in the damp conditions. They were standing on a peat bog, which promptly ignited. By the following morning there was a giant column of acrid smoke, and to escape they had to run through it for fifty metres holding their breath.

They eventually climbed the mountain on their second attempt, taking two days to reach the summit of Batian from the south. On the first day they crossed Mount Kenya's largest glacier, the Lewis Glacier which spills down between Point Lenana and the two main summits, then climbed an arête on the lower side of Nelion. On the second day they ascended the Darwin Glacier using steps in the ice they had cut on their earlier attempt, and climbed a rocky rib coming down from the western corner of Nelion. They discovered a smaller glacier below the Gate of the Mists, the saddle between Batian and Nelion, which they named the Diamond Glacier on account of the hardness of its ice. It took them three hours to cut steps up it, but from the saddle it was a short scramble to the summit of Batian. They arrived there too late to get a decent view. The Gate of the Mists lived up to its name and from the summit they could only get fleeting glimpses of the land below. Mackinder described the summit as a stunted tower arising from ruins, and crowned by low turrets.

My objective wasn't the fearsome rock peaks of Batian and Nelion, but the much gentler Point Lenana which would be a good warm-up for Kilimanjaro. It was first climbed in 1899 by one of Mackinder's companions, Campbell Hausburg. Its most daring ascent was made in 1943 by two Italians, Felice Benuzzi and Giovanni Balletto. Finding themselves interned in a British prisoner-of-war camp on Mount Kenya's slopes during the Second World War, they contrived to escape for a couple of weeks, make an attempt on Batian, bag Point Lenana as a consolation, then return to camp and hand themselves back in for the remainder of the war.

I wasn't imprisoned in camp, but I arguably had the next closest thing when I found myself sharing a tent with a former semi-professional rugby league player called Mark Dickson, who was built like a rhino, and whose conversation alternated between razor-sharp wit and disconcerting frankness. He also seemed able to drink prodigious quantities of alcohol. In addition to a good pair of boots, one thing I was going to need on this trek was a sense of humour. Mark was on gardening leave – which meant he had quit his job, but instead of asking him to work out his notice period and run the risk of upsetting anyone, his employer had frog-marched him out of the door and sent him home on full pay. I soon understood why.

Our view from the grounds of the Naro Moru River Lodge, where we stayed on our first night, must have been very similar to the one Eric Shipton gazed upon when he arrived in Kenya as a 21-year-old, fully intending to spend the rest of his life as a tea planter.

The whole northern horizon was filled with a gigantic cone of purple mist. The cone was capped by a band of cloud. Above this band, utterly detached from the Earth, appeared a pyramid of rock and ice, beautifully proportioned, hard and clear against the sky. The sun, not yet risen to my view, had already touched the peak, throwing ridge and corrie into sharp relief, lighting here and there a sparkling gem of ice.[23]

With hindsight it's easy to glimpse Shipton's future career as one of the great mountain explorers in this statement, and conclude that tea planting wasn't really his thing. Mark was equally impressed, but rather less romantic.

'That's a big fucking mountain,' he said.

Later that morning we stopped at a signpost marking the Equator, by the side of the road to Nanyuki. We got out of the bus and watched a man claim to demonstrate the Coriolis Effect using a basin of water. As he drained the water through a plug in the bottom of the bowl we watched it circle in an anticlockwise direction; then he refilled the bowl and walked twenty metres to the south, where we watched it drain clockwise.

Mark was laughing. 'That's a clever magic trick,' he said. 'Of course, it's got nothing to do with the way he's rotating the bowl!'

We approached Mount Kenya by the Sirimon Route, which passes through jungle and bamboo forest by a dirt track on its northern side. I chatted with one of our local guides, Francis, who pointed out silver-haired and bushy-tailed colobus monkeys swinging in the trees high above us, and the occasional green splash of the Jardine's parrot flying past.

'There was much to fill the heart in the days that followed,' Shipton remarked as he set out from Chogoria on the eastern side of Mount Kenya. I felt a little of the same sense of anticipation, and I have often felt it since on the first day of a trek or expedition; though unlike him I didn't have the same admiration for 'the sight of the naked Masai porters, erect and lithe, swinging along in front of us'.[24]

We reached the top of the forest that first afternoon, then for two days we trekked through the unusual open landscape Mackinder marvelled at (and set fire to) during his first ascent of Batian more than a hundred years earlier.

Above the forest the lower slopes of Mount Kenya were covered with long grass, giant heathers and the strange giant lobelias erupting from the grass like enormous natural fertility symbols. Beyond the brow of the hill the twin towers of Nelion and Batian were the only summits visible until halfway through the second day, when gradually we became aware of the peaks and valleys around us. On the third day we crossed one of these hillsides into the broad Mackinder Valley, and the landscape became stranger still, with isolated giant groundsels standing sentinel like scarecrows.

Mount Kenya's history is full of stories of climbers ascending in glorious sunshine only to find themselves in thick mist on the summit, and we were to experience this characteristic weather pretty much every day. The morning would begin bright and sunny, but by early afternoon it invariably clouded over. There were frequent showers. Fortuitously, I had the good sense to try and keep up with Mark as we were ascending the Mackinder Valley. We managed to reach the shelter of Shipton's Hut at the top end of the valley just as the heavens opened, but the rest of the group were drenched like a bath of wet towels when they arrived half an hour later.

Shipton made two attempts on Mount Kenya from where we camped on the north side. On the first, with Percy Wyn-Harris in 1929, they were trying to make the first ascent of Nelion, but took one look at the North Face and decided it was unclimbable. They then tried to reach the Gate of the Mists via the north wall of Batian, but were stopped by an overhanging bulge just beneath the summit, and retreated to look for Mackinder's route from the south. Shipton returned with Bill Tilman the following year, and the two great mountain explorers completed the first traverse of both summits via the West Ridge, an intricate route that involved skirting two giant rock towers (or *gendarmes*) jutting up from the ridge.

We nearly needed two attempts on the mountain ourselves, even though we were only aiming for lowly Point Lenana. We spent the afternoon huddled in the shelter of the hut and began the card games which each day were to become increasingly violent. As the afternoon became colder the rain turned to snow, and long before nightfall the campsite was covered in a two-inch carpet of white. Our trek leader Simon told us if the snow continued all night we would have to abandon the climb. My main focus was Kilimanjaro, so I wasn't too disappointed, but Mark felt otherwise.

Mount Kenya's two rocky summits of Nelion and Batian rise above the giant lobelias and grass landscape that Halford Mackinder's party set fire to

'I came here to climb both,' he said.

This time Mount Kenya's reliable weather patterns worked in our favour. In the evening the sky cleared, and by the next day it looked like we had another beautiful morning ahead of us. The snowfall only made our ascent of Point Lenana more picturesque, although we weren't to experience the same quality of scenery as the early explorers. In 1929 Shipton described a glacier-capped Point Lenana, but there's no longer a permanent ice cap on Mount Kenya's third highest peak. He foresaw this when he climbed the West Ridge with Tilman. They crossed an ice sheet called the Joseph Glacier, which was named after one of Mackinder's Courmayeur guides. 'Cesar has been immortalised by a similar slab of ice further to the east,' Shipton remarked, before going on to explain that, 'immortalised is perhaps hardly the right word, for I fancy all the glaciers of Mount Kenya are dying'.[25]

He wasn't wrong. Although the Joseph Glacier still survives, a report by the US Geological Survey concluded that seven of the eighteen glaciers present on Mount Kenya when Mackinder surveyed it in 1899 had disappeared by 1986, and the total area of the mountain covered by glaciers was only 25% of what it was then.[26] Some scientists have predicted Mount Kenya will be free of ice within thirty years. It's a similar tale for other glaciers in Africa – a sad story for everyone except perhaps readers of the *Church Missionary Intelligencer*, who may feel vindicated for their scepticism, albeit two centuries late.

It took us only four hours to reach the top of Point Lenana from Shipton's Hut, on a rocky trail past the pleasant Harris Tarn, which nestled in a small combe. By the time we reached the summit at ten o'clock it had already started clouding over, and we couldn't see the African plains below us, never mind Kilimanjaro 350km away. The red rocky triangle of Nelion dominated the view across the Lewis Glacier, obscuring the slightly higher Batian behind it.

Predictably we were overtaken by a snow storm as we

descended to Mackinder's Camp in the Teleki Valley to the east. Impatient with the slow pace as we descended, I started running down a giant scree slope, only to find Mark sprinting past me, determined not to be beaten. We hurtled down the slope, but I realised I didn't have a chance of keeping up with an ex-professional rugby player. I ambled into the hut at a more leisurely pace a short while after him, knowing I could avenge myself at cards later in the afternoon.

Mackinder's Camp in the Teleki Valley offers one of Mount Kenya's classic viewpoints, with the twin-humped bulk of Batian and Nelion dominating the scene, and the dramatic rock needle of Point John rising up to the right. Most photographs also include a giant groundsel in the foreground just for good measure and to leave you in no doubt which mountain it is. Just in front of Point John is a smaller tower of rock known as Midget Peak which was the scene of one of Shipton and Tilman's more nerve-jangling adventures. Tilman knocked himself out during a fall, and ended up dangling on a rope below an overhang in an incident reminiscent of Joe Simpson on Siula Grande. This time Shipton was belaying from above, and was in a rather more secure situation than Simon Yates. He didn't have to resort to his knife, but lowered the unconscious Tilman until the rope reached its maximum length and then began descending, using the friction of the rope against the rock to prevent himself falling. To his relief he hadn't descended very far before Tilman came to rest on a ledge and the rope slackened. By the time Shipton descended to the overhang and peered over the edge, a decidedly groggy Tilman had begun to come round.

We had one more day of travel on Mount Kenya, descending its western Naro Moru Route through an infamous section of mud known as the *Vertical Bog*. I quite enjoyed it, mainly because I managed to stay on my feet, and had fun watching other people fall over every few seconds. I don't know what the Swahili is for *fuck*, *shit* or *bollocks*, but by the end of the descent our Kenyan guides would certainly have known the words in English. Back at the Naro Moru River Lodge that evening we washed away the mud and enjoyed a few bottles of Tusker beer in the peaceful garden as we anticipated the greater climb ahead of us.

Two days later we found ourselves at the village of Londorossi on the western slopes of Kilimanjaro. Our campsite was on a football pitch, but a more potholed and rutted surface I had never seen in my life. It had a submerged dirt track running through the middle of it, and was fine for a campsite, but less good for football. On the equally rutted adjacent pitch a very important match was taking place between Londorossi village and a team of government officials. It was so important there were around 500 people on the touchline, and none of them seemed remotely interested in the western trekkers who had turned up to camp. Most of the spectators were wearing Arsenal shirts, but if you're wondering who won, I have no idea.

The next day we discovered the dirt track through our campsite led right up to the Shira Plateau, halfway up the mountain at 3,500m. There are seven main routes on Kilimanjaro; five of these are ascent-only routes, one is a descent-only route, and one, the Marangu Route, is both a descent and ascent route. In 2002 the Marangu Route, which approaches the mountain from the south-east corner, was disparagingly known as the Coca Cola Route, because it was by far the most popular and many people believed it was also the most boring. But our Shira Plateau Route must surely have made Coca Cola taste like red wine. The Machame Route, which approaches from the south, has now caught up with the Marangu Route in terms of tourist numbers. It passes through primeval cloud forest with striking crested turacos fluttering through the trees, and is known as the Whiskey Route. By contrast we seemed to have chosen the Stagnant Water Route.

We completely bypassed the cloud forest, instead striding through an immature conifer plantation on the fringes of the village. The road was so dusty it was much better to walk at the front so you didn't have to breathe in the dust churned up by the people ahead of you. I did my best to keep up with Mark as he pushed the pace to stay ahead of the group; and as we strode ahead confidently, our Tanzanian guide Andrew tried in turn to keep in front of us because, well, he was a guide and that's what guides are supposed to do. This resulted in everybody walking more quickly to keep up with him, and our trailing dust cloud grew ever bigger. Those at the back found they had acquired Hitler moustaches, with dust clinging to the suncream on their top lips.

Poli, poli, the Swahili for *slowly, slowly* had been a common cry throughout the trip whenever our guides were leading too quickly. A *poli, poli* pace is essential when you've come up from sea level and are in the process of acclimatising, but *poli, poli* was nowhere to be seen that day. It's not a good idea to rush so quickly at high altitude, and had we not been pre-acclimatised from Mount Kenya, then it's likely we would have suffered more than just an awkward resemblance to evil dictators.

At last the conifer plantations merged into the moorland zone of shoulder-high heather and St John's wort. Gradually this thinned out and gave way to scrubby dry grassland as we arrived on the Shira Plateau, a huge plain stretching between Kibo and the western summit of Shira. A fine day had become overcast, and Kibo was hiding in cloud. The road eventually petered out and we camped in the middle of the plain, where I managed to find what seemed to be the only bit of river with water in it, and cleaned off all the dust that clung to my skin.

In 1889, roughly 113 years before we camped there, a German geologist called Hans Meyer stood on the Shira Plateau and looked up at Kibo. He saw an enormous glittering ice cap more than 2,000m high covering the entire volcanic cone and extending all the way down to the plateau. His feeling of satisfaction must have been great. Along with his companion, the Austrian Ludwig Purtscheller, he had just completed the first ascent of Kilimanjaro all the way to its highest point, and he was nearing the end of what had been a great feat of African exploration. His journey had been a difficult one, and he thoroughly deserved to bask in his achievement.

When he set off from Zanzibar on the coast of East Africa a few months earlier, the few Europeans who had tried to climb Kilimanjaro since Rebmann first saw it in 1848 had experienced very little success. At least six attempts had been made, and Meyer himself made three more. His first in 1887 was almost successful. He reached an altitude of nearly 5,500m before encountering a fifty-metre wall of ice barring the way up Kibo, and realised he would need alpine climbing equipment to tackle it.

He returned the following year, but had only just started out from the coast when he and his companion Oscar Baumann were captured by the Arab Sheik Bushiri and clapped in chains. They were eventually released after paying a heavy ransom, but the expedition was ruined. All their equipment and the goods intended to last a caravan of 230 men for two years were lost.

Most people would have given up at this point, and resolved never to return to Africa. Personally I prefer to avoid countries where I might get taken hostage, and I'm yet to find a travel insurance policy that would cover equipment for 230 men. But Meyer would doubtless be puzzled at the security even our most intrepid adventurers require in the 21st century. He had peered into volcanoes in Indonesia, penetrated jungles in the Philippines, sailed up rivers in China, and made his way up the east coast of Africa. He wasn't going to let the small matter of a spot of mild terrorism in Tanzania thwart his ambition to climb Kilimanjaro.

Meyer and Purtscheller travelled from the coast at the head of a large caravan which included a guide, six Somali guards, two Swahili headmen, and an unspecified number of porters, who were sufficiently well paid they were able to subcontract their services by employing porters for the porters.

The life of leader of a large caravan crossing relatively unknown territory was very much to Meyer's liking.

It was Africa once more – the red arid soil, the dry thorny bush, the parched grey-green grass, the pure dry air, the cooing doves and chirping cycadae of our promised land of travel and adventure. Once more I was in the midst of the familiar hum and bustle of the free caravan life.[27]

A similar experience can be felt by the modern-day trekker starting out on a large camping trek with local guides, kitchen crew and porters.

Meyer started his ascent of Kilimanjaro from Marangu in what was clearly the very first ascent by the Coca Cola

Route. His experience in 1887 convinced him of the need to establish both a base camp and a high camp. The base camp was placed just above the forest zone, and Meyer, Purtscheller and their attendant Mwini moved up to high camp on the Saddle, an area of high-altitude tundra between the 'white ice-helmet of Kibo and the jagged crown of Mawenzi.'[28] Here Mwini stayed for several days looking after the camp while Meyer and Purtscheller made their ascents and exploration of the mountain.

It took them two attempts to climb the white ice-helmet up the Ratzel Glacier east of Stella Point, the place where modern-day trekkers climbing from the south arrive on the crater rim. On the first occasion they set out at 2.30am and ascended scree slopes until they found a firmer ridge to the east. By 8.15 they were already above the height of Mawenzi, and could see a mist creeping up from the forest zone towards the Saddle. They reached the start of the ice cap at around 5,500m. It was 10.30, and while Purtscheller was able to put on 'climbing-irons' (crampons), Meyer had only a pair of strong nailed boots, which meant they had to ascend the glacier using good old-fashioned step cutting. The ice was hard as glass and it took twenty strokes of the axe to cut each step. They crossed a section of crevasses using fragile snow bridges, and at 12.30 they arrived at the bottom of the last wall of ice at an altitude of 5,700m. The final part of the ascent passed through an area of ice pinnacles, and at two o'clock they burst onto flatter slopes and found themselves looking down into a giant crater – the first westerners ever to do so (though, as Hemingway pointed out, not the first representatives of the animal kingdom).

They realised they were not on the summit of the mountain, as several higher points lay further around the crater rim, but they didn't think they would be able to get up and back down safely in the remainder of the day. They decided to return to camp and come back another time – a wise decision. It took them two hours to descend the precarious ice slopes, and they crossed the Saddle in a state of exhaustion in the gathering twilight. It was pitch black when they reached camp at seven o'clock after nearly seventeen hours of climbing, but Mwini was waiting for them with a roaring fire, hot tea and brandy.

Their climb taught them that they needed to arrive on the crater much sooner in the day. After resting for two days, they climbed up to a convenient hollow between rocks at 4,700m, where they bivouacked for the night and started out at 3am. Not only were they better acclimatised from their previous climb, but they knew the way and found the steps they had cut still in place. They were much quicker, and reached their previous high point on the crater rim before nine o'clock.

They reached the highest of three humps on the rim at 10.30, planted a German flag, and named it Kaiser Wilhelm Peak in honour of their emperor. It was renamed Uhuru Peak in 1961 when Tanzania gained independence – appropriately enough, since *uhuru* is Swahili for *freedom*.

Back at camp that evening Meyer expressed his sense of satisfaction at their successful ascent.

We were in a very amiable frame of mind ourselves, and, notwithstanding all the toil and trouble my self-appointed task had cost me, I don't think I would that night have changed places with anybody else in the world.[29]

It's a universal sentiment that has been shared by thousands of successful summiteers since.

In one important respect, the mountain Meyer climbed in 1889 no longer exists. From where I stood on the Shira Plateau there was little evidence of the 'glittering ice-cap' he described in his book *Across East African Glaciers*, a title that would make no sense for any modern book about Kilimanjaro. All I could see were two small wisps of white on the very top of Kibo, like unsightly strands of grey on a thick head of raven hair. The thousands of trekkers who climb Kili every year believing it to be a walk up might be worried by Meyer's description of the ascent. The step cutting and crossing of crevasses and snow bridges give the impression of a true alpine climb.

But the Ratzel Glacier which Meyer and Purtscheller climbed on their first ascent no longer exists. Like those on Mount Kenya, Kilimanjaro's glaciers are shrinking frighteningly quickly. Meyer returned there in 1898 and was shocked to discover the glaciers which gave them so much trouble had receded a hundred metres in just a few short years. The statistics are almost unbelievable. According to Meyer's rough survey, there were $32km^2$ of glacier in 1889. By 1912 this had shrunk to less than $20km^2$. In 1953 there were just $11km^2$, and by 2003 less than $4km^2$.[30]

Scientists currently believe the main reason Kilimanjaro's glaciers are disappearing so quickly is not because global warming is causing the ice to melt more quickly, but because there is less snowfall replenishing them. It's a trend which has been going on for centuries as part of the Earth's natural climate cycle, but it has also been accelerated by human activity. In the last century there has been much deforestation to make way for fields and houses, causing the air to be less humid, and resulting in less precipitation.

Kilimanjaro's environment had been altered beyond recognition by human activity, and I knew I was making my own small contribution. In a dull moment during his trek in

1889, Hans Meyer totted up the number of westerners who had been to Kilimanjaro since it was discovered by Rebmann in 1848. It was forty-nine, and he could name them all. By the end of 2007, more than 40,000 tourists were visiting per year.[31] There could be little doubt its status as a trophy mountain was helping to fuel this growth, but my feelings changed as I climbed.

It's easy to see the negative consequences. Much of the landscape was man-made. We had spent the last day walking up a dirt track wide enough for a vehicle and arrived at a campsite with a green tin hut for the national park rangers. Had I been trekking along the Marangu Route, I would even have been staying in huts instead of camping. Bill Tilman got a bit snotty about these things when he climbed the mountain solo in 1933, objecting that the local climbing club had erected signposts on the crater rim to label each of the summits. He called them *tin insults*. He also saw a herd of twenty-seven eland (a type of antelope) on the Saddle. Meyer climbed the lower slopes of the mountain by following elephant tracks, but the chances of seeing large mammals on Kilimanjaro these days are about as high as hearing poetry recited on the pitch at Old Trafford. This isn't to say they've been exterminated, but if I were an antelope I reckon there are places I'd rather be than a hill with 40,000 humans plus their guides and porters traipsing over it every year.

Many armchair travellers would look at this and say it has to be stopped; it's probably what I would have thought myself before I climbed it. It's easy to be critical when you have no interest. But climbing the mountain gave me a better understanding of the issues, and I could see there were many positives. Trekking on Kilimanjaro is tightly regulated. You have to pay a daily national park fee just for being there, and an additional fee to stay in a hut or campsite. It's illegal to climb solo, and every climber and trekking agent has to hire local guides, cooks and porters. This money gets spread around and benefits a great many people. Reducing the number of tourists would have a big impact on people who are already extremely poor.

Of course, we have a responsibility to minimise the impact of our trekking, but if you're going to dress up as a rhino and do something silly for charity, there's no reason you shouldn't climb a mountain in Tanzania rather than run around tarmac in Central London for twenty-six miles.

For the next two days we crossed the Shira Plateau and began to skirt the southern side of Kibo. We reached the end of the plateau on the first day and stayed at Shira Huts, a campsite in an elevated location looking west over a sea of cloud. A short distance away, the dark trapezium of Mount Meru rose above the cloud like an island. Only occasionally when hill walking had I experienced the morning valley fog known as a *cloud inversion*, when I climbed above a thin layer of cloud and saw it in the valley below me. It was always a satisfying experience, but this felt different. I didn't know whether it was the same phenomenon, but I had a real sense of elevation, like I was high in the sky and had climbed above the clouds themselves, rather than a thin layer of fog.

As we climbed the next day, the scrubby grassland of the plateau gave way to alpine desert. Giant heath bushes were replaced by weird rock sculptures including a black tower of lava and strange mushroom-like rock formations. Kibo had become a forlorn wall of dark rock towering over us to the left, with a clutch of sorry-looking glaciers hanging from its crown. We descended back into the vegetation zone to spend a night at Barranco Camp, looking out over a lush valley of giant groundsel.

Here our violent card games reached their zenith. We arrived early, and spent most of the afternoon in the dining tent playing a marathon game of Pig, the card-playing equivalent of musical chairs. It involved grabbing a plastic cup off the table at the end of the game. There was one more player than cups, so the slowest person to react ended up cupless. The most violent incident involved me, the ex-rugby player Mark, and Jeremy, the youngest member of our group. Mark was quickest to react at the end of the round, but in the act of picking up his cup he flicked the other one behind him. This meant he was now sitting between us and the cup – a less than convenient position. Jeremy scrambled over me to reach it, and I had no option but to push Mark off his chair and dive over him. The three of us sprawled into a heap on rocky ground, two of us wrestling over a single cup, and the other one trapped underneath. All the other card players had jumped out of their seats and were roaring with laughter.

I don't recommend starting a climb nursing cuts and grazes from an afternoon of card madness, but in some ways the game our trek leader Simon introduced me to the following day was a more rash one to play on the eve of a summit attempt. A wall of dark rock called the Barranco Wall rose for 300m above Barranco Camp. From below it looked nearly vertical and extremely daunting, but a well-trodden path zigzagged up it, and the scrambling was sufficiently easy that it made Crib Goch on Snowdon seem like the North Face of the Eiger. Simon certainly didn't feel we'd be in any danger climbing it.

He called his competition the *Hundred Game* and the idea was to climb without using our hands. We started with a hundred points, and every time we put a hand down we lost one (a point that is, not a hand). It made the ascent a good deal trickier, but not impossible, and it certainly helped to improve my balance. I arrived at the top feeling pleased with my 92 points – until Simon told me he'd once scored 96 on Crib Goch.

It was still a fine day when we reached the top of the Barranco Wall. Above us Kibo looked forlorn with its diminishing glaciers dripping from shelves like cream on chocolate pudding, but Mount Meru rose majestic to the east above a veil of cloud. We continued hiking through a sparse landscape of giant groundsels standing at wide intervals. We descended into the Karanga Valley, a narrow cutting in the side of the mountain that offered a last opportunity to fill our bottles with running water. We were surprised to find the porters had erected our ugly blue dining tent beside the river, and we stopped for a long lunch. We were still in the land of sparse vegetation, and beyond our valley the trail rose up a steep slope of knee-high rocks and waist-high heather.

The afternoon was miserable. To our left Kibo disappeared into cloud and the terrain became increasingly barren. The groundsels were gone, and the heath and tussock grass soon followed. The last remnants of vegetation in that high-altitude desert landscape were the clumps of tiny silver flowers known as *everlastings*. A film of rain clung to us as we entered the clouds, and by the time we reached Barafu Camp at 4,500m, the launch pad for our summit attempt, it was raining heavily.

It was much the busiest campsite we stayed in, and sprawled up a band of rock for a hundred metres or more. We were right at the bottom of camp, and would have a longer summit day, nearly 1,400m of ascent in total. The longdrop toilets were unpleasant and needed emptying out. There was a story about a woman who fell in to one of the pits and died. Although there are deaths on Kilimanjaro every year, this seemed a terribly melancholy way to go, and not very heroic.

Summit day on Kilimanjaro was my first experience of climbing at night; in fact, it was my first experience of a lot of things. We left at one o'clock in the morning. Our guide Andrew led the way through the sprawling campsite by the light of our headlamps. The first hour was the easiest as we plodded *poli, poli* up a rocky trail that zigzagged up a ridge, but altitude sickness played on my mind. I rigged up my hydration bladder by tucking it into a layer of clothing against my chest. This was a collapsible water bottle with a drinking tube, enabling me to drink as I walked. There was a theory that it made you drink more frequently, therefore making you less likely to suffer from dehydration and altitude sickness; but the tube could freeze in cold conditions, causing you to drink nothing. To counter this I coiled up the tube and stuffed it down my front. It seemed to work, but we had to stop every hour anyway for everybody else to drink, and I was always bursting for a pee. *The Three Cs* had been Simon's mantra throughout the trip: clear, comfortable and copious. If my pee was all three of these things I could be happy I was staying hydrated and helping myself to acclimatise. While I could be sure about the third C, the darkness really didn't help me with the first, and I was doubtful about the second. For various reasons I've stopped using hydration bladders now, and am content to get a little dehydrated on summit days.

After an hour we stopped in the darkness and Simon looked at his altimeter. He said we were at 4,800m, which meant we had ascended 300m, but there was still a long way to go. The next three hours were the worst. I could see nothing but the dark zigzag of the trail ahead of me, broken only by the dapple of stars overhead and the jagged silhouette of Mawenzi behind us to the right. There was little

I could do but count out the minutes stretching into hours as I concentrated on the repetitive task of putting one foot in front of the other, angling my way up the slope. It was painful, and a mental battle as much as a physical one. Every step of the trail was a struggle for oxygen, and it was hard to gauge our progress. When we stopped for a drink I looked across at the silhouette of 5,149m Mawenzi to see if we were above it, but its outline didn't seem to change. Simon's altimeter came to the rescue, and he told me we were ascending at 200 metres an hour. As we climbed higher, my one relief was that I wasn't experiencing the high-altitude headache I had assumed would strike at any moment.

The next time we stopped Simon had dropped too far behind to give an altimeter reading, but Andrew produced a welcome flask of hot water. When we continued I realised the picture had changed. I looked behind me and saw the sun peeping above the jagged outline of Mawenzi. After four hours of trudging monotonously in the dark I could see how close we were to the top. A soft orange glow spread around Mawenzi's crown and revealed a carpet of cloud far beneath us. Gaps in the cloud provided tantalising glimpses of a green landscape even further below. These were sights I had never experienced before, not even in my imagination. From a state of determined uncertainty I was suddenly in the position of knowing for sure I was going to make it.

A wave of satisfaction came over me and I realised I was no longer tired. When athletes talk about *second wind* they don't mean the side effects of a tin of baked beans, but a new burst of energy just as they are becoming overwhelmed by fatigue. I had mine now as Andrew pointed out Stella Point just above us, our entrance to the crater rim. It was about a hundred metres away, but I was no longer thinking of a hundred vertical metres as half an hour's trudge. We were nearly there and I still had plenty of energy left. I turned to

Mark and assumed he would be just as happy.

'Come on then,' I said. 'I'll race you. Last one up's a sissy.'

'You can race if you want,' he replied with less enthusiasm. 'I'm fucked.'

He could have produced a pair of ladies' panties from his trouser pocket and put them on over his Gore-Tex and I would have been less surprised. The ex-professional rugby player, much the strongest of us all, who was impossible to keep up with and could drink twice as much as anyone else was ... well, you heard what he said. I was walking second-in-line behind Andrew, and hadn't been paying attention to anyone else. Now I looked around me and could see they were all exhausted. Every one of them wore a haggard expression, and I realised my excitement must be as welcome as Ozzy Osbourne at a fundraising evening for the Bat Conservation Society. I followed Andrew up to Stella Point, and the others staggered onto the crater rim behind us. One lady in our group was in tears, and Jeremy walked towards the crater to throw up.

I was expecting it to be boring up there compared to Mount Kenya, but it was amazing. The crater was enormous, and we looked down to the barren dry earth inside it, the red glow from the morning sun just starting to fade into brown. I could have been on the surface of the moon, so alien was the landscape, but for two white smudges of Kilimanjaro's dying glaciers painted across the opposite side of the crater. The lunar brown of the crater floor contrasted sharply with the pale cerulean of the sky. It was like no landscape I had ever seen. Behind us, clouds hung in the Saddle between Kibo and Mawenzi like a carpet of whipped cream. It almost looked like there was a vast ice cap down there, but I knew there couldn't be. Beyond Mawenzi's jagged crown a layer of cotton wool clouds stretched to the far horizon. The scene far exceeded my expectations, and it was hard to believe I was really there.

But I wasn't *there*, at least not yet. I looked back into the crater. To the left I could see the rim curve round and rise up to a high cliff, which Andrew said was Uhuru Peak. It took us another forty minutes to reach it. I walked behind the others and watched Mark stagger like a drunk in front of me. I had seen him walk like that after a few bottles of Tusker beer in the Naro Moru River Lodge, but never on the trail. He was by no means the worst of them. As we approached the summit I put on a burst of speed and caught up.

It may sound like I'm gloating – *look at me, I'm so much fitter than everyone else* – but that's not my intention at all. Many times since then I've been so exhausted on the summit of a mountain I haven't been able to appreciate my surroundings. I was expecting to feel like that on Kili; so many people said it would be the hardest thing I had ever done in my life. It was higher than I had been before and I was sure I would have a headache. But I felt fine, and I was amazed.

Looking back, I need not have been so surprised. I was trekking for most of the year, which meant I was mountain fit. Each time I returned to high altitude I acclimatised more quickly, and was generally in better shape. I was benefitting from recent treks.

The summit of Kilimanjaro had a home-made sign made from four old planks and two bits of bamboo, which looked like somebody's granddad had hammered it together in the back of his garage. Written in yellow paint, which probably fell off the back of a lorry, was the legend:

Congratulations: you are now at

Uhuru Peak, Tanzania, 5895m AMSL.

Africa's highest point, world's highest free-standing
mountain

One of world's largest volcanoes. Welcome

A year earlier Mark was sitting behind a desk, and now here he is
beside a home-made sign on the roof of Africa

AMSL, in case you're wondering, stands for *Above Mean Sea Level*, and serves to remind us that in some respects heights of mountains are arbitrary. The sea sloshes around quite a lot and changes with the moon. Somebody decided sea level would be the place we measured heights of mountains from, but they could just as easily have chosen the bottom of the ocean, or the centre of the earth – or perhaps, more usefully, the bottom of the mountain. Had they done this, then what we define as a high mountain would be very different. I had climbed the highest mountain in Africa but what did that really mean? It was a timely reminder that what mattered to me was the scenery and an appreciation of the beautiful natural world around me.

A year earlier I was sitting at a desk in an office, looking at the same confined space for eight hours a day that I'd been looking at every day for years. OK, I moved offices a few times, but the view was essentially the same, and it certainly hadn't got any more exciting. I liked to get out into the country at weekends and walk up hills, and that was exhilarating, but it hadn't prepared me mentally for this.

The bulk of Kilimanjaro's few remaining glaciers were confined to the outer side of the crater rim, and had a curious structure of interlocking columns like a church organ sculpted from ice. Beyond it the carpet of cotton wool clouds was beginning to disperse, providing a tantalising glimpse of the African plains far beneath us. The dark triangle of Mount Meru was no longer floating on air, as it had been throughout our trek, and now I could almost see to its base. When I looked down into the crater I could see the gap in the crater wall just beyond Uhuru Peak known as the Western Breach, best known as the most direct and toughest route to the summit. At the top of the breach the tiny Furtwangler Glacier rested incongruously, a strange chunk of ice lying on a desert lunar crater. When most of this landscape was ice, like it had been in Meyer's day, it wouldn't have looked at all out of place; but now it seemed weird, about to retreat over the edge at any moment, which isn't far off the truth. Beyond the Furtwangler Glacier the land rose again, to what I assumed to be the opposite side of the crater rim. It was only later I learned it was another crater. In fact Kibo contains three concentric craters: the outer oval one I stood on, about 3km long by 2km wide, and the inner one known as the Reusch Crater, measuring 1.3km in diameter. Inside this is an even smaller one known as the Ash Pit, just 140m wide.

When Bill Tilman climbed Kibo solo in 1933 he

descended into the crater to find a bivouac site for the night under a large overhanging rock. Before going to sleep he walked up to the Reusch Crater and looked down into the Ash Pit, where he saw sulphurous fumes rising up from the lip. He took some rock samples, but his claim of seeing volcanic activity was disputed by others who had been there, including the same Richard Reusch after whom the inner crater had been named. His story was convincing enough to persuade the vulcanologist J.J. Richard to climb up to the crater in 1942, and Richard discovered clear evidence that Kilimanjaro was not extinct, but dormant.

Tilman's main concern wasn't that he might get blown to smithereens by a sudden eruption, but the tedious names of some of Kilimanjaro's features: Hans Meyer Point, Kaiser Wilhelm Spitze, Gillman's Point, and the Furtwangler Glacier.

I have not discovered who Gillman was. Hans Meyer …
deserves to be remembered, but whether that can be said of
the fourth name is open to doubt. Furtwangler, I am told,
was the first to use skis on Kibo.[32]

Clement Gillman, incidentally, got as far as the crater rim in 1921, but no further. Kaiser Wilhelm Spitze is now known much more appropriately as Uhuru Peak, and Tilman would doubtless have been delighted to learn that Stella Point was named after the wife of Dr Latham, the man who discovered Ernest Hemingway's leopard.

As for all the bits of Mount Kenya now named after his old mate Eric Shipton, heaven only knows what Tilman thought.

I left the summit long after the rest of my team departed, and caught up with Mark and Andrew at Stella Point. Andrew showed me an alternative trail back to Barafu Camp down a giant scree slope. There's a growing consensus that scree running, where you allow the carpet of loose rocks to slide beneath you and aid your descent as you literally run down a slope, is bad for the environment and leads to rapid erosion. Certainly, on a mountain as busy as Kilimanjaro, which has 40,000 paying visitors a year, you don't need to be Albert Einstein to realise that if everybody runs down, moving a size-ten boot's worth of stones a metre down the slope with every step, eventually all those loose stones will end up at the bottom. I've been on slopes where this has happened, and what remains is a hard surface of sloping rock with a thin layer of dust and tiny pebbles. Imagine yourself walking downhill on tiny marbles and you get an idea of just how treacherous such a surface is to descend.

But I didn't consider any of this when I climbed Kili: all I knew was that scree slopes are great fun to run down and this was the biggest one I had ever seen in my life, nearly 1,400m of vertical descent. In Britain that would be an entire mountain. I took out a single trekking pole to assist my balance, and I legged it. It took just fifty-eight minutes to convert six hours of plodding ascent into a return journey. At no point did I stop for a breather, and I was sure I would be the first back, but just short of Barafu Camp I caught up with Jeremy and we arrived back together. Mark was slowly improving and wasn't far behind us.

We still had a long way to descend that day to our lower campsite on the top edge of the forest zone, so after a welcome mug of tea at Barafu, I left with Mark on the final leg of our summit day. We descended by a trail known as the Alternative Mweka Route (also known as the Kidia or Rau Route) which no longer exists. It was open for about a year to allow parts of the normal Mweka Route to regenerate and recover from the pounding of a thousand feet.

I don't remember very much about our descent, for the

simple reason that Mark had made a full recovery. He was determined to make up for his uncharacteristic summit fatigue with a thorough demonstration of his newly restored athletic prowess. Most of the next two hours involved a gentle descent on a dusty trail through moorland of knee-high groundsel and heather. There were quite a few loose rocks and roots sticking out, and all my concentration was needed to avoid tripping over as Mark hared along like an Olympic walker being stalked by a rhino. There were moments of respite when I heard a stumble in front of me, and looked up to see him staggering like an inebriated gorilla making a last-gasp effort to lunge for the try line with a rugby ball. This happened quite frequently, and I was dying to see him crash into the heather and land in a sprawling heap, but he always made some improbable manoeuvre at the last moment and stayed on his feet.

At last we reached Rau Camp to find our blue tents had been erected while we were absent on our summit bid. Mark disappeared for a moment. I put down my pack and found a comfortable rock to sit on while I looked up at the distinctive cone of Kibo rising above the gentle slopes of heather. It seemed a long way off, and it was hard to believe we had been on the top only a few hours earlier.

'Kilimanjaro or Safari?' Mark said when he returned. We were due to go on safari after our climb, and I was looking forward to it.

'Safari, of course,' I replied. 'I'm not going back up there again!'

But, of course, he was talking about alcohol. *Kilimanjaro* and *Safari* were the two local Tanzanian beers, and Mark had discovered they were selling both at the rangers' hut adjoining the campsite. It was reassuring to see he'd made a full recovery.

We were on our third bottle when Andrew arrived with

the rest of the group.

'Kilimanjaro or Safari?' Mark asked him.

Andrew knew exactly what he meant.

'Safari, of course. I cannot drink my office.'

And what an office he had. An African walking guide might not get paid as much as a digital project manager, but the working environment was a big improvement on a room full of computer screens in Central London. I had only recently started on my travels, but I was learning very quickly that poverty comes in many shades. I spent much of the year living in a tent, wearing the same set of clothes for days on end and defecating into a hole in the ground – but how much more enjoyable it had been than all those years experiencing the comforts of the developed world.

I was no longer a boring city office worker, and felt like I had become a real adventurer.

I expect some of you are thinking, *so you climbed Mount Kenya and Kilimanjaro on a guided commercial trek. Big deal, there's nothing very intrepid about that.*

You're right, and that's precisely the point. I didn't consider myself to be very intrepid, and a year earlier I'd never dreamed of visiting these places. Climbing Kilimanjaro sounded like travelling to the moon, and it was the security of a group trip that gave me the confidence to do it.

I might have felt like I was following in the footsteps of Shipton and Tilman, but my journey was a world away from theirs and still left much to the imagination. Every step of the way I was walking where somebody had been before, and I was in very little danger. By contrast Shipton, Tilman, Mackinder and Meyer were journeying into the unknown, unsure if they would be able to return.

For example, in his account of the first ascent of Nelion with Percy Wyn-Harris, Shipton described an incident where he found a narrow crack in the rock above a sheer drop. The holds were smooth and sloped outwards, and his progress was extremely slow. He didn't like it at all, but he continued onwards because 'the prospect of beating a retreat was even more repugnant than climbing on up.'[33]

The words *burning* and *bridges* spring to mind. Luckily they were able to come back down the same way without as much difficulty, but this was in doubt as they moved upwards.

This is why first ascents of mountains are much more impressive than subsequent ones. While many high-profile *firsts* are nothing more than contrived and over-used marketing devices (we're still waiting for the first gay Ruritanian female with a wooden leg to climb Kilimanjaro), genuine pioneers deserve respect. Shipton remarked upon this after they considered using Mackinder's old route down the Diamond Glacier, a route they really didn't fancy.

I have since repeated the climb several times, and each time I was more amazed, not only that we should have thought of such a desperate alternative, but that we should have regarded the ascent of Nelion as so very difficult. Each step became so engraved on my memory that it seemed commonplace and perfectly straightforward ...

This experience of repeating a climb, the first ascent of which I had made myself, showed me very clearly how it was that mountains in the Alps, which had resisted the attacks of the pioneers for so long and had appeared to them such desperate ventures, should come to be regarded as quite easy. To a lesser extent, too, this illustrates the main difference between 'guided' and 'guideless' climbing.[34]

But let's not forget all things are relative, and even these intrepid explorers were happy to accept outside assistance when it was available. Shipton travelled from Nairobi to Mount Kenya in a lorry, and hired porters to carry his equipment to the foot of Nelion. Thirty years earlier Mackinder had to walk from Nairobi and negotiate with native tribes for safe passage as he travelled through their territory. On the other hand, he was able to travel by train to Nairobi from the coast, and his African staff included ninety-six Kikuyus, sixty-six Swahilis and two Masai.

This insight into the lives of explorers might surprise some people, but they wouldn't be the first. Hans Meyer, who wasn't even able to catch the train like Mackinder, nevertheless needed plenty of help and made this very point after he returned from Kilimanjaro in 1889.

Stay-at-home folks are often greatly exercised to know how the traveller in unexplored countries like Central Africa is able to find his way from place to place; and when you tell them, simply by means of the native paths and the native guides, they assume an air of aggrieved surprise, as if you had done them a mortal injury by mentioning such commonplaces in connection with a region where they have been taught to expect only the marvellous and unusual.[35]

I've never been kidnapped by Arab tribesmen like Meyer, and I hope I never will, but set against this perhaps my contentment to explore the world by the convenience of modern commercial group travel isn't so shaming after all. It certainly never bothered me that in some people's eyes I might be cheating. The important thing was that I was going there at all. The world is getting smaller and it's becoming much easier to travel, but that's not necessarily a bad thing if it means ordinary people like me can visit such extraordinary places.

I still wasn't satisfied, though. I had climbed Kilimanjaro without as much hardship as I anticipated. I certainly wasn't going to let it finish there, but to get up bigger mountains I was going to need some different skills. Kilimanjaro is a trek, and I was still very much a hill walker.

To move on to the next step I had to become a mountaineer.

4 ICE AXE AND CRAMPONS

The year 2002 marked a turning point. I made the transition from office worker and part-time hiker, who headed for the nearest hills whenever he could spare some holiday, to high-altitude trekker who had hiked among the most beautiful peaks on Earth.

It happened because I had the good luck to receive a bonus from an internet startup, which gave me the confidence to quit my job and go travelling. But if any of you are looking at me enviously, and wondering how you will ever be able to afford to follow the same journey, then please don't; I believe it's a journey within the reach of most people fortunate enough to be born in the developed world. Depending on your salary and holiday entitlement it may take longer, but this is not a race, and the longer the journey the more time you have to savour it.

I crammed a lot into that one year, including two long treks in the Himalayas and Andes, and two weeks in Africa. But I didn't need to do it that way. With hindsight it wasn't necessary to receive a large bonus and take a year off to embark on the journey. In 2014 the average annual salary for most countries in Western Europe was over US $25,000.[36] A group trip to Everest Base Camp can cost as little as $2,000 plus flights, and prices are similar for treks in the Peruvian

Andes or an ascent of Kilimanjaro.

Good quality equipment isn't cheap, but it can last for years. A decent pair of hiking boots can set you back $300, but should last three or four years with a lot of wear and tear. My first down sleeping bag cost me over $500, but it was ten years before I had to buy a new one, by which time I had lost count of the number of warm and cosy nights I'd snuggled within it. One trek a year is achievable for many people in the developed world, and after three years they will have made good progress along the path.

For me there was much more to come, but by 2003 I had spent a good chunk of my windfall and was looking for a job, just like any normal person. I would have to continue the journey using only my annual vacation allowance, but there was no hurry, and I had time to save up money again.

In any case, at that point I had other things to worry about which might not be a factor for many of you. When I first started on this journey, I didn't have a very good head for heights. It was so bad that on Swirral Edge my brother described me as a *big girl's blouse,* and on Crib Goch I thought I was going to die. When I saw some rock climbers making their way up a sea stack off the coast of Scotland, I assumed they must be clinically insane. To put it another way, the thought of clinging to a vertical cliff face with a gaping drop below me, nothing but a narrow sliver of rock to put my toes on, and only a slender length of cord tied to my waist for security, had about as much appeal as a night in the lion enclosure at London Zoo.

The correct name for a fear of heights is *acrophobia*, and while it's not ideal for a hill walker, it's a genuine drawback for a mountaineer. Acrophobic mountaineers are right up there with claustrophobic potholers and necrophobic undertakers on the *Times Top 100* list of the world's silliest lifestyle choices. I wanted to climb bigger mountains, but in order to do so I needed to learn a few technical skills – because sooner or later I was going to come across an obstacle too steep to simply walk up. But if I was going to climb steep objects, I also needed to conquer my fear of heights. It wouldn't do to get halfway up a rock face and freeze like a stone. It was time for me to learn how to climb, and gain competency with the technical equipment that came with it.

My first experience of wearing crampons came in early 2003 during a trekking holiday in Patagonia. The mountains in that part of South America are relatively low in altitude but extremely dramatic, rising in a series of rock towers above lakes and glaciers. I wanted to get close to one of the most dramatic, Cerro Torre, a narrow finger of impossibly vertical rock rising above the Southern Patagonian Ice Field, and to do this I had to walk up a glacier for the first time.

It was good weather and the surface of the Torre Glacier consisted of hard, dry ice. This made it easy to walk up, and meant we could see crevasses more clearly and steer clear of them. It was only much later in my journey that I learned how newly fallen snow can hide crevasses and make a glacier more dangerous to cross. We weren't roped together, and walked with trekking poles rather than ice axes, but before we stepped onto the glacier we strapped crampons to the soles of our walking boots to provide grip as we walked up the ice. I found walking in crampons remarkably easy, especially uphill – easier than walking up a similar gradient on normal terrain without them.

Halfway up we stopped beneath an ice cliff on the glacier and did some ice climbing. This involved walking up vertical ice by kicking in the front points of our crampons. We had an ice axe in each hand to drive in to the ice above our heads as we climbed, but I learned that the bulk of the climbing was done with our feet rather than with our arms.

It felt a bit like climbing a ladder, and it was impossible for me to fall off because a harness around my waist was attached to a rope which looped through an anchor at the top of the cliff, and I was held in place using a technique known as *belaying*. One of our guides stood at the bottom and held the other end of the rope using a metal ring known as a belay device. As I climbed he drew the rope through the device, keeping it tight above me, so that if I fell I would immediately be held in place. This gave me total confidence to climb, and my head for heights wasn't challenged because I didn't need to look down. When I reached the top I leaned back and walked backwards down the cliff as the guide gently lowered me by means of the belay. It was my first taste of ice climbing, and I realised I could do it without difficulty.

Not everyone warms to ice climbing. The Scottish mountaineer and writer Tom Patey was alleged to have quipped 'ice is for pouring your whisky on' when asked whether he preferred ice climbing or rock climbing. But most high mountains (and many smaller ones) contain snowfields and glaciers, and if you want to get up them safely you need a technique for climbing these obstacles.

Alpine mountaineering developed in the European Alps throughout the 19th century. The most important piece of equipment was the ice axe, whose predecessor was the shepherd's *alpenstock*. Although it's undergone a few innovations in the last hundred years, it's essentially used in the same way today. For much of the time the ice axe is used as a walking stick, with a spike at the end of the shaft to dig into the ice. The head of the axe consists of two tools: a pick for climbing and arresting in the event of a fall, and an adze for cutting steps. For most of the 19th century the adze was the more important tool, as steps needed to be cut up every steep snow slope, making climbing a lengthy and tiring process.

People have been strapping spikes to their feet to cross snow for hundreds of years. When Mark Beaufoy became the first Englishman to climb Mont Blanc in 1787, in addition to a pole for walking he took with him 'Cramp Irons for the heels of my shoes'.[37] The British mountaineer Oscar Eckenstein is credited with designing the first modern ten-point crampon in 1908, which was made commercially available by the Italian Henry Grivel. Essentially a spiked metal frame that strapped to the bottom of the boot, it revolutionised mountaineering by enabling people to walk straight up snow and ice slopes without having to cut steps. It was a while before all mountaineers adopted them, and we have already seen that Bill Tilman was still struggling with step cutting on Annapurna IV as late as 1950.

In 1929 Laurent Grivel added *front points* to his father Henry's crampons, two horizontal spikes sticking out of the toe of the boot. These enabled climbers to scale steeper sections of ice much more easily, and ultimately led to the birth of ice climbing as an activity in its own right. In the 1960s Yvon Chouinard shortened the shaft of his ice axe and added a curve to the pick, enabling it to bite into vertical surfaces more firmly. Nowadays, some of the more technical ice tools have reverse-curved picks and don't look much like axes at all. They are used in pairs and function as extensions to the climber's arms.

As you can see, if I wanted to become a mountaineer I needed to get myself togged up with lots of new equipment and learn how to use it. One way was to join an alpine skills course where I would learn how to walk and climb in crampons, use an ice axe for ascending and arresting a fall, walk up a glacier roped to other climbers, and rescue a climber who has fallen into a crevasse. But I wanted to learn in an enjoyable way that didn't feel like going back to school, a way that felt more like a holiday than a lesson. Many adventure travel companies offered trips to climb Mont Blanc, the highest mountain in Western Europe, which included enough training for beginners to attempt the climb. These trips were at the higher end of the grading system, but after a *moderate* trek in Nepal, a *tough* one in Peru, and a *challenging* ascent of Kilimanjaro, the next logical step was to try something *bear-gryllsian*. It was time to scratch my paws on a real mountain.

In many ways 4,810m Mont Blanc was an appropriate choice for my first foray into mountaineering. It became the birthplace of modern mountaineering when Michel Paccard, a doctor from Chamonix, and Jacques Balmat, a farmer, reached the summit on the 8th of August 1786. The seeds were sown in 1760, when Horace-Benedict de Saussure, a student at the Geneva Academy, travelled to Chamonix and was so enchanted by Mont Blanc that he offered a reward to the first person to climb it. He hired a guide, Pierre Simon, and they travelled and climbed together in the Alps. Saussure wrote extensively about his travels, and his influence generated a great deal of interest in climbing Mont Blanc. He climbed it himself the year after Paccard and Balmat with a party of seventeen people, including Balmat as guide. Mountain climbing as a hobby and pastime for tourists was born, and Saussure is sometimes regarded as the father of mountaineering.

While Balmat and Paccard undoubtedly achieved the first ascent of Mont Blanc, they gave conflicting accounts and argued over the details, rather like a married couple going through a divorce. Paccard claimed to have led the crucial pitch from the Grand Plateau up to the summit between two ribs of red rock called the Rochers Rouge, but Balmat said he guided Paccard through the more difficult sections. He even claimed to reach the summit an hour before Paccard and went back to fetch him, though observers with telescopes in Chamonix saw them step onto the summit together.

Their feud didn't enhance the reputation of either man. When Saussure climbed Mont Blanc the following year he arrived on the summit at 10.00am and spent the best part of a day carrying out experiments, not leaving until 3.30 in the afternoon. Those were the days when exploration and adventure needed to have a solid scientific purpose in order to be considered valid. This meant Paccard and Balmat could be accompanied by a brass band to the summit, and serenade people across the border in Italy to the tune of the Marseillaise, but without science it would have all the respectability of a policeman in a leotard. When Saussure returned from his ascent in 1787 he received far more plaudits than his two predecessors. Mont Blanc had finally been climbed and the sport of mountaineering was born.

Saussure, Paccard and Balmat all made multiple attempts to climb Mont Blanc before they finally reached the summit. I also failed to climb it at my first attempt in 2003, for entirely unexpected reasons.

My preparation was good. I decided to acclimatise in Morocco by trekking for a week in the Atlas Mountains and climbing 4,167m Jebel Toubkal, the country's highest peak and an easy walk up. It was August, Morocco was hot and dry, even at higher altitudes, and I frequently found myself walking in temperatures in excess of 30ºC. When I returned home, London was enjoying one of its hottest heatwaves on record, with temperatures close to what I endured in

Morocco. I found the humid, sultry conditions oppressive, but there was one consolation: I felt in good shape for Mont Blanc. As long as I learned the basic mountaineering skills in those few days of training at the start of the week, then I should be in a good position to reach the summit. I knew that a week of high winds, cold temperatures and snow might stop us climbing the mountain, but as long as the weather remained warm and sunny then we would surely get up?

I was wrong. Since Paccard and Balmat first climbed Mont Blanc via the Grand Plateau, the easier route for novice climbers like me had become the Goûter Route, over two subsidiary tops north-west of the main summit, the Aiguille and Dôme du Goûter. The main obstacle on the first day is a section of rock scrambling known as the Goûter Corridor which crosses a narrow couloir (or gully) susceptible to rockfall. Climbers usually cross it by wearing a helmet, putting their head down, and running as quickly as they can.

I had a pleasant surprise at Geneva Airport when I bumped into Brian, my tent-mate from Peru, and discovered I would be climbing with him. In Chamonix we met our leader for most of the week, Sandy Allan, a veteran mountain guide from Scotland. He was the first person I ever met who had climbed Everest, and a few years later he would win the Piolet d'Or, mountaineering's equivalent of an Oscar, for his epic ascent of Nanga Parbat in Pakistan by a new route. He bought a round of drinks and sat us down in our hotel lobby for a *wee chat*.

The news wasn't good. The heatwave was causing a lot more rockfall than normal; the ice which usually held the rocks in place was melting. Sandy explained that the couloir on the Goûter Corridor usually threw down fist-sized chunks that could be easily avoided, but this year they were seeing rocks the size of cars and even houses. It was unlikely the situation was going to change in the next few days, and the authorities had taken the unusual step of closing the mountain. We would still be able to do our skills training and acclimatisation on the Mer de Glace and Glacier du Tour, but instead of climbing Mont Blanc at the end of the week, we would drive underneath it through the Mont Blanc Tunnel into Italy, and climb a mountain called Gran Paradiso about fifty kilometres further south.

The following day we boarded a funicular railway up to the Mer de Glace, the largest glacier in the Chamonix area. Its name translates variously as *sea of ice* or *shit ice*, depending on your ability to read spaces. Our training mostly involved ice climbing up a couple of prominent folds in the glacier, and walking up and down on the ice behind our guides as we became accustomed to the feel of the crampons on our feet. We spent the next three days in a region of high glaciers on the France-Switzerland border, staying in mountain huts and practising the skills we had learned. We ascended the steel-blue ice of the Glacier du Tour between the slate-grey rock cathedrals of the Chardonnet and Aiguille du Tour, descended an ice cliff into Switzerland and crossed the wide open spaces of the Plateau du Trient. The following day we scrambled up the rock peak of Aiguille du Tour and looked along the Chamonix Valley to the broad snow mass of Mont Blanc, the mountain we would no longer be climbing.

Although the views were magnificent, and I loved being among the otherworldly scenery of the high Alps, I wasn't a natural climber. The skills came slowly to me, and my poor head for heights was proving an impairment. Our crossing into Switzerland involved descending a vertical ice cliff onto a precipitously steep snow slope whose angle gradually lessened. We were lowered over the vertical section by means of a belay, but once I arrived on the snow slope I began to have problems. Released from the rope I had to descend on my own without falling, and my heart was pounding. I could manage to descend backwards by facing into the slope, securing myself with my ice axe in the wall above me and climbing down using the front points of my crampons, but my descent was painfully slow.

Skills training on the Mer de Glace

One of our guides caught up with me and ordered me to speed up by facing out of the slope and walking down, but as soon as I turned around and saw the drop below me I panicked. I lost control, fell and slid the remaining fifty metres on my backside. This would have been a good moment to practise my ice axe arrest technique, but it was a skill I had yet to learn, and as I was enjoying my impromptu toboggan ride a lot more than my tentative down-climb, I allowed myself to slide all the way to the bottom. I was rewarded by learning some colourful words in French I had never heard before.

I had an even more unpleasant descent the following day, when the same guide started lowering me down another steep ice slope. I quickly realised my harness was badly positioned, causing my entire body weight to rest on my most tender region. Hearing my anguished cries, he stopped lowering after five metres and shouted down the slope.

'Eet is trapped on your bollocks, *oui*?'

'Yes, thank you,' I grunted tearfully.

He shrugged his shoulders and continued lowering. I held my breath and descended for thirty metres until I arrived on firmer ground, barely able to stand. If there's a better method of contraception, then I'd like to hear it.

Squashed testicles is one of the more unusual mistakes for a novice climber to make, but between us we made plenty of the classics during those two days on the Glacier du Tour. A common error beginners make is to trip over their crampons by getting the points of one caught in the straps of the other. A similar mishap occurs if the rope between climbers isn't kept tight while walking roped together. If the person walking behind you follows too closely then the rope beneath your feet can become looped, causing you to trip over it. It's important to keep the rope tight to react quickly if someone falls into a crevasse, as most of us did at least once. We didn't always see the crevasses, and sometimes snow on the edge can be firm for one person but give way for the next. But falling into a crevasse isn't a problem if you're roped together, because others on the rope can hold you in place while you climb out again. I expected our guides to be patient with us while we learned the techniques, but this wasn't their way at all; every time somebody made a mistake a Gallic ear-bashing was the usual reward. I remember thinking it was like being back at school. The last thing you want after suffering the humiliation of falling flat on your face is for some tanned

Adonis to rub your nose in it with a stern lecture.

But we had learned enough to attempt Gran Paradiso, and were more confident climbers when we set out from the Val Savarenche in the Graian Alps of Italy. We had a pleasant hike up 1,000m through forest and grassy moorland to the well-equipped Rifugio Chabod on the flanks of the mountain, which looked more like a grand stone hotel than a mountain hut. At the huts in France and Switzerland we slept crammed together on palettes fifty centimetres wide, and a whole line of people woke up every time one of us rolled over. But here we had proper beds of a girth that would have given an older Elvis Presley a good night's sleep – not that we had much time to rest, and we were up at 3.30am for a night-time start. It's common to make these early starts on glaciated mountains, because many routes become prone to rockfall and avalanche when the sun comes up and the ice starts melting.

The route from Rifugio Chabod climbed across a scree slope before reaching a glacier beneath Gran Paradiso's summit ramparts. Most of the climb was a straightforward glacier walk until we reached a col beneath the summit. Here an aluminium ladder led onto an elevated summit mushroom, where some zigzags up a steep snow slope took us onto the exposed summit ridge. We took our crampons off for the last part, which involved scrambling over rocks with steep drops on either side. It was a test for my gradually improving head for heights, but I tried not to look down. At the summit there was a small statue of the Virgin Mary, which one of our guides found useful as an anchor for lowering his rope team off, allowing them to bypass the queues of people forming on the summit ridge. It was far from a leisurely descent as the sun started to warm the slopes. They rushed us to put our crampons on when we got back to the snowline, and one of Brian's came off as we descended.

Photography is difficult when you are climbing as part of a rope team, because everyone has to stop for you to take a picture. The scenery was too good to miss, and I expected to be shouted at every time I asked our guide to halt, but he understood the need for photos. This seemed to be the only time he was happy to be patient. Once we were off the glacier and out of the area most at risk from rockfall, the urgency ended and we made a more leisurely descent. It wasn't Mont Blanc, but I had climbed my first alpine peak.

My week in the Alps had served a purpose, but it hadn't possessed the magic of my treks in Nepal, South America and East Africa. This might seem surprising, because the alpine environment provides mountaineers with a landscape very different from anything seen by those who don't climb. I remember getting my first view of an ice cap when I walked up a rocky trail to Paso del Viento during my trek in Patagonia, and looked out across the Southern Patagonian Ice Field. I couldn't imagine there would be anything exciting about looking across a large featureless sheet of ice that would in any way compare to Patagonia's dramatic needle-like mountains of Cerro Fitzroy and Cerro Torre, but I was wrong. It wasn't just the boring sheet of white that I imagined – it contained many hues of blue and grey, which shimmered as the shadows of clouds moved across it. It was never smooth, but cracked, streaked and dappled with rocks and pebbles. It stretched to the far horizon, but in many places its level surface was interrupted by rocky outcrops and vast mountains rising above the plain. It was like nothing I had ever seen before, and it was the highlight of the trek for me, even more than the piercing rock spires.

There were moments when I had a sense of this during my three-day exploration of the highlands of ice on the Glacier du Tour, but they were only fleeting, and for various reasons I didn't appreciate the experience as much as I should have done. It's harder to immerse yourself in the scenery when you're concentrating on new techniques, swallowing your fear, making mistakes and getting shouted at. To make matters worse I always felt like we were being rushed, with never an opportunity to relax and enjoy the moment. Last of all I found the Alps to be a scarred landscape, with ski lifts, cable cars and electricity pylons on every hillside, and busy roads nestling in the valleys. While it's sometimes nice to finish a day out in the mountains with a cold beer in a lively bar, I realised it was the remoter parts of the world I enjoyed the most.

I was longing to return to the Himalayas, and Nepal offered my next logical step. On the way home from my first Nepalese trekking holiday with the Ludlow ladies I remember reading an article in the Qatar Airways in-flight magazine by someone who had just climbed Mera Peak, a 6,476m mountain south of Everest. Most of his ascent was up a steep snow slope wearing crampons, and at the top he needed to complete a short ice climb, but from the summit an unbelievable mountain panorama stretched before him which included five of the six highest mountains in the world. It sounded like a real mountaineering expedition, but the writer made it clear he was a trekker rather than a climber. Although it was physically very tiring, he hadn't found it an insurmountable technical challenge.

When I returned home and flicked through adventure travel brochures in search of my next holiday, I noticed a few companies offering Mera Peak as a trip. At the time I imagined it to be way out of my league, but a seed had been sown, and it remained in the back of my mind as a target to aim for in the distant future. Barely two years later, having climbed to 5,895m on Kilimanjaro and picked up a few basic technical skills in the Alps, I realised I was ready for it. And I was longing to revisit my many happy memories of Nepal.

Mera Peak was one of a group of mountains the Nepalese government had classified as *trekking peaks* – a misleading term which said nothing about their technical difficulty. Mera was one of the easier ones, but I knew it still needed an ice climb to reach its summit. It was first climbed on the 20th of May 1953 by Jimmy Roberts and Sen Tenzing, a Sherpa who accompanied many of the British Everest expeditions of the 1930s and was given the nickname *The Foreign Sportsman* on account of his flamboyant dress sense.

Roberts helped to organise the logistics for the 1953 Everest expedition which put Edmund Hillary and Tenzing Norgay on the summit. His responsibilities ended when his porters delivered the final supplies to their depot at Tengboche.

'I now had about six weeks to roam, explore, and climb as the spirit might move me,'[38] he said in his account of what followed, and you can feel the sense of anticipation he must have experienced.

He chose to explore directly south of Tengboche, because it was an area neither Eric Shipton nor Bill Tilman had explored during their earlier reconnaissance trips. He crossed a high pass called the Zatr La directly above Lukla, the village now famous for its scary airport, and passed through pine forest into the high alpine Hinku Valley. Mera Peak towered nearly 3,000m above them: a giant wall topped by a regal crown of three summits, a formidable obstacle the most ambitious climber would twitch at. Two days later he had skirted the west and north sides of the mountain and was standing on the Mera La, just 1,000m below the summit of Mera Peak. From there he could see a straightforward route up the Mera Glacier.

From the north Roberts described Mera as a rambling mountain with a mass of false summits. There were no real technical difficulties, but they didn't reach the true summit, and Roberts knew it:

The summit ridge, running from west to east, consists of three or four large bumps and we chose the eastern one. To our west a semi-detached wave of ice hanging over the southern precipices may have been about 100 feet higher.[39]

In fact, they were standing on the 6,461m summit of Mera Central. Mera North, Mera Peak's true summit, is just fifteen metres higher. After climbing Mera the party descended into the Hongu Valley to the east, one of Nepal's loveliest, full of alpine lakes and meadows. From here they headed north, crossed another high pass into the Imja Valley, and completed a circuit by returning to Tengboche. This is a route which is now commonly used by commercial expeditions to both Mera and Island Peaks.

As we have seen, Jimmy Roberts organised Nepal's very first commercial trek, and although he wasn't the first to lead clients up Mera Peak, it is quite possible this little reconnaissance – an insignificant postscript to the giant media story that was the first ascent of Everest – sowed the seeds of commercial trekking in Nepal.

In October 2004 I was absurdly excited to be returning to Nepal again. Of all the places I had been to, it was the one where I felt most at home, while at the same time being the most exotic. I know that makes no sense, but I will try to explain.

The landscape of the Himalayas was like nothing back home in Britain. Our miles of rolling, featureless farmland, of giant fields criss-crossed by hedgerow bore no comparison with the precipitous hillsides of Nepal, piled high with row upon row of rice terraces. Our pockets of colourful woodland flushed with spring bluebells are a haven, but put them beside the Tolkienesque bamboo and rhododendron forests of Nepal, which carpet entire mountainsides and sweep through narrow gorges curtained with massive crashing waterfalls, and you might as well be comparing Surrey with Mordor. And as for the mountains themselves, even the most dramatic of Scottish peaks would be no more than a grassy knoll if dropped into the Himalayas. Such hillsides can be found overlooking every village, and are so insignificant beneath the mighty snowcaps that they're not even dignified with names.

When it comes to the culture, like the remote villages bereft of modern luxuries and the chaotic bustle of Kathmandu, I can't even begin to describe the differences. Yet for all the unfamiliar landscape and way of life I felt welcome and relaxed there. The living was comfortable and affordable, and the pace of life transported me away from all the stresses of the modern world. I didn't mind sleeping on a wooden palette in an unfurnished stone hovel, or washing myself from a bucket every few days, but I quite liked that I didn't have to walk very far before coming across a teahouse with a balcony overlooking a heart-stirring valley, where I could buy a meal and a beer. People were keen to learn English, so communication was rarely a problem.

Apart from three hours of monotonous trudging in the dark, I found Kilimanjaro much less exhausting than I had expected; but if I thought Mera Peak would provide an easy transition I was in for a surprise. It was by far the toughest thing I had ever done in my life and took me far out of my comfort zone. I had to dig deep into reserves of energy and determination, and uncover resources I never knew I had. But it was worth it, not only for the sense of achievement it gave me at the end, but the many moments of enjoyment along the way. This is the essence of adventure. If all you get out of it is the ability to pat yourself on the back afterwards and say you've done it, what's the point? That's like the man who holds the world record for smashing the most eggs against his forehead in under a minute. I bet he felt a sense of achievement as well, but really? You've got to enjoy it too.

For someone who is a hill walker rather than a climber, one of the great things about mountaineering in Nepal is that you nearly always have to walk for days just to get to the mountain. I enjoy trekking as much as climbing, and if you choose the right route then the trek to Mera Peak is as picturesque as any. Many people get straight off the plane in Lukla and climb over the Zatr La into the Hinku Valley. That's certainly the most direct way, but when Roberts took that route in 1953 he had already walked all the way from Kathmandu and ascended to Tengboche at 3,800m, so crossing a 4,500m pass was no problem for him. People thinking of flying from Kathmandu to Lukla at 2,800m, and going straight over the Zatr La, may wish to consider preparing themselves for the experience by drinking five pints of Belgian Trappist ale and running for six hours on a treadmill while their personal trainer smashes their head with a tea tray. To put it another way, altitude sickness is quite likely.

I took an alternative route which heads south from Lukla and joins the Hinku Valley further downstream. There are few teahouses on this route, so it was a camping trek. The first five days were undulating, sometimes gentle and sometimes steep as we followed paths which wound around hillsides high above farmland. We hiked over ridges, dropped down sharply into valleys to cross rivers, and climbed back up again. We saw our first views of Mera Peak after crossing the 2,850m Pangkongma La on the third day of the trek. On the fringes of the temperate zone, this was the altitude where rhododendron trees began to grow, and we were high above the Hinku Valley looking across a canopy of trees. On the horizon was an impressive snow-capped crown of summits rising above a sea of forest green: Mera North, Mera Central, and a third, gentler trekking summit. The South Face of Mera rose almost sheer for 2,000m in a wall of dark granite streaked by flutes of ice. It looked like a proper mountain, and it was hard to believe I was even contemplating standing on its summit, but I could see from the contours of my map the ascent was much gentler from the north.

Over the next few days our trek took us down into subtropical woodland to cross the Hinku Khola river, then back up through bamboo and rhododendron forest into grassy moorland. We camped in a spectacular setting on a ridge, watched the sun go down behind mountains to the west, and passed a series of sacred lakes in a swirling atmospheric mist. Three days after descending into the subtropics we woke up to a thin carpet of snow in a high moorland bowl nestling in a hanging valley between mountainsides. Our walk that day was spectacular, on a narrow path slender as a thread, crossing scree slopes more than 1,000m above the Hinku Khola. The river was so far beneath us we couldn't even see it, never mind hear it crashing through the valley.

Eventually the trail descended steeply through primeval forest. Huge fir trees laden with green woolly sheets of lichen spilled their ancient roots over giant boulders, and it felt a bit like something out of *Lord of the Rings*. I imagined being gently lifted off the ground to find myself peering into the eyes of Treebeard the Ent.

Below Mirkwood we rejoined the Hinku Khola, but were now over 1,000m higher than where we originally crossed it. The transition from forest to flood plain was immediate, and grey banks of fine pebbles formed an apron between the forest and the rocky valley floor. It provided stark evidence of a flood a few years earlier. In September 1998 an earthquake caused a 100m by 300m section of ice which had been damming a glacier lake, Sabai Tsho, to break off. A $2,000m^2$ hole was formed, and within ten minutes a deluge filled the Hinku Valley with a ten-metre wall of water, rocks and ice. Smaller floods followed. Within three hours of the dam bursting, the water level had risen to the level of the houses in Tangnag, which sits just beneath Sabai Tsho. Miraculously the damage in Tangnag was small. Two houses and three yaks were swept away, and no more casualties were reported, but the effects extended a hundred kilometres downstream. Bridges and houses were swept away and many people were killed.

Most of Kote, the village where we stayed that night, had been built since the flood. It was a stronghold for the Maoists, who had been waging an insurgency against the government since 1996. While they had terrorised the local population in many rural parts of Nepal, they generally left tourists alone. We were affected briefly on my previous visit, when they called a general strike and we had to travel by road a day earlier than planned. Drivers lived in fear of their lives if they broke a strike by working, but tourists trapped in urban areas found themselves inconvenienced at worst. The main effect for trekkers was a *tourist tax* we had to pay if we hiked through Maoist-controlled areas. This happened to me when I trekked the Annapurna Circuit in 2006. We passed a Maoist checkpoint where a well-spoken rebel politely asked us to hand over a hundred rupees per day for our trek, and presented us with a receipt to show to any other guerrillas who might stop us along the way.

Kote was my first overt encounter with Maoists. People were strutting around with Kalashnikovs, and the buildings were scrawled with Maoist slogans. Our sirdar Kaji, normally a cool and calm person, looked decidedly harassed. They told him he was carrying a dodgy receipt and needed to pay another 3,000 rupees for each member of the group. Our poor Sherpas felt intimidated, but as Kaji negotiated a compromise we were left free from harassment to continue our card games in the dining room of a teahouse.

Our group included three Scottish friends who were Scout leaders with better navigational skills than our guides. The oldest, Graeme, had such a strong regional accent that sometimes we had to ask his friends for a translation, but he turned out to be the sanest of us all. The youngest, Craig, helped to break the ice by producing a party game called *Pass the Pigs*, which involved tossing a pair of model pigs onto a table and trying to get them to land in various sexual positions. The third, David, sported a fine moustache, and his two friends were delighted when someone pointed out his strong resemblance to the man on a tube of Pringles.

Mera Peak looked daunting from Kote. The South Face rose 3,000m above a side valley, the upper reaches of its South-West Pillar just visible beyond a ridgeline. When Mal Duff and Ian Tattersall made the first ascent by this route in 1986 they completed the final half dozen rock pitches in a hailstorm. 'We climbed to survive,' Duff later said, 'individual moves no longer fun, just a necessity.'[40] Some of you may disagree, but I think this neatly illustrates my point about smashing eggs against your forehead. We stared up the giant wall of rock and ice as we left Kote, and I tried not to think about the gruelling climb ahead of us, or that we hoped to be up there ourselves in a week's time.

Above Kote the trail passed through pleasant yak pastures, alive with bearded rhododendron and dwarf juniper. There were many colourful wild flowers, gentians and cinquefoil, and it was an oasis of life beside the flooded mass of boulders that scarred the course of the Hinku Khola. But it was gradually collapsing into the river. When I passed that way again in 2010 the trail had been diverted along the barren valley floor, bypassing this wild haven of shrinking alpine meadows.

We spent two days acclimatising and resting in the village of Tangnag, in a wide flood plain where the valley narrowed, steepened, and swung sharply to the east to pass around the north side of Mera Peak. At 4,400m, Tangnag stood on the fringes of the vegetation zone. Many of its buildings were seasonal teahouses catering to trekkers climbing Mera. The setting was dramatic, nestling in the place where the valley was at its widest beneath three huge mountains: Kusum Kangguru to the west, Kyashar to the north, and Mera to the east.

We climbed up the flanks of Kusum Kangguru on an acclimatisation walk and reached over 5,000m along a rocky spur. I was beginning to suffer from splitting high-altitude headaches the likes of which I had never experienced before. They afflicted me every day until we came back down. Aspirin became my staple diet. I took one every morning when I woke with a headache, and another when I arrived in camp. It provided brief respite, but the headache always returned. Even so, I decided I'd rather suffer than take the local cures. On the way down from our acclimatisation walk, one of our Sherpas, Mingma, gave us what we thought was a sweet to suck on, but was in fact yak cheese. It was rock hard with an unpleasant taste, and impossible to chew. It felt like frozen plasticine; I noticed David and Graeme wincing, and as soon as Mingma turned his back to head down the hill, we glanced at each other and spat our mouthfuls into a patch of juniper. They say a female yak is called a *nak*, and the word *yak* signifies a male. If this is true I can confirm if you're ever offered yak cheese you definitely shouldn't eat it.

Beyond Tangnag the trail diverted steeply to the east up a narrow river valley. We could see a gap in the wall of rock at the valley head in front of us – the Mera La pass. Beneath it was a shelf of ice, the start of the Mera Glacier which formed a gentle frozen highway all the way to the summit. We reached the village of Khare, a community of teahouses at 5,000m, and camped in a grassy dip just above it. This marked the end of the easy trekking I so enjoyed. Beyond this we had to put on plastic boots and crampons – the climbing had begun.

But it wasn't just the conditions underfoot which changed. These I could deal with. I knew how to use my ice axe and crampons, and I didn't have any problems with the terrain, but one thing none of my previous experience prepared me for was the harsh environment of high-altitude camping. In the Alps I stayed in mountain huts rarely above 3,000m, where hot meals were served at tables. In Peru I camped for several days at 4,000m, but always in lush meadows when I was well acclimatised. Even on Kilimanjaro I had spent only one night at 4,500m, and got up in the middle of it to head for the summit. Mera was different. Our 5,000m camp at Khare was comfortable enough in a grassy hollow, but it was bitterly cold. Our two higher camps, at 5,400m beneath the Mera La, and at 5,800m on a rocky ledge just off the Mera Glacier, were decidedly harsh. In time I would become accustomed to these mountain camps, but in 2004 they pounded my brain like an elephant wielding a sledgehammer.

The Mera La was bleak and miserable. A drizzly sleet fell

all afternoon and a cold mist clung to my skin whenever I stepped outside. Our kitchen crew served us dal bhat in the porch of our tent. This felt like the height of laziness, but we had no dining tent up there, and the alternative was to sit outside in the cool wet spray – not a good idea when resting for a summit climb. My appetite was suffering and I could only manage a few mouthfuls before leaving the rest to go cold.

We roped up for the climb from the Mera La to high camp, though the Mera Glacier seemed relatively free of crevasses. We stopped frequently because the view was amazing. It was a mountain panorama unlike anything I had ever seen before, with giant snowcaps all around, too numerous to name, though I'll give just a sample. To the north-west a tangle of peaks stretched to the far horizon, the jagged outline of Ama Dablam and the giant dome of Cho Oyu behind it. To the north was the crumpled rock wall of Nuptse and Lhotse, crowned by the black pyramid of Everest, while to the north-east Makalu rose dramatically. The sharp-eyed were able to see the crinkled outline of Kangchenjunga in the far distance on the Indian border. Directly behind us, and towering over the Mera La, was a prominent rock peak known as Peak 41.

People who talk about a room with a view are unlikely to have been to high camp on Mera, perched on a ledge on the side of the mountain, with the Naulekh Glacier hundreds of metres below. The contrasting shapes of Makalu and Chamlang were most prominent across the Hongu Valley to the north-east. The former, the fifth highest mountain in the world, appeared as a perfect rock pyramid on the far horizon. The latter was just as impressive, but looked more like a sheer disc of ice embedded in the ground. At dusk an eerie purple glow lit the sky behind them, and clouds billowed up from the valley beneath.

It was without a doubt the most spectacular place I had ever spent a night, but I was suffering. I still had a crashing headache, and it was so cold I shivered like a washing machine on its final spin. I spent the afternoon curled up in my sleeping bag and didn't even feel like reading. I had only pecked at my food for the last few days, but inevitably this was the moment when I needed to clear my bowels. I summoned up the energy to drag myself outside. There were rows of tents before me and nowhere I could see with any privacy. I followed the ledge as it curled and narrowed around a pillar of rock, and as soon as I was out of sight of the tents I knew I had found my way to Poo Corner. The ground beneath my feet was covered with frozen turds which, for all I knew, had been there years.

Some of you may be wincing as you read this. The issue of human waste and other litter on high mountains has become a hot topic of debate in recent years. Everest is often described as the *world's highest garbage dump* in articles that go on to describe how mountaineers routinely jettison oxygen cylinders, tents and other garbage on their way to the summit. Often modern climbers are compared unfavourably with pioneers like Edmund Hillary and Tenzing Norgay who, the articles claim, would be astonished by what a dumping ground their mountains have become.

The reality is slightly different. Until that moment I had never had to hover so closely over the remains of someone else's meal before. On all my previous treks and climbs our crews had dug pits for toilet tents, or we had used existing longdrop toilets. As for our other rubbish, it had always been packed away and carried out with us until it could be disposed of somewhere more appropriate. I encountered litter from time to time, of course, but to describe any of the mountains I visited as garbage dumps would be distorting the truth.

It wasn't always so. After returning to their high camp from the summit of Everest in 1953, Hillary and Tenzing stuffed some personal gear into their packs and continued down, leaving their tent and oxygen cylinders on the South-East Ridge. Hillary later admitted that in those days they had no awareness of environmental matters.

I wasn't thinking of them either at that moment. I did what I needed to do with the grandest scene before me, but it's hard to appreciate these things when you are terrified of toppling over. Everything took so much effort, and I had never been so exhausted completing the simple task of relieving my bowels. I staggered back and begged some soap and water from the kitchen crew. I was panting so heavily they may have wondered if I was dying.

But nothing was wrong, and the fresh air and exercise had done me the power of good. It was better than languishing in a tent – I had warmed myself up, shed some ballast and washed my hands for the first time in twenty-four hours.

'Job done,' I said to my tent-mate Huw as I climbed back into my sleeping bag.

But the job was far from over. Oh no, if I only knew what the next day would bring.

It was -30ºC when we set out at 1.00am that night, the sort of temperature that would make even a yeti put on a pair of thermal long johns. I wore two pairs of trousers, two pairs of gloves, and three layers on top – including a down jacket – but still I had no real appreciation of the cold as we set out into darkness up the glacier. Huw and I shared a rope with our guide Narender, who was in his forties and had been on Everest four times, including once above the South Col. We started strongly and made good progress up a simple 30º snow slope with a firm surface beneath our feet. Although the terrain was featureless and the twin summits of Mera Central and Mera North were no longer visible in the darkness, I was able to measure progress with my wrist altimeter.

I had woken up with the usual banging headache, but it disappeared as soon as we started walking. Narender set a gentle pace, and we stopped frequently to drink water and get our breath back. We were beyond halfway, at 6,200m, when the problems started – and they happened very suddenly. The slope became steeper, the snow more powdery and soft. We started sinking to our ankles, and for every two steps forward I slid another one back. The cold was starting to seep into my fingers and toes, but on the whole it wasn't too bad. More uncomfortable was my crotch, which I had accidentally spilled hot water over as I was getting ready in our tent at midnight. It was pleasantly warm at first, but the agreeable sensation of heated underwear didn't last long; now the wet patch was so cold that if I closed my eyes I could imagine myself being pleasured by a polar bear.

We stopped for another rest, which we were now taking every forty or fifty paces, but this time it was different. We waited for five minutes. Narender didn't move; I started to feel the cold. I shouted up the rope to ask if we could continue, but there was no response. The bitter air cut right through me and I started shivering uncontrollably. The wait continued, and it was exasperating.

We remained stationary for twenty minutes in total. I didn't understand why we had waited for so long, but I later discovered Graeme was wearing a pair of ancient crampons even George Mallory's grandfather would have sold to an antique dealer. They had worked loose as we climbed, and Narender had helped him to put them back on. But Narender was only forty-five years old. Graeme's crampons were from an era when mountaineers were scientists, and awkward technical equipment posed no problem for them. Had we stopped to complete a Rubik's Cube instead, then we would have been moving much sooner.

As soon as we started climbing again I knew I was in trouble. The path was flattening out, but my hands were killing me. I took off my gloves and was horrified to discover my fingers were black. I put them down my front and held them against the skin of my chest to try and warm them up. There was no warmth in them at all and it felt like someone had stuck a dead penguin down my front. I had never seen black fingers before, and I didn't know how serious it was, but there was still a long way to go and they were only going to get worse. I knew I couldn't go on without getting some life back into them. I called to Narender and he came to warm them with his mittened hands. Huw stared at me blankly and I kept apologising for holding him up.

Somehow Narender managed to get the blood flowing again, and we continued. I tried to keep my hands warm by swapping my ice axe from one to the other, and put the unoccupied hand inside my down jacket. We were walking with more urgency now. Narender led without stopping. This suited me, and I walked in a daze, knowing there was no turning back. Time vanished from memory. Suddenly dawn was breaking and all three rope teams stood beneath the summit dome of Mera Central. We had a thirty-metre snow wall to climb, and I could see members of the first team were already on their way up, kicking the front points of their crampons into the wall and steadying themselves with their axes. They reached the top and I heard cheering, but I didn't feel like celebrating. I was bitterly cold, and kept having to beat my hands together to keep them warm.

I climbed confidently when it was my turn, but after a few metres the rope became taut and somebody above shouted for me to stop climbing. A few minutes of confusion followed as I waited for the instruction to continue. Gradually my calf muscles began to ache and it became painful to maintain my position. I was in agony, and it felt like an actual calf was kneeling on my legs.

I could stand it no longer, and cried out to the Sherpas waiting above me.

'Can we start climbing again please – I think I'm going to fall!'

They looked down at me in alarm, and it didn't take me long to realise they had misunderstood. There was a tug on the rope and I was hauled upwards like a harpooned whale. The sudden flurry of movement left me exhausted. I was wheezing like a cat with a hairball as I flopped onto the summit.

I stood up to walk across the summit dome, and Graeme greeted me with an enormous bear hug. Only then did I shed my worries and appreciate what we had achieved. The whole team was there. We had all made it.

I was on a ridge of snow about fifty metres long and ten metres wide. The greater view was to the north of us, across the whole of the Khumbu, and showcasing four of the highest mountains on Earth: Cho Oyu, Everest, Lhotse and Makalu. A fifth, Kangchenjunga, loomed on the horizon to the east. To the south were a few smaller mountains, but beyond them the land dropped away to the lowlands. We were right on the edge of the Himalayas, and we had the grandest view of them.

But I was shattered and freezing, and unable to appreciate the scene as much as I might. I was like my companions had been on Kilimanjaro. I tried to take pictures, but my camera was frozen.

When Jimmy Roberts stood there in 1953, he looked across at the twin dome of 6,476m Mera North, and suspected (correctly) that it was slightly higher. I was too exhausted to even notice this second peak a short distance away. Like most commercial clients, I had been led up 6,461m Mera Central, believing I was climbing the true summit of Mera Peak. Had I known it then, I probably wouldn't have cared. I was higher than I had ever been before, standing on a proper summit. We had it to ourselves for twenty minutes, and I remember a vague feeling of contentment.

A shattered Mark on the summit of Mera Central, unable to acknowledge the camera, with Makalu and Chamlang behind (Photo: Huw Davies)

The sun had been up for a while by the time we climbed down from the summit and ran down the snow slopes which had been such a struggle to ascend in the dark. I felt warm again, and I had a chance to appreciate the view to our north. I was rueing my frozen camera, but our achievement was beginning to sink in. We reached high camp at 8.30am. Our tents were still pitched and we were able to snatch some rest before continuing the descent to Khare. I went to the kitchen tent to fill my hydration bladder with hot water. Although I was thirsty, drinking water wasn't my first need. My fingertips were still numb and I wanted to warm them on the surface of the bottle.

Back in the tent I discovered that my worries paled beside Huw's. His hands had been as cold as mine, but he hadn't bothered to warm them like I had. While mine had returned to their normal colour, his were now purple and in a far worse state. In the golden age of mountaineering, these were the situations when a tent-mate would sit for hours bashing his comrade's fingers with a bit of old rope to get the circulation going again. There were stories of mountaineers putting hands and feet down each other's trousers to get some body heat into them, but Huw and I had only known each other for two weeks, and I was afraid he might misinterpret it if I proposed such a solution.

'Here, try holding onto my warm Platypus,' I said as I handed over my hydration bladder.

It took us another four hours to descend to our campsite above Khare. We arrived in the middle of the afternoon and flopped out on the grassy banks, where a flock of snow cocks had taken advantage of our absence to make their home among some sleeping bags that had been put out to air. We had a magnificent view across the head of the valley to the three summits of Mera. It was much more satisfying to look at them now that we'd been up there.

Craig the Scout leader was a trauma nurse by profession, and he examined Huw's frostbitten digits. The left hand seemed to be all right, but the right one had come up in blisters the size of his fingers. After I completed the important task of photographing Huw's frostbitten hand with Mera as a backdrop, Craig drained the blisters, dressed them, and told him to wear a glove at all times – advice that would make him look like a James Bond villain in the bars of Kathmandu.

Our campsite was a hundred metres above the teahouses of Khare. When we stayed there on the way up, we discussed the possibility of doing a beer run down to the village if we reached the summit. It seemed like a good idea at the time, but after an exhausting summit day the prospect of descending a hundred metres to buy a crate of beer, and lugging it back up the hill, seemed as realistic as lassoing a couple of wild yaks and staging a rodeo. I didn't feel like drinking beer anyway, so I kept quiet and hoped that nobody remembered our conversation. To my great distress a couple of enterprising shopkeepers had other ideas. They turned up at dinner time with a range of alcoholic drinks in a bucket. The three Scotsmen bought Tuborgs and made me drink one (through clever use of peer pressure rather than actual violence). Celebrations were muted; we had been up since midnight and were shattered. I waited for the Scots to go to bed, then gave my beer to one of the porters.

My ascent of Mera Peak was by far the toughest thing I had ever done in my life. I wasn't prepared for the cold. One of my little toes went black, and I experienced a numbness in my fingertips that lasted six weeks after I returned. My weight had been over eighty kilograms when I started, the heaviest I had ever been, but when I arrived back I was ten kilograms lighter.

My only exercise was regular walking, and I was one of the only members of the team who didn't keep fit by going to the gym. I knew if I wanted to climb harder mountains I would have to start a regular programme of exercise.

But overall I had enjoyed it a great deal. It had been another amazing experience, and I knew in my heart that I did want to climb harder mountains. I started running for the first time since I was a student, when I played in a

Sunday league football team, and soon I was looking for my next peak.

5 EXPEDITION STYLE

It was after I came back from Mera Peak in 2004 that I first started to think about climbing Everest.

I was realistic. I knew the idea was no more than a tiny seed that would probably never germinate. I thought about the experience I still needed, and the mountains I could climb to gain it. I needed to improve my methods for dealing with the extreme cold I had encountered on Mera summit day. My alpine skills were rudimentary, and I would need to climb more technically difficult peaks to improve them. Mera Central, at 6,461m, was a long way short of Everest's 8,848m. I needed to continue my gradual progression in altitude.

Finally I had no experience at all of *expedition-style* mountaineering. This involves establishing a series of camps that can be used in sequence during a multi-day summit push. The theory is that you acclimatise while carrying loads up to supply these camps, and return to a base camp at the bottom of the mountain to recover between each carry before establishing the next camp. Once the camps are in place you return to base camp and wait for the right weather to climb to the summit. The alternative to expedition-style mountaineering is known as *alpine style*. With this method camps are not established in advance, and the climbers simply go straight up. Alpine style is quite sufficient for smaller peaks, but it only works at high altitude if the climbers have acclimatised to the altitude in advance, and are strong enough to carry all the equipment for a multi-day summit push with them as they climb.

Everest still seemed an impossibly distant dream for me. I focused on the more realistic aim of a five-year plan to climb an easier 8,000m peak, such as Cho Oyu. I had no idea whether I could cope with the trials that would be coming my way, but of one thing I was certain – I was determined that my mountaineering holidays would be enjoyable, and not become an obsession. If I reached a point where they became an ordeal which I looked forward to as much as my first day back at work wading through 200 emails, then I would stop. But as long as I still enjoyed them I would continue building on my experience by doing tougher climbs. This last point is important. Although Everest was a destination at the end of the road, the journey to get there mattered just as much. If I didn't reach the end it was because I found a place along the way I liked more. I was open to any possibility.

I decided to climb Aconcagua, the highest mountain in South America. At 6,962m it was the next logical step up from Mera Peak in altitude, and it offered a couple more things I was looking for: extreme cold and expedition-style mountaineering. How would I cope with sitting around at base camp for days on end, and would I be capable of carrying heavy loads at very high altitude? I had no idea, but I wanted to find out.

One thing it wouldn't offer was a chance to improve my climbing skills. Aconcagua's standard route offered no technical challenges at all, and it had a reputation for being the highest mountain in the world you can just walk up. Like Kilimanjaro it was one of the Seven Summits (a list comprising the highest mountain on each continent), and a trophy bagger's peak. People were attracted to it because of its name and reputation rather than for its interesting climbing.

Aconcagua lies wholly within Argentina, in a region of high, desert peaks a short distance from the Chilean border. A pass crosses the Andes between the Chilean capital Santiago and the Argentine city of Mendoza. Aconcagua is accessible to the north up a couple of wide river valleys. The lack of rainfall means that, despite its high altitude, Aconcagua is surprisingly free of glaciers. Its giant South Face rises nearly 3,000m in a tumble of snow chutes and seracs (large vertical blocks of ice). It has long been attractive to extreme alpinists who need a liberal sprinkling of danger with their climbing. One of the routes is named after Reinhold Messner, who did for high-altitude mountaineering what Evel Knievel did for driving. On the eastern side the gentler Polish Glacier offers a slightly more straightforward alpine climb, but the northern and western approaches to Aconcagua are bare of permanent snow, and their giant scree slopes offer nothing more technical than one-foot-in-front-of-the-other plodding.

The American writer James Ramsey Ullman once described Aconcagua as 'an intolerably monotonous slag-pile'[41]. The people who remember it as an ugly mountain are those who attack it from the north-west side and spend days walking up and down the giant 1,000m scree slope above Plaza de Mulas, base camp for the so-called Normal Route, and another scree slope higher up called the Gran Acarreo, which literally means the *great haul*.

The first recorded ascent was made on the 14th of January 1897 by the Swiss guide Matthias Zurbriggen, during the large self-financed expedition of Edward Fitzgerald, an American who lived much of his life in

Britain. At the time it was the highest mountain ever climbed. Fitzgerald intended to make the first ascent himself accompanied by Zurbriggen, but he rarely climbed above 6,000m without experiencing breathing difficulties. The story of their expedition is a good lesson to anyone who thinks climbing Aconcagua is easy just because there are no technical difficulties. They endured many hardships which included difficult terrain, extreme cold, frequent blizzards, and a number of perilous river crossings just getting to the base of the mountain.

After initially exploring the Vacas Valley, which these days forms the approach to the eastern side of the mountain for those attempting the Polish Glacier and False Polish Routes, they found a way up the Horcones Valley to the west. They established a base camp at 4,250m beside the snout of the Horcones Glacier, close to what is now Plaza de Mulas. They started up the scree slope on their first attempt, but for every two steps forward they slipped back another. Fitzgerald suffered from nausea and didn't sleep at all during their first night on the mountain. He decided it was much too cold to make a summit attempt unless they carried up wood to cook hot meals. They pitched a camp at 5,700m inside a cleft in a rock to the left of the Gran Acarreo. Then they retreated, but not before Zurbriggen went a little higher on a short reconnaissance.

They were beginning to appreciate the vast scale of Aconcagua. Features which they thought were nearby turned out to be huge distances away. Zurbriggen walked for two or three hours, apparently making no progress at all. He expected to reach one spot quickly only to discover it was nine or ten hours away.

On their second attempt they zigzagged up the scree rather than climbing directly, to limit the amount of back-sliding. They arrived in camp parched with thirst, but everything was frozen and they were unable to find a drop of water to drink. They had difficulty lighting their firewood. Although they managed to melt some water for tepid soup, they were unable to get it to boil, which meant they couldn't cook.

They left at the crack of dawn the following day. The summit looked so close they even talked of reaching it in five or six hours – but they were in for a shock. Fitzgerald noticed Zurbriggen was speeding up, and when he asked why, Zurbriggen said he could no longer feel his feet and wanted to reach high camp before they froze. Fitzgerald ordered him to stop and take his boots off, and was horrified to find the circulation had stopped completely. He tried some novel methods of warming them, first by rubbing them with brandy, and then snow (which is a bit like trying to cure chronic diarrhoea with hot curry). Eventually they got the circulation going again, but Zurbriggen was in so much pain that some of the other guides had to hold him down. They had no option but to return to their lower camp.

The following day Zurbriggen's feet were better and they waited for the sun to come up before leaving for another attempt. This time they tried ascending by the firmer ground of the North Ridge, but by 2.15 it became too windy and they had to retreat again.

Back at camp they were so depressed about the extreme cold Fitzgerald ordered a retreat up the Horcones Valley to the relatively balmy altitudes of Puente del Inca, a resort with a guest house on the main route between Santiago and Mendoza, where they could rest and recuperate. Zurbriggen's bad luck continued; he almost drowned fording a river. Crossing on muleback, his mule lost its footing, and both steed and rider were swept away by a powerful current, somersaulting over one another as they went. A large rock stopped them, but Zurbriggen found himself pinned by his mule, partially submerged. Fitzgerald and a muleteer reached the rock in time to push the mule back into the flow and drag Zurbriggen out. He was unconscious, but Fitzgerald revived him with his favourite cure-all, brandy.

By the time they returned to the mountain for their third attempt, two of the guides, Nicola Lanti and Joseph Pollinger, had been hard at work stocking the higher camps with wood, provisions and blankets. This attempt was again curtailed when Fitzgerald felt nauseous at around 6,000m. He sent Zurbriggen ahead to prospect the route, and the Swiss guide climbed all the way to 6,800m, to the saddle between the two summits, now known as Cresta del Guanaco. In other words, he nearly reached the top, but came down again because his employer wasn't with him.

Zurbriggen had gone far enough to see that the easier north peak was the highest. They decided to have another go the following day. This time they all started feeling nauseous after drinking a tin of sour milk for breakfast. Fitzgerald made it to 6,400m, but then he tripped and fell, and was violently sick. They all turned back again, but after lunch at high camp Fitzgerald felt better and the weather was fine, so he went for a little stroll up the mountain to get 'hardened and habituated to the conditions'.[42] He made it to the same point they had reached earlier in the morning without any difficulty, and with renewed hope he returned to camp and ordered an immediate fifth attempt the following day.

Poor Fitzgerald. His altitude problems appeared to be psychological rather than physical. Under no pressure to reach the summit that afternoon he achieved 6,400m without trouble, but he was unable to get so high on any of their determined summit attempts without feeling sick.

I've often witnessed this curious psychological altitude sickness in climbers who are going to high elevations for the first time, and it's one reason why I recommend the seven-step journey to Everest. Only with experience do you learn that minor symptoms, such as headaches and appetite loss, are part of the acclimatisation process and nothing to worry about. By climbing only 500 metres higher than I had been before, I was always confident of my ability to acclimatise.

In Fitzgerald's case it wasn't just that *he* hadn't been to that altitude before: *nobody* had. The previous altitude record (as far as anyone knew) was held by Edward Whymper and his Italian guides Jean-Antoine and Louis Carrel, who reached the 6,310m summit of Chimborazo in Ecuador in 1880.

Some people believe Zurbriggen made the first ascent of Aconcagua by climbing straight up the scree of the Gran Acarreo, but in fact they kept to the east side of the North Ridge in order to shelter from the wind, climbing between the boulders above the plateau of Nido de Condores on a route which must have been very similar to the one climbers on the Normal Route use today. Some distance up they stopped to light a fire and have something to eat. While they rested, Fitzgerald – who had been feeling fine until that point – gradually became nauseous again, an event he attributes to the sudden discovery of a broken bottle of champagne in Pollinger's knapsack.

'Though we might have known that this would happen, yet … it discouraged us greatly,' he said.

Luckily I've never been turned back on a mountain because of a missing bottle of champers. I imagine it must be pretty devastating, but this was some excuse.

To Fitzgerald's credit he realised his bouts of nausea were getting a bit silly and in danger of jeopardising the main purpose of the expedition, so he sent Zurbriggen on alone.

Scarcely more than four hundred yards separated me from

the goal; but after my long journey and my many attempts
I felt that I should never reach it myself. I got up and tried
once more to go on, but I was only able to advance from two
to three steps at a time, and then I had to stop, panting for
breath, my struggles alternating with violent fits of nausea
... black specks swam across my sight.[43]

He descended to high camp with the other two guides, reaching it at five o'clock. Zurbriggen returned from the summit at 6.30, having made the first ascent of Aconcagua.

Aconcagua and the featureless scree slope of the Gran Acarreo rise for
over 1,000m above tents at Nido de Condores

The lack of technical climbing has led many people to underestimate Aconcagua, believing it to be just another trek like Kilimanjaro, only a bit bigger. Strictly speaking you can't argue with this – but the *bit bigger* is crucial. You could say a cow is like a steak, only a bit bigger, but I've never seen anyone sit down with a knife and fork and eat a whole one.

More people die on Aconcagua every year than on any other mountain in South America, usually from altitude sickness, exposure, or both. The weather is often appalling, with impossible winds and extreme cold a common occurrence. There are many loose boulder fields above 6,500m, and although it's possible to get all the way to the summit walking only on rock, after a lot of snow an ice axe and crampons are needed. Unlike Kilimanjaro, there are no porters to carry your equipment to the high camps and pitch your tents for you. Its status as a trophy peak means many people who try to climb it have no idea what they're letting themselves in for.

I was under no illusions. There was a moment on my Mera Peak summit day when I looked at my hands and worried that I would lose fingers. I was in a daze on the summit, so exhausted that I didn't fully appreciate my surroundings. Crucially, although it felt like a great achievement, for much of summit day I hadn't really enjoyed myself. I wanted to experience the same delight on my summit days as I did on the trek, when I was able to relax completely and appreciate every moment of walking in some of the most beautiful scenery on Earth.

I had always relied on my natural fitness as a regular hill walker to get me up mountains, and had never trained for anything, but my experience on Mera clearly demonstrated this would only get me so far. I would have benefited from some training beforehand. For Aconcagua it was going to be essential.

In early 2005 I started running again, and although I hated it, I discovered that running into work in Central London is a million times more pleasant than crowding into a sweaty tube train during rush hour, or waiting twenty minutes for a bus which arrives so full the driver continues without stopping. Running into work had the double advantage of providing my daily exercise and getting me into work faster.

I was working in the City of London at the time. At eight o'clock on a Monday morning it's one of the most crowded square miles of land anywhere on the planet. The roads are busy, and every footpath contains a seething tidal wave of sharp-suited businessmen and women, sweeping anything caught in their path onto a new trajectory.

It's surprising how many commuters don't watch where they're going. Annoying as they are, I can understand people who feel they must reply to a text message as they walk. I'm less able to fathom what goes on in the mind of someone who walks among hundreds of people on a crowded footpath, casually reading a newspaper. There are few things these people deserve more than an unexpected sweaty embrace from a man in shorts. They got one. My morning runs would also have been good training for rugby players – I became very good at side-stepping.

Other aspects of my training were more unusual. I worried about the load-carrying I needed to do on Aconcagua, but I have an aversion to gyms, and bench-pressing had about as much appeal as Prince Philip in jodhpurs. The best method was to head for the hills for a weekend of backpacking and wild camping. Not only did I improve my hill walker's leg muscles, but I carried a big pack like I would be doing in Argentina. Living and working in London made this harder; Britain's best hill-walking destinations were at least five hours' drive away, and I could only go occasionally during the weekend.

I decided to alternate my daily runs by walking into work with a backpack full of weights, but it was a time of increased vigilance against the threat of terrorism. That same year fifty-two people were killed when four suicide bombers walked onto the London transport network carrying backpacks full of explosives. I was working in the communications team at City of London Police, and every day I worried whether I would face the embarrassment of a stop-and-search by one of my colleagues.

Snow or no snow on Aconcagua, it was going to be cold up there, and I would be walking for long periods in heavy mountaineering boots. As well as carrying heavy loads, I decided I needed to do something to strengthen my ankles. While carrying a big pack into Central London during rush hour was one thing, I was less sure about wearing my mountaineering boots. The days were long gone when one of my colleagues in the police might throw a man into the cells and beat him with a truncheon for an innocent fashion crime, but if you saw the boots in question you might feel it was justified.

To avoid any potential embarrassment for either myself or my workmates, I bought a pair of ankle weights. These were strips of material I wrapped around my ankles and secured with Velcro straps. They were adjustable, and I could alter the amount of weight each ankle was carrying, but no matter how much weight I put in them, or how much I tightened them, they started rubbing as soon as I walked any great distance. Many years earlier I'd had an operation on my left ankle to repair an Achilles tendon, ruptured playing football. The operation left a scar which never fully healed, and after several days of wearing the ankle weights, the scar reopened. Strips of flesh were torn from my ankles, and they looked hideous. I consigned the ankle weights to the box of items I no longer had any use for, alongside my comb and hair-drier.

With a marvellously sophisticated training regime in place, I turned my attention to finding the best operator for my Aconcagua expedition. I had done most of my previous trips with a British adventure travel company called Exodus. I had few complaints with any of the treks I did with them, but I was moving into the realms of mountaineering and felt I needed someone more specialised. I decided to climb Aconcagua with Jagged Globe, a UK company with a reputation for mountaineering expeditions rather than treks.

Recognising that many people who joined their expeditions didn't know what to expect, they prepared us by organising a pre-expedition weekend in Snowdonia, involving an equipment briefing, slideshows, lectures on altitude and health, and a day on the hills to provide a crash course in any skills which might be needed on the mountain.

That was the theory – in practice it was mainly a social weekend for like-minded people in a hotel. There were about forty of us booked onto a range of trips, and we whetted our appetite for adventure by watching slideshows of all of them: Kilimanjaro via the Western Breach, Uganda's Mountains of the Moon, and an ascent of Mount Vinson in Antarctica which included a trip extension called *The Last Degree*. This one involved dragging a sledge from 89ºS to the South Pole over miles of flat and featureless ice. I met someone booked onto it who told me he trained by dragging tractor tyres around his village, which made my own antics through the City of London seem quite conventional.

People wandered freely between the lecture room and the hotel bar, and there was a fair amount of banter. Many of the trip leaders making the presentations fancied themselves as stand-up comedians. I had no idea what they were like as mountain guides, but hopefully much better.

'They've built a great big monument to the Equator in Ecuador,' one leader said, 'but they put it in the wrong place. The real Equator goes through this bloke's garden.'

He showed us a photo of a man in a Panama hat collecting money outside his front door.

'Do you see that giant bottle of ketchup in the corner of the photo?' said another leader, who was promoting a climbing holiday in Uganda. 'That's the sauce of the Nile.'

This was the moment some of us decided to start heckling.

'One of the clients on last year's Aconcagua trip was an ex-jockey. He was fit and healthy, but HAPE can affect anyone, and he developed a bad cough,' said Jagged Globe's managing director Simon Lowe during his presentation on altitude sickness.

'Was he feeling a little horse?' someone shouted at the back.

Simon wasn't going to go down without a fight. He started hitting back at the audience.

'Has anyone here ever experienced hyperventilation?' he asked.

I had, and I felt it was a topic I knew something about. Hyperventilation is when your breathing rate increases through anxiety. It's a purely psychological condition, and as soon as you consciously slow down your breathing, you recover completely. In my case, when we called an ambulance to whisk me away to hospital, a paramedic said it was likely there was nothing wrong with me. He told me to relax and slow down my breathing. He was right – I stopped hyperventilating almost immediately.

I tentatively raised my hand.

'Yes, we know all about yours,' Simon said, pouncing upon me like a crocodile attacking a wildebeest. 'You were like that politician who was found in a hotel room wearing women's underwear. Did you have an orange in your mouth at the time?'

It's generally not good practice for a managing director to accuse one of his clients of bizarre sex acts in front of an audience, but for a reason I can't explain, I felt at home among these people.

My main drinking buddy that weekend was Dan. I'd not met him before, but we were booked onto the same Aconcagua trip and had roughly the same amount of climbing experience. He also lived in London, and two weekends later we went on a training walk along the Seven Sisters on England's south coast, a chain of steep sea cliffs which rise and fall over seven distinct summits. It's the nearest thing to a hill walk a short train ride from the capital.

We were both keen to try out our new plastic mountaineering boots before we left for the expedition. We agreed to simulate an Aconcagua load by carrying fifteen-kilogram packs. I felt a bit of an idiot in my bright red boots as we walked through the coastal town of Eastbourne, a sleepy place famous for its many retirement homes for the elderly, but luckily Dan's boots were orange, so I walked behind him and tried to keep a low profile.

The footpath is picturesque, and is one of my favourite day walks near London. It passes over Beachy Head, Britain's highest chalk sea cliff which rises 162m above the English Channel, and continues on lush grass over the undulating brows of the Seven Sisters. It was a clear day, and the contrasting blue, green and white of the sky, grass and cliffs made a colourful picture. The dog walkers were giving us funny looks, but we were full of anticipation for Aconcagua, and we didn't care.

We were tired and exhilarated by the time we reached the attractive market town of Alfriston, with its timber-framed cottages and cobbled alleyways, and we still had five more kilometres to reach the station. It was November, and dark by four o'clock, but we'd come prepared with head torches. We took off our boots and staggered into the Star Inn, where we slung our bulky packs into a couple of spare seats. Six pints later we strapped on our head torches and staggered out again like a pair of polar explorers heading into the depths of the frozen Antarctic winter. By that stage we weren't very steady on our feet, and everybody in the pub was laughing at us.

While the pints may not be something a personal trainer would recommend for a fitness programme, I completed more preparation for Aconcagua than any mountain I had climbed before, and felt I had done all I could to maximise my chances of success. It was the most eagerly anticipated of all my trips to date, and everything seemed to be falling into place.

I met most of our team at the pre-expedition weekend, and the banter continued as soon as we got on the plane to Argentina in December 2005. Much of it was directed at an IT project manager called Steve. Since we met in Snowdonia he'd chosen to have his hair cut in the manner of the cricketer Kevin Pietersen. His hair stood up like the spines of a startled hedgehog and he had a bleached strip down the middle which made it look like he'd been lying in a high street when the road-marking truck drove by. Meanwhile, despite having a thorough briefing about outdoor equipment, Dan arrived wearing a furry beaver-skin hat that looked more like a Russian tea cosy than an item of clothing.

Aconcagua is famous for its high winds. The chill factor makes already bitter temperatures positively Arctic. We may find ourselves hunkered down for days in a snow storm, but snow at the right time was more likely to help than hinder us. The crux of Aconcagua's Normal Route is a fearsome scree chute know as the Canaleta, which leads up to the Cresta del Guanaco between the two main peaks. It would be an easier proposition in snow because we would be able to climb it using crampons on a much firmer surface, instead of sliding on the loose stones Fitzgerald described as a *breathless struggle*, but which have since been described by climbers in much more colourful terms. The wind and the resulting low temperatures are the deal breaker on Aconcagua.

After my narrow escape from frostbite on Mera Peak I was impressed to see our expedition leader Chris Groves take the risk of frozen digits much more seriously. He carried out a kit inspection at our hotel in Mendoza, paying particular attention to boots and gloves, and arranged last-minute shopping for anyone whose mitts were considered inadequate. I was taking no chances. As well as my new red boots I had a pair of down mitts the size of my forearms; I felt sure my extremities would be much warmer this time.

Our head guide for the expedition was a young Argentine called Lionel, who had summited Aconcagua ten times. I sat next to him at dinner on the second evening, and found him polite and dignified. He told me he spent four months a year guiding. This enabled him to earn enough money to climb for pleasure the rest of the year. He was very quiet, and I spent most of the meal speaking to the more garrulous Trevor – a slightly balding banker in his early forties with a mop of crazy hair which gave him the appearance of an eccentric professor. He was extremely bright, but seemed to have a mischievous streak lurking beneath the surface. When I asked him about his training for Aconcagua, he said he hadn't done any. He didn't seem concerned by this, and when I told him I'd been carrying a backpack full of weights to work, he shrugged his shoulders as if to confirm his suspicion that the world is full of fools.

Mendoza, the gateway to Aconcagua, is a neat city of leafy squares and broad tree-lined avenues which sits on a huge plain on the eastern side of the High Andes. It has a wonderful temperate climate in the heart of Argentina's main wine-growing region. Far more tourists visit Mendoza for booze-ups (commonly known as wine-tasting tours) than to climb mountains, and as a happy consequence the city has a large number of high-quality restaurants. It's only a day's drive to Aconcagua's national park entrance along a tarmacked highway that crosses the High Andes into Chile.

We had our first view of Aconcagua up the Horcones Valley two days later, as we stood beside the ranger station. A giant 3,000m wall of rock and ice, the fearsome South Face appeared as an incongruous smudge of white between the brown desert hills which had been our constant companion since leaving Mendoza. The explorer and mountaineer Martin Conway, who came here in 1898, said that 'a climber beholding the mountain from this side would hardly be likely to choose the Horcones Valley for his first attempt'.[44] But after Mera Peak I was getting used to mountains which looked ridiculous from one side, yet offered a relatively straightforward way up from another. I had no doubt this mountain would present me with few technical difficulties.

I was yet to experience failure to climb a mountain through sheer exhaustion, but I lived in fear of the weather – particularly the wind – and I hoped it would be kind to us. I was optimistic because our itinerary allowed for a couple of spare days should the weather be poor on our intended summit day. As I had on Mera, I took a photograph of the South Face on the off chance somebody might take a look at it and say, 'you didn't really get up *that*, did you?'

One technical advance which has made Aconcagua much

easier to climb since Fitzgerald's day is the presence of bridges. Zurbriggen, the scientist Stuart Vines, and Fitzgerald's pack pony all fell in the river and were swept away during their many treks up and down the Horcones Valley. Zurbriggen was lucky to survive. The Rio Horcones swept noisily down the valley ahead of us in a torrent of deadly cascades, but we hardly noticed its power as we wandered up the path on a bank alongside it. A sturdy suspension bridge had been erected at the only crossing place and we strolled nonchalantly over to the other side.

We spent our first night at Confluencia, a large semi-permanent camp of giant dome tents erected to provide kitchen and dining facilities to expedition teams on their way to base camp. We were at an altitude of 3,400m, so we spent two nights acclimatising there. During our rest day we walked up the side valley to get a closer view of the staggering South Face. It looked truly terrifying, with tiers of giant hanging glaciers bulging over vertical walls of loose rock.

The following day we walked along the broad featureless flood plain of the Horcones Valley to reach Plaza de Mulas at 4,400m, base camp for Aconcagua's Normal Route. It was a tedious walk over loose stones, but the angle of ascent was gradual and at least we didn't have any of the murderous river crossings Fitzgerald had to endure. We also had our first experience of Aconcagua's famous *nieves penitentes*. These curious icicles protrude from the ground and range from knee to shoulder height. They are formed by the action of the sun on deep, consolidated snow, and disappear and reappear with the seasons. They form in thick clusters and neat rows, and it's often difficult to find a path which is wide enough to thread your way between them. The name is derived from their appearance; from a distance they are thought to resemble a procession of penitent monks. Charles

Darwin first described them during his travels in South America, but it's not known who coined the term *penitentes* or whether they had been drinking.

Plaza de Mulas lay on an elevated table at the head of the Horcones Valley. It was a sizeable village of substantial marquees providing restaurant facilities for the various expedition teams attempting the mountain. There was even a line of portable toilets on the western end of camp. These were emptied regularly by a helicopter which flew over and departed down the Horcones Valley with the toilet drum dangling from a rope. It was wise to stand well clear during this process. There are no good ways to die while mountaineering, but to be speared by a shaft of frozen urine dropped from a great height would be a particularly ignominious one.

A triangular rock peak called Cerro Cuerno rose above camp to the north, at the top end of the valley and surrounded by glaciers. Directly above the eastern side of camp, Aconcagua looked like a crumpled heap of brown rocks sheltered by a small penitentes field. The contrast with its towering South Face could not be more stark. It was not an impressive mountain from this new angle, and its lower slopes seemed to consist of one vast, featureless mass of scree. It was easy to see how Fitzgerald had been deceived by the scale of Aconcagua. There was more than 2,500m of mountain above us – but it didn't look like it.

Our first duty on arrival at Plaza de Mulas was to visit the base camp doctor for a mandatory health check. This was controversial. While most people are happy to visit their doctor when they are ill, we would probably object to a doctor who ordered us to visit when we're feeling fine, only to tell us we could be better.

The health check involved having our blood oxygen level, heart rate, pulse and blood pressure taken to see whether we were fit to climb. But taking the readings after we had just arrived in base camp – 4,000m higher than Mendoza where we had been relaxing comfortably a few days earlier – was misleading. While they are still acclimatising, a person's heart rate, pulse and blood pressure increase sharply because their heart is working harder to pump oxygen around the body. This is perfectly normal – as are various minor symptoms of altitude sickness such as headaches, nausea and loss of appetite.

People acclimatise at different speeds. Slow acclimatisers are going to have readings at the high end of the scale, suggesting they are less healthy than fast acclimatisers, but this doesn't mean they're going to perform poorly once they're fully acclimatised. We've already seen how Edward Fitzgerald's fear of altitude sickness helped to bring it on, and it's perfectly possible that a base camp doctor who takes readings that worry a healthy person may – ironically – make their patient worse. It reminds me of the political rally I once attended, where one of the candidates noted that his rival liked to use the title *Dr* rather than *Mr*.

'He's the only doctor who makes you sick just looking at him!' he said to his cheering supporters.

I had been to 6,461m already, and knew there would be plenty of time for me to acclimatise. I feared the base camp doctor much more than I did the altitude, so I took an aspirin to ease my headache and reduce my blood pressure. It seemed to work; the only thing I suffered as a consequence of my medical examination was abuse from the rest of the team.

The doctor was young, female and quite attractive.

'What is your age, please?' she asked.

'34,' I replied.

'Really? You look much younger.'

She took my heart rate and blood oxygen level.

'These are very good,' she said. 'Are you an athlete?'

I was tempted to lie, but I could see another member of our team, Matt, waiting his turn in the queue and trying his best not to laugh.

'She obviously fancies you,' he said as we returned to camp. 'I think you should go back there tonight and pretend you have a genital rash.'

When I confessed to taking an aspirin, I was accused of being a drug cheat. One of the genuine athletes in the team was a triathlete and marathon runner who was likely to perform much better than me once he was fully acclimatised. The doctor had put him on medication and instructed him to return the following day for further checks. He was furious.

'She's useless,' he said. 'What a waste of time. She's made a complete cock-up of the examination.'

'I thought she was excellent,' I replied with as much sincerity as I could muster. 'One of the best doctors I've ever seen.'

Aconcagua was my first experience of expedition-style mountaineering. I spent plenty of time sitting around at base camp, staring up at the mountain. Much of it I spent lying in my tent reading, but we also played a lot of card games in the dining tent. Occasionally this life of leisure was interrupted when we found we had work to do, like washing garments which had become encrusted with fine dust in the dry and windy atmosphere of base camp. We practised pitching the tents we would be using higher up the mountain.

It's not a lifestyle for people who are easily bored, but I found I didn't mind it. For me, beach holidays are no more enjoyable than office team-building days, and I find it hard to take my mind off the stresses of working life unless I'm active. I didn't know how I would cope with the days of doing nothing – but I was focused on an objective, and I knew every day spent at base camp helped me acclimatise and increased my chances of achieving my goal. There aren't many times in life when sitting on your backside doing nothing has a sense of purpose, but this was one of them. In any case, I'm always happy reading, and I wasn't in any danger of running out of books.

We climbed up nearby mountainsides and carried equipment to higher camps, returning to base camp in the same day. While this might seem like an exhausting version of Snakes and Ladders, it served an important purpose. Gradually our bodies were adapting to lower oxygen levels by following the traditional mountaineering principle of *climb high, sleep low*. When you climb to a higher altitude where the air is thinner, it triggers your body to generate more red blood cells, which in turn help to circulate oxygen around your system. Your lungs gradually increase their capacity, and when you return to a lower altitude these changes to your body are still there, ready to be used when you go back up again. Performance improves so dramatically that in other sports you would have the anti-doping testers coming round to your tent. An exhausting six-hour plod can easily become a straightforward four-hour waltz.

From our position at the base of the mountain, it was difficult to get a sense of scale or even identify the features on Aconcagua's Normal Route. Two days after we arrived at Plaza de Mulas we had our first opportunity to study them in detail when we ascended Cerro Bonete, a 5,000m glaciated peak on the opposite side of the Horcones Valley.

It was a tiring day, even though we weren't carrying loads, but it was my first chance to try out my big plastic boots in a realistic setting. This time we didn't have to worry about dog walkers giving us funny looks; nevertheless, Dan's green beaver-skin hat was still a topic of discussion.

'I keep wanting to stroke your head,' Trevor said, reaching towards it.

'It looks like an old lady's furry muff,' Steve remarked.

Trevor quickly withdrew his hand.

We soon had other things on our minds. The route alternated between scree slopes and penitentes fields, and it was awkward going. The separation between icicles was often small, and it was easy to become wedged between them. The ice was slippery underfoot; I fell over several times and found my backpack trapped between pinnacles of ice. When that happened I couldn't get up without shrugging my pack from my shoulders. On one occasion Dan needed to help me stand, and it was humiliating to be rescued by a man I'd just belittled for wearing a tea cosy on his head.

We arrived on the summit after some easy scrambling and a lot of zigzagging up scree slopes – good practice for later. Aconcagua towered above us across the valley, bare and brown and nondescript, but nevertheless utterly impressive in scale. A smudge of white cloud like a goose's feather whipped off its summit, indicating deadly winds, and we could see nearly all of the Normal Route. We were looking at the West Face, composed of rock strips laid out in tiers. A number of gullies ran vertically down – possible lines of ascent for competent rock climbers.

Our attention was drawn to a giant scree slope, the Gran Acarreo, which ran from the ridgeline below the summit, all the way down to Plaza de Mulas more than 2,000m below. At the very top of the scree slope a jumble of rocks appeared to bar access to the summit, but somewhere hidden from view the scree continued up the gully called the Canaleta to the summit ridge. The scree slope itself had two distinct parts, divided by Nido de Condores (literally *Nest of the Condors*), a 5,600m col at the bottom of the ridgeline to its left. Above Nido, the Gran Acarreo could be bypassed by ascending a band of rocks on the ridgeline, but a long traverse was required beneath the summit rocks to gain the entrance of the Canaleta. The Normal Route weaved up firmer ground somewhere through this rock band on a line similar to the one taken by Fitzgerald in 1897.

For over 1,000m below Nido there was no way the scree slope could be avoided. Its featureless surface was broken in only a couple of places. As the rocks of the west face merged into the scree of the Gran Acarreo, a small outlying crag known as Plaza Canada rose at around 5,000m. This was to be our Camp 1, with Camp 2 at Nido, and Camp 3 somewhere in the rock band above it.

It was satisfying to reach the top of Cerro Bonete, and we felt in good shape, but one thing was clear: when James Ramsey Ullman described the mountain as a slag-pile he was probably being generous. It wasn't going to be a fun climb, unless scrabbling around on spoil tips tickles your fancy.

Two days later we did our first load carry up the featureless scree slope to Plaza Canada. Lionel led the way at a slow, even pace which enabled us to build up a rhythm. The West Face of Aconcagua may be as exciting to look at as a bank manager eating a burger, but Plaza Canada turned out to be a beautiful campsite on an airy perch halfway up the lower scree slope. It was sheltered behind a large rock which bore a passing resemblance to a wizard casting a spell, and we called the rock Gandalf (there may have been funny ingredients in our drinking water).

The camp's elevated position and west-facing aspect allowed us to watch a splendid sunset behind the mountains of Chile on the opposite side of the Horcones Valley. The scree slope behind us glowed a burnt orange. As the light dimmed, it cast shadows across the nearby peaks of Cerro

Cuerno and Cerro Catedral, one a glaciated horn and the other a rock cathedral (I'll leave you to work out which was which).

Collecting water wasn't easy on the dry desert of Aconcagua's West Face. There was a short penitentes field which gradually melted in the afternoon sun five minutes from Plaza Canada. Snowmelt trickled between pinnacles of ice, providing running water to fill our bottles. It was our first night on the mountain, and we acquainted ourselves with the rules about waste disposal. Many people who have spent time camping in the wilderness have a story about lifting a rock to bury their poo only to find somebody else's hidden underneath. It's estimated around 4,000 people climb Aconcagua every year, and as most stay at the same campsites, the likelihood of it happening would be quite high. But national park rules make it compulsory for climbers to pack their waste out. That includes faeces.

At Plaza Canada, Lionel gave us a practical demonstration of how to shit on Aconcagua (though thankfully he left some of it to the imagination). The technique involved crapping onto a sheet of kitchen paper weighed down by stones on its four corners. The stool was wrapped in the paper and stashed in a black bin bag. Each individual turd bag was put into a turd master bag for tying to the outside of our packs and carrying with us. It may seem unpleasant, but this was no picnic. With our poo bags swinging behind us we kept a good distance from our companions on the trail, and were careful about how we tied our ice axes to our packs.

The following day we completed a load carry up to Camp 2 at Nido. Plaza Canada lay to the right of the scree slope, and to get to Nido a path slanted across the slope up to the col. It didn't look far, but the ascent was nearly 600m and it was a monotonous climb. As we crossed from one side to the other, the featureless expanse of the Gran Acarreo stretched above us. Again I was reminded of how Fitzgerald had been confused about distances. The temptation to start up the great haul must have been strong. The top of the scree slope, where the route traversed beneath the summit rocks, didn't seem so very far away, but it was over 1,000m vertically.

Nido was a vast multi-level plateau with tents spread over large distances, and there was room for hundreds more. A horizon of high peaks could be seen to the north, including the gentle snow-sloped armchair of Mercedario, a mountain nearly as high as Aconcagua. Above us the Gran Acarreo looked straightforward and not at all steep, with only a few rocky outcrops breaking its even surface. How easy it looked, and how very different reality would prove to be. The first time you see a Baileys you might think you're looking at a glass of milk, but try drinking a pint of it. Then have another one. By the time you've drunk six you might be in a similar state to a climber approaching the Canaleta. It's not easy. We cached equipment, had some lunch, then returned to Plaza de Mulas to rest and recover.

We expected to be gone at least five days the next time we left base camp, for our summit push. The weather had been fine every day, and although wispy clouds shooting off the summit were a permanent feature, everywhere else was cloudless. At Plaza Canada the penitentes field we had hacked water from was drying out, and it took a long time to fill up my bottles from the one clean trickle I could locate with my ice axe. I picked up all the kit I had left there, and the following day continued to Nido carrying about fifteen kilograms. It may not seem much, but my pack was full, and I had all sorts of equipment strapped to the outside.

We spent two nights at Nido acclimatising, and completed another load carry to Camp 3 at a place called

Berlin. Beyond Nido the Normal Route bypassed the Gran Acarreo by ascending firmer ground between the rocky outcrops of the North Ridge. At last there was a change from the monotony of the giant scree slope which had been our only objective for days on end.

Berlin was a long-established camp in the shelter of rocks, with three battered A-frame huts in various states of disrepair. The most recent was named Berlin by German climbers after a friend died on the mountain, but the name is now applied to the whole campsite. Although they were called huts, in reality they were no more than garden sheds pitched at 5,900m on one of the windiest mountains on Earth. They reminded me of the wooden house which collapses in the opening sequence of the 1970s BBC comedy series *The Goodies*. They had stood for many years, but I expected them to fall over at any moment. I was glad I had a tent. The area had been used as a campsite since long before the rules about waste disposal were introduced, and it wasn't the most pleasant environment to camp in.

Before returning to Nido for a second night we walked a little further up the ridge above Berlin for some extra acclimatisation. I was wearing my ordinary gloves and hadn't brought my down mitts. By the time we reached Piedras Blancas, an outcrop of white rocks above 6,000m, my fingers were perishing. I could sense them going through the red-to-purple-to-black stage I experienced on Mera Peak. When I sat down and removed my gloves, my fingers were just starting to turn a shade of indigo. I rubbed my hands together and put them under my armpits in a desperate attempt to get some warmth back into them. I resisted the temptation to stick them down my crotch, and eventually they warmed up enough to get some feeling back, but it left me nervous about summit day. Although I would be wearing my down mitts, we would be climbing at night when it was even colder, and I wasn't willing to sacrifice fingers.

Back at Nido, the weather seemed to be changing; the wind was picking up, and for the first time since we arrived in base camp the upper reaches of the Gran Acarreo were obscured by clouds.

Nevertheless I was relaxed as I walked up to Berlin again the following day. I felt in good shape, we were now in position to have a shot at the summit, and we had a three-day weather window if we needed it.

The climb that day was short. We arrived before lunch and had many hours to rest before our summit attempt. Later in the afternoon I emerged from my tent to see Dan's head poking up behind a rock a few metres away.

'What do you think, Dan – are you feeling confident?' I shouted over to him.

He looked uneasy. 'Windy, isn't it?' he replied after what seemed like a struggle.

Steve and Matt emerged from their tent and joined our conversation.

'I think it's going to be cold, Dan,' Matt said.

'What's that?' Dan replied.

'I said I think it's going to be cold.'

'Come over and talk to us, Dan,' Steve said. 'What are you doing over there?'

'What the fuck do you think I'm doing?' he replied.

It was only then we realised he was relieving his bowels.

Dan may have felt awkward, and so did we when we realised – well, OK, perhaps highly amused is a better description than awkward – but soon *awkward* would be a memory. The following day we might be anything from very uncomfortable to suffering uncontrollably. We were mountaineers now, and if we wanted to climb big mountains then we were going to have to get used to trivial discomforts like relieving ourselves in public.

It was 4.30am when I awoke the following morning and started to get ready for our summit climb. The thermometer at Berlin read -20ºC, but a sharp wind blasted across us and it felt much colder. I gulped down a couple of mugs of tea outside the hut which Lionel and our other guides were using as a kitchen, and we left for the summit at six o'clock.

It was still dark, but sunlight soon started to illuminate the trail as we threaded our way between the rocky outcrops of the North Ridge. Although it was technically a ridge because the terrain fell away on both sides, the angle was very gentle, and often the path ascended in zigzags as it had on the scree below. Thankfully the ground was now much firmer. We passed Piedras Blancas and I was pleased to discover my forearm-sized down mitts were doing their job. My fingers were warm as toast, and when I removed the mitts to get at my water bottles, my hands warmed up as soon as I put them back on. My toes were not as comfortable, but by wiggling them inside my bright red boots I could keep them warm enough.

Above Piedras Blancas the trail slanted up another dry slope to the next outcrop, Piedras Negras. We laboured on. I stuck firmly to the heels of Lionel as he led the way. I was used to plodding along at the back, but this time I was determined not to be left behind if the group became separated. Behind me was Trevor, the mischievous professorial banker, who told me in Mendoza that he hadn't done any training. He seemed to be the only one of us who wasn't struggling. Despite his nonchalant appearance he was a natural athlete. Every time we continued after a break, he held out a hand to let me walk in front, like a distinguished English gentleman holding the door for a lady.

It was a long time before Lionel stopped again. The next leg of the journey took us over a stony section of lightly sprinkled snowfields. I took in nothing of my surroundings, and concentrated on putting one foot in front of the other and wiggling my toes to keep them warm. I lost track of time, but suddenly I looked up and saw the top of a battered A-frame hut like the ones at Berlin. I recognised it from photographs, and knew at once we had arrived at Independencia. The hut lay in a broad, sheltered balcony between rocks, and at 6,400m it was close to the halfway point for summit day on the Normal Route. On the opposite side of the balcony the North Ridge rose sharply up steep crags, but our path led across a short slope to the right which took us up to the long traverse across the top of the Gran Acarreo, the part of the trail we had studied many times as we acclimatised at base camp.

I felt quite tired and feasted on snack food to get my energy back. I hadn't realised how cold it was until we stopped moving. We rested at Independencia for twenty minutes, as we had done on Mera Peak, and once again the bitter wind blasted against me, but this time I was properly equipped and my hands and feet felt comfortable.

It wasn't so for everybody. Some started complaining of the cold and others spoke of turning around. There seemed to be some doubt about whether we would continue, and we appeared to be waiting for a guide from another group to ascend the slope above us and assess the wind conditions on the traverse. With great relief I watched him reach the top and wave for us to come on.

I resumed my position behind Lionel, unaware that behind me five members of the team had quit. At the top of the short slope above Independencia the view opened out and we stood above the Gran Acarreo at long last. We could see the traverse ahead of us beneath Aconcagua's summit rocks, and I felt a new breath of life seep through me, as I had when I saw Stella Point on Kilimanjaro. I was buzzing.

For the first time since we left camp I felt like the summit was within our grasp.

I knew we could do this, and it was an exhilarating feeling.

We reached a finger of rock a short way along the traverse and took shelter from the wind. There were only six clients and three guides remaining. I hadn't noticed Trevor was no longer behind me, having turned back when he realised his toes were becoming frozen. Chris and Lionel were deep in conversation as they studied the route to the foot of the Canaleta.

Then Lionel looked back at us and spoke a single word that floored me.

'Sorry!'

I knew it was cold and windy, but until that moment I hadn't been aware that our group was shrinking. Because my fingers and toes were much more comfortable than they had been on Mera Peak, it didn't occur to me that our guides were having serious doubts about whether conditions were safe enough to continue. Although we were climbing in beautiful sunshine they were looking up and seeing suspicious wispy clouds like the ones we saw batter the summit from Cerro Bonete.

'It is five hours to the summit,' Lionel said when he saw my surprise. 'And there is no more shelter.'

We were at 6,460m. Chris waited for me as I took some last photographs from the highest point we reached. I didn't argue with the decision to go down, because I knew that if we went very much further I would be too exhausted for another attempt on our two spare summit days.

'We can have another go tomorrow,' I said.

'I don't think that's the deal,' Chris replied.

This was also unexpected, and I sank deeper into despair. I felt like we were giving up too easily and I needed to compose my thoughts.

I lingered on the descent back to Berlin in a way I had been unable to during the ascent, and I took many photographs. The line of ochre peaks dusted with snow was so far below us I felt like I was standing on a cloud. The view from the summit must be magnificent, but would I ever see it?

Chris was waiting for me to catch up, and I asked again about the possibility of another attempt. He was more thoughtful now, and appeared to be weighing up the options.

'Let's get back to Berlin, talk to Lionel, see how everyone is feeling and take it from there,' he said.

There was a glimmer of hope. I rushed back to camp and rounded up the rest of the team to see if anyone else was interested in another shot. Six of us were willing to give it another go, and we had nothing to lose by trying. Everything was in place, with plenty of food, and tents pitched in a sheltered location at 5,900m. It was still only eleven o'clock; we had the rest of the day to recover.

It was down to Lionel. As soon as Chris arrived he went over to the hut to speak to him.

But Lionel was already beginning to pack up, and his response was immediate.

'No, one attempt only,' he said.

And that was that.

Although Chris was in charge, and was willing to make another attempt, he needed the help and experience of our Argentine guides for us to succeed.

Utterly deflated, we were determined to prove we still had bundles of energy. We packed up our tents and equipment there and then, descended to base camp, and completed the twenty-five kilometre trek along the Horcones Valley to the roadhead the following day.

Aconcagua was a bitter experience for me, but it was a lesson I needed to learn. Failing to reach the summit, for whatever reason, is part and parcel of mountaineering – and it's something every mountaineer needs to accept without feeling the crushing sense of disappointment I had on that occasion. More often than not failure is due to the weather, or dangerous conditions on the mountain. For many it could be because they are not strong or skilled enough, while for others it may be due to an unfortunate accident or injury. And for those of us who sign up to be led, sometimes we have to accept the decision of our guides however much we may disagree with them.

Many years later I can look back on that Aconcagua expedition without emotion. My impressions are mixed. On the one hand, I realise it was very unlikely we would have reached the summit had we continued that day. It was bitterly cold and the winds were strong, and although my hands and feet were still comfortable when we turned back, there were many hours of climbing ahead of us. The winds would have been even fiercer closer to the top. I also know that no one reached the summit on subsequent days, so it's likely we would have failed had we tried again on our two spare summit days.

Despite this, I still believe we gave up too easily. We had trained hard and expended emotional energy to be there. We spent a lot of money on the expedition, took a month off work and used up most of our annual holiday allowance. On the mountain itself we spent days patiently waiting. The work to get everything in place for a summit attempt was physically very hard. I know now that failure on a mountain is easier to bear if you keep trying, and only admit defeat when all your options are exhausted. We still had options when we packed up and left.

But if I had a third hand, that would be holding the most important knowledge of all: that reaching the summit is just one satisfying moment of an experience that has lasted much longer. Many times since, I have sat in a tent cursing the weather, only to pinch myself and remember where I am. I could be sitting in a meeting room listening to someone droning on about how one of the directors was upset about not being asked for his opinion; or rushing to compile statistics for a manager who needs them immediately (and preferably yesterday); or swearing at a computer screen because the network has just gone down and if the report I'm writing isn't finished in an hour then the company will go bankrupt and everyone will die. I could be sitting behind a desk, worrying myself sick about my endless duty to be doing more and more in less and less time.

For most of our working lives we have to deal with these stresses and worries which, from a distance, seem contrived. Instead I'm away from all that, enjoying the easy pace of expedition life, surrounded by breathtaking mountains that not even Thomas Edison could have invented. What matters is not reaching the summit, but just being there and enjoying the moment.

I've since been to many beautiful places with Jagged Globe and have many reasons to be grateful to them. What happened on Aconcagua all those years ago is no longer important. I learned much from the experience, and blame no one. I still keep in touch with Chris from time to time. He has gone on to become one of Jagged Globe's most experienced high-altitude leaders, and has led successful expeditions to the 8,000m peaks.

And in one very tangible respect I owed them all a favour. Had we reached the summit, then I would have gone home with Aconcagua ticked, and the memory of those days on end spent staring at – and trudging up and down – that monotonous scree slope. Perhaps I would have lived the rest of my life thinking Aconcagua was a boring climb.

But then I would have forgotten the South Face, and the fact that mountains have many aspects and I just needed to find the right one.

Five years later I returned there and climbed the eastern side on the False Polish Glacier Route. With its gullies, plateaus and snowfields, and with the scenery changing from hour to hour, it could have been a completely different mountain – and a very beautiful one. I was lucky to climb with a Peruvian guide called Augusto Ortega, who had summited South America's highest peak over fifty times, more than anyone else. Instead of making what seemed like the half-hearted attempt of my first visit, we fought and defeated everything the mountain threw at us, battling through a blizzard on summit day, approaching the top with Augusto breaking trail through knee-deep snow. I was another climber – more experienced, yet more prepared for failure too. It was one of my happiest and most satisfying expeditions, and I may never have experienced it had I reached the summit first time around.

Even though I failed to reach the summit at my first attempt on Aconcagua, I still made progress and learned many important lessons. I discovered that the expedition lifestyle of passing the time at base camp, looking up at the mountain and gradually making progress in a series of load carries, was one that appealed to me. The west side of Aconcagua wasn't the prettiest mountain face to spend weeks staring at, but if I could cope with that, what about spending weeks camped at the foot of a stunningly beautiful one?

Best of all, I was still enjoying myself and wanted to

climb higher.

But big expeditions are not easy to accommodate into a working life. I managed to take a month's holiday to climb Aconcagua by going at Christmas, when businesses close and employers are more open to granting extended leave. There are other times when asking my boss for a three-week holiday felt like asking if his 18-year-old daughter needed a climbing partner. As for getting two months off to climb an 8,000m peak ...

Some companies allow their employees an extended unpaid career break if they have worked there long enough, but it's usually a one-off. I had just learned that however well prepared you are, you can never guarantee to reach the summit of a mountain. Imagine how much worse the disappointment would be if I knew I was investing in a one-and-only opportunity. Everest was still a long way off. It was unlikely I would ever gain enough experience, and it seemed big expeditions were a pipe dream for all but the lucky few who were able to make a career out of it. I was certainly not in that league and knew I never would be.

My discovery that expedition life lay within my reach came quite by chance. For a second time my job became intolerable, this time through the simple uncontrollable circumstance of reporting to a new line manager who was not so sympathetic to my aspirations. I was overlooked for promotion and found myself in a dead-end job. On the day I was rejected, I sat in my office feeling deflated, trying to summon up the motivation to continue with my work, when a senior executive walked in and expressed his sympathy.

'There's always a silver lining to these things,' he said.

At the time I didn't understand what he meant, but I now know they were the wise words of a man who had taken a few falls. There are places in the world where people are born into unfortunate circumstances, and there's little they can do to change them, but for most of us lucky enough to be born into a democracy, we have options. I was in a job I didn't enjoy, but that's trivial compared with what some people have to endure.

The suffering was mostly in my head. I remember writing down three things that would make life better if I changed the way I thought about them. The first was craving for something I couldn't have (a promotion); the second was taking work home with me (why stress about what happened earlier in the day when you're sitting at home reading a good book?); and the third was worrying about the future.

The last of these was the most important one. The solution is usually in our own hands, and life has a way of sorting itself out if we remain positive. Unpleasant events can be the kick up the backside we need to make changes; so it proved for me. Had it not been for a fall in my previous job I would never have discovered high-altitude trekking. Now I was being offered another chance to escape from the soul-destroying environment of office politics that becomes a daily routine for so many of us.

Being overlooked for promotion isn't so bad when it sends you somewhere else, and I wouldn't have swapped the place it sent me for anywhere in the world. It was the signpost that eventually led me to Everest.

If I met that line manager again, I might even shake her hand.

A few months later I was back in the Himalayas enjoying a feeling of complete freedom. I had quit my job and had nothing to occupy my thoughts but the days ahead, travelling through the wide-open spaces of Tibet, surrounded by azure skies, sandy brown hills and dazzling snow-capped peaks. One Friday I was running about, frantically trying to tie up the loose ends in a job I no longer cared about, and three days later I was in one of the most peaceful landscapes on Earth. If it was possible to know what a dung beetle feels like coming up for air from inside a particularly unpleasant cow pat, then I think I came close.

Reaching the summit of Everest was still far from my thoughts, but its lower slopes were very close indeed when I renewed my acquaintance with Mark Dickson in April 2007 in the tranquil leafy garden of the Summit Hotel, Patan (one of the three cities of the Kathmandu Valley). We hadn't seen each other since we'd climbed Kilimanjaro together five years earlier. I recognised him immediately, but things had changed in the intervening years, and I suspected he didn't remember me quite as well.

'What's your name again?' he said. 'I thought you had more hair.'

'I did,' I replied, crestfallen. It was true; my hair was receding, while Mark still had more hair than tact.

With Aconcagua long since forgotten I joined another Jagged Globe expedition to climb Everest's North Col. If all went to plan we would be following George Mallory's footsteps up the East Rongbuk Glacier, then climbing up a steep wall of seracs to 7,000m. It was a climb that would take me above the altitude I had hoped to reach on Aconcagua, and provide me with some technical climbing experience as well.

Our guide was a cheerful Australian called Mic Rofe, who was a good ten years younger than the rest of us.

'It's going to be interesting spending the next month with you guys,' he said. 'Between you, you've been to every continent except Antarctica, and climbed some great mountains. Cho Oyu, Spantik, Denali, Aconcagua …'

I glanced around me; most of the group were looking quizzical. In fact Mic could have expressed himself more concisely by omitting the words *between you*, as he had simply reeled off Mark's peak list. When I met him in Africa, Mark had quit his job and was on gardening leave. Like me, rather than returning to work afterwards he had taken a year off to travel the world. Unlike me he hadn't returned to a normal job with limited holiday. He had become one of three partners running their own investment banking firm, and had convinced the other two they only needed him to work six months a year. He spent the other six months climbing mountains.

As he explained this to me, two thoughts crossed my mind. The first was *what a wanker*, but the second was more positive. I had just resigned for the second time in my life after becoming hacked off with my job. Another period of extended travelling lay before me, and it occurred to me that if Mark was able to arrange a life that enabled him to have more than a few weeks' holiday a year, why couldn't I?

Another of our companions that day was on his own journey towards a life of adventure. Ian Cartwright was a contract surveyor who worked offshore on boats and oil platforms. His contracts were intensive, involving long hours, no days off and a great deal of stress, but they were short, paid well, and gave him plenty of time off between jobs.

Our trip to the north side of Everest started with a flight across the Himalayas to Lhasa, Tibet's capital, and from there we drove for three days across the wide open spaces of the Tibetan plateau. It was my first visit to this once-secretive land of mediaeval monks and Bon black magic. I was surprised to discover the old Lhasa had all but vanished. Apart from the amazing Potala Palace – former residence of the Dalai Lama which sprawls across a hillside in the middle of town – it's just another modern Chinese city. But its geography ensures Tibet will remain a harsh land long after China's government has a change of heart and invites the Dalai Lama back again. While Lhasa lies at a relatively balmy altitude of 3,500m, the majority of the land is at well over 4,000m. This makes average temperatures more than 20ºC colder than at sea level. Its position north of the Himalayas means prevailing weather systems have deposited their rainfall by the time they reach it. The land is a desert, with very few plants and trees, and the cold dry winds are legendary.

When the first British expeditions explored Everest in the 1920s, it took them several weeks to trek there from Sikkim in north-east India. Instead we drove along the Friendship Highway for three days in Toyota Land Cruisers. The road was once a dirt track linking Lhasa and Kathmandu, but the Chinese were intending to carry the Olympic torch to the summit of Everest the following year, and they were in the process of paving it at an alarming rate. The road was as smooth as Bobby Charlton's forehead. The 4x4 Land Cruisers were hardly necessary as we drove in convoy through vast dusty valleys and over high passes, with horizons disappearing into infinity. It was a land made for giants – and it was easy to see why the Tibetans believe in so many mountain deities.

Occasionally the setting was profaned when our drivers pulled up by the side of a wide road and we all jumped out to pee in a line. We stopped in Shegar, a small village a few kilometres off the highway, where a ruined dzong (or fort) stood on the very pinnacle of a pointed summit. It was a place Sandy Irvine used to test his newly modified oxygen apparatus during the 1924 expedition, and we followed in his footsteps to a tangle of Buddhist prayer flags among the ruins at the top of the hill. Here we had our first view of

Everest fifty kilometres away, crowning a line of snowcaps which included Makalu and Cho Oyu rising above a foreground of dusty brown hills. It was probably my imagination, but the clearness of the deep azure sky was astonishing.

Shegar had become a popular tourist stop for people on their way to Everest Base Camp. No sooner had we climbed out of the vehicles than we were mobbed by a gaggle of tiny children begging for money. Ian gave them a handful of yuan to guide him up the hill, and they shot off at breakneck speed, laughing as he struggled after them. The rest of us took it more leisurely. We were still acclimatising, and we knew it was wise to walk slowly up the hillside.

More of a surprise was Tim, the oldest member of the party, who was in his early sixties and had taken up mountaineering after he retired a few years earlier. He had one of those genial faces, with short grey beard, big red nose and a glint in his eye, which made people want to laugh at him even when he hadn't said anything funny. We wondered whether he would be able to keep up with the rest of us. When he announced at breakfast he had pulled a muscle in his back while sleeping and was staying at the hotel to rest, our fears were confirmed. It was a surprise when he appeared at a col on our way down from the hill, leading an entire playground of schoolchildren like the Pied Piper of Hamlin. Having sat upright against a flask of hot water for an hour, he decided his back was much better, so he strapped on his climbing helmet, hitched a ride from a Tibetan on a motorbike along the rutted dirt track to Shegar, and rushed up the hillside to catch up with us.

The view of Everest from the north is far more distinctive than from the Nepalese side. The Rongbuk Valley could have been designed as a landscaped feature to frame the mountain's splendour as you approach, like the gardens of the Taj Mahal. The summit was hidden in cloud on the day we arrived, but Everest was so familiar to me from photographs that as we drove up the valley I began to recognise its lower features. Although the summit pyramid wasn't visible, the West Ridge to its right was unmistakable: an angle of 45º rock descending to meet a horizontal ridge of snow. I realised this must be the snow slope Mallory climbed during the 1921 reconnaissance, when he looked down into the Western Cwm and provided the name that is now so familiar to Everest climbers.

I saw Everest in its full glory the following morning. The Norton Couloir scarring the left-hand edge of the summit pyramid was perhaps the most distinctive feature, but the route up the East Rongbuk Glacier in front of Changtse was also quite obvious. It was this highway to the North Col that Mallory famously overlooked during the 1921 reconnaissance expedition. Everest towered above the top end of the Rongbuk Valley like a giant fortress, but part of its North Face was obscured by the smaller peak of Changtse standing in front. The two peaks are linked by the North Col, and while studying the mountain from a distance Mallory had already identified a route up the North Ridge from the col. This route joins the North-East Ridge, which can be followed all the way to the summit. If they could find a way onto the North Col then Mallory knew they would have found a practical route to the summit.

From the Rongbuk Valley there were two obvious options: round the left-hand side of Changtse to approach the North Col from the east, and round the right-hand side to approach it from the west. The right-hand route was the more prominent, and involved heading straight up the main Rongbuk Glacier to the foot of the North Face. Mallory tried this one first, but decided the climb to the North Col from there was too difficult for porters laden with equipment.

The left-hand route involved branching off up the side valley of the East Rongbuk. Although it wasn't as prominent as the main Rongbuk Valley, it was still pretty blindingly obvious, but apparently not to Mallory. After rejecting the first option he retreated to base camp and beyond to make a massive semicircle some distance from the bottom of the mountain to see if he could find another route up to the North Col from the east side. To give him credit, he succeeded in finding one over a high pass, the Lhakpa La, but by then a more meticulous survey of the area had been completed by the surveyor Oliver Wheeler. He described and mapped the obvious approach up the East Rongbuk Glacier that Mallory had missed but I could see as clearly as if it were a big signpost saying *Everest this way*.

Mark Horrell beside the puja platform at Everest Base Camp. Behind him the smaller peak of Changtse rises in front of Everest's North Face. The East Rongbuk Valley, which Mallory failed to spot, clearly branches off to the left.

These days Mallory's oversight would probably have led to him obtaining sponsorship from *Specsavers.*

I was still at an early stage in my journey to becoming a mountaineer, and I learned much while we acclimatised at base camp. Mic took us onto a small icefield on a nearby hillside to teach us some technical skills. The most difficult part of the expedition would be the climb from Advanced Base Camp up the North Col Wall. This whole section of mountain would be strung with ropes which were anchored into the ice at every rope length, enabling climbers to use the ropes as a handrail. Indeed, people climbing even higher would find that teams of Sherpas had put these fixed ropes in place all the way to the summit.

Our training mostly involved learning how to move up and down the fixed ropes safely and efficiently. We learned how to use a jumar, an ascending device which slides up a rope but locks in place when pulled from below. We learned how to attach carabiners and Prusik cords to the rope for extra safety, and how to abseil down again.

Some climbers will tell you such training is inadequate and that use of fixed ropes and jumars isn't proper climbing. More recently these arguments have given rise to the belief that climbing Everest is easy. It's certainly true that fixed ropes and jumars on the steeper sections have made Everest easier and safer to climb for less-gifted mountaineers. Because the jumar slides up the rope but locks in place when tugged from below, it provides two benefits. The first is safety – if the climber falls it will hold them – and it also enables them to climb a difficult technical section more easily by hauling themselves up. But *easy* and *easier* are two different things.

As for whether it's proper climbing, that depends where you stand on the concept of *alpinism*. This philosophy promotes a 'pure' style of climbing, fast and light, on new routes and with a minimum of support. Alpinism places more importance on the style of ascent than whether the goal is achieved. It emphasises pioneering, risk and uncertainty over established routes and well-trodden paths, and puts great value on self-sufficiency. Alpinists, as their name implies, climb alpine style rather than expedition style, and many alpinists and aspiring alpinists see commercial expeditions which used fixed ropes, bottled oxygen and guides as anathema. While many alpinists see nothing wrong with guided commercial mountaineering, and simply look upon it as a different activity to the one they pursue, many object to it. At its extreme fringes the arguments about climbing ethics and style can resemble religious fanaticism.

There is no doubt that alpinists deserve far more respect than commercial climbers for their boldness and climbing ability, and for sticking to their principles, but then you can say Pelé deserves far more respect for his three FIFA World Cup winners' medals than my mate Ade does for winning the John Smith's Yorkshire Brewery Pub Trophy in his local Sunday league tournament. Ade was certainly excelling at his hobby in a way that was beyond me, and I was in awe of all the people at base camp who were hoping to climb Everest. The successful alpinists are the professional footballers of the climbing world; they do not need to be critical of commercial mountaineers, who are simply doing it as a hobby, any more than Lionel Messi needs to belittle Ade for not being good enough at keepy-uppy.

In any case, I was unaware of many of these nuances and was unlikely to have cared if I had known. My ambition was not to become a skilful climber, but to enjoy the scenery and learn enough to reach places I wouldn't otherwise get to. I had no qualms about using a jumar, any more than I would hesitate to eat my meal with a knife and fork, or wipe my backside with tissue instead of using my fingers.

It was also my first experience of a *puja* ceremony, an essential part of any Himalayan expedition which uses Sherpa support. The Sherpas believe summits are the abode of gods who must be appeased before a mountain can be climbed. The ceremony takes place beside a platform built from rocks in a prominent location at base camp. The platform contains a small furnace for burning juniper branches and incense, and climbers put their axes, crampons and other technical equipment beside it to be blessed during the ceremony. The puja is usually conducted by a monk who chants mantras and makes offerings to ask the mountain gods for safe passage during the climb. At the end of the ceremony the Sherpas hang prayer flags from a pole and spread them to all corners of camp like spokes of a wheel.

Our puja on this occasion was a bit different. We were taken to a *gompa*, or small monastery, called Zarongbuk on a hillside near base camp, where twenty exuberant pilgrim women dragged us down a trapdoor into an underground cave with a Buddhist shrine. Two of our Sherpas, Nima and Pasang, murmured prayers for three minutes before the women hauled us back out again amid hoots of laughter. I never did discover what they found so funny, but hopefully the mountain gods were pleased.

One of the older members of our team was a Czech called Petr whose professional career made the rest of us look as exciting as a cheese sandwich. One day at base camp I asked him what he did for a living, and after talking fluently for twenty minutes about his career over forty years – which included working as a software engineer, agricultural wholesaler, stonemason, builder, and property tycoon – he turned to me with a helpless expression and said:

'When people ask what I do for a living, I don't know what to say. I do whatever comes, and I am happy.'

Petr had another thing to be happy about: his daughter

Klara was hoping to become the first Czech woman to climb Everest. He joined our expedition to be near her for some of the climb, and she visited us at base camp. She had already been there three weeks and climbed as high as 7,700m. She was much younger than we were and I remember thinking she looked in remarkable shape for someone who had been above 5,000m for so long.

Shortly before we left to ascend the East Rongbuk Valley I wandered over to a mound of moraine which housed the base camp memorials. Several dozen cairns of differing shapes and sizes had been erected for the bewildering number of people who had died on Everest. I spent a few sobering moments contemplating the stones and stopping briefly as I recognised the names of famous climbers. I knew most were far greater climbers than I would ever be. They included Joe Tasker and Pete Boardman, the two British climbers who went missing on the North-East Ridge in 1982; and Marco Siffredi, a French snowboarder who made the first ever descent from the summit by snowboard in 2001, only to disappear attempting a harder route the following year.

Incredible as these feats of mountaineering were, I couldn't help feeling a sense of hubris too. Boardman and Tasker were both in their early thirties and Siffredi was just twenty-three. All of them had achieved a great deal in their lives, but still they wanted more. Had they over-reached themselves on routes the mountain gods had forbidden?

During the 1924 expedition they called the route up the East Rongbuk Valley *Via Dolorosa*, after the street in Jerusalem that is believed to be the route Jesus took on the way to his crucifixion. Whether that was how mountaineers felt on their way up Everest I didn't know, but it certainly involved some arduous terrain. Towering ice pinnacles presented an impassable barrier on the way up the glacier.

Unlike the penitentes on Aconcagua, which were no higher than a man and formed by sun and wind over the course of a single season, these were dozens of metres high and created by the pressure of the glacier crushing its ice into ridges as it gradually flowed down the valley. We called them *sharks' fins*, and they seemed a terrifying proposition to skilled climbers, never mind Tibetan porters carrying heavy loads.

But there was also a not-so-secret route which was so straightforward it enabled yaks to ascend as high as Advanced Base Camp (ABC) at 6,400m. This was a strip of medial moraine the British expeditions had found in the 1920s which ran right up the middle of the glacier for much of its length. Although the tumble of jagged rocks and boulders made for difficult terrain underfoot, it presented a strenuous walk rather than a difficult climb. This moraine seems so remarkable it has become known as the *Magic Highway*. It took us three days of laboured plodding and two intermediate camps to reach ABC, and it was easy to forget we were walking to the same altitude as the summit of Mera Peak, still the highest I had ever been.

During the week we spent at ABC my head was pounding so badly it felt like Metallica was rehearsing in the tent next door. Leader of the 1924 expedition Edward Norton described ABC as a 'truly horrid spot'[45] and reminisced about the hatefulness of the evening meals. I think I know how he felt. Cows spend their lives chewing grass just to survive, and at ABC it was a bit like that with me and potatoes. At dinner I spent long hours chewing and chewing then chewing some more, and the spuds steadfastly refused to go down until I washed them away with tea. I even struggled with staples like soup and corn flakes. I took liberal quantities of aspirin for my headaches, but I might just as well have taken alcohol for all the good it did.

We were often blessed with sun in the mornings, when

lying in a hot tent was a comfortable experience, but in the afternoon the clouds closed in, wind whistled through camp, and the only way to stay warm was by curling up inside our sleeping bags. In his great comic novel *The Ascent of Rum Doodle*, W.E. Bowman described this state variously as *tent lassitude*, *base camp lassitude* and even *stopping-for-the-night lassitude*. I discovered the best way to alleviate it was with activity. Mic gave us plenty of opportunity by taking us onto the glacier every day to practice our rope skills. These sessions may not have turned me into a great climber, but after a few days I was able to jumar with the best of them. Miraculously, the discomforts of Rum Doodle lassitude disappeared for a few hours as I warmed up, lost my headache and enjoyed the view.

And the view was pretty special. It was a very different Everest from the black rock pyramid you see in most photographs. Looking across the crumbling ice of the East Rongbuk Glacier the fearsome Pinnacles took centre stage – a jagged line of knife-edge rock Mallory dismissed as impossible when he looked up at them from the Kharta Valley on the east side in 1921. They marked the place where Boardman and Tasker went missing in 1982, and were an obstacle which thwarted all attempts to climb the North-East Ridge until Russell Brice found a way past them in 1988. From ABC the Pinnacles looked like the highest points on the mountain, but the true summit peeped up on the horizon just behind them and could usually be identified by the plume of cloud which appeared to be issuing from it. The two ridges, the North-East and the North Ridge converged above the Pinnacles. The latter was clearly a much easier proposition to climb, but below it stretched the apparently sheer ice cliff of the North Col Wall. This was the feature that drew most of our attention because in a few days' time we would be trying to climb it.

Everest was the only focus for the majority of people camped at ABC. A smaller peak on the opposite side of the valley may have escaped the attention of many of them, but not us. The difficult North-East Ridge descended to a gentle col, the Rapui La, and on the other side of it the land rose again to a small trapezium of snow, 7,045m Lhakpa Ri, first climbed by Bill Tilman in 1935, and photographed by Mallory's team when they crossed the Lhakpa La on their roundabout route to the North Col in 1921. After a few days of headaches and rope training at ABC we crossed the glacier to climb it ourselves.

The phrase *snow slog* can be applied to quite a few climbs in the Himalayas, and there were few more appropriate times to apply it than this one. We set off into a wide snow basin in relatively benign conditions just as the sun was rising, but the snow began to fall in giant flakes as we climbed, laying out an ever-thickening carpet beneath our feet. It was tiring enough for me, but for Mic and our two Sherpas, who were sharing the trail-breaking at the front, it must have been exhausting. By the time we reached the Lhakpa La, where Mallory looked across to the North Col for the first time and realised Everest could be climbed, ABC had disappeared from view and we ascended into a whiteout.

We continued, but our pace slowed to that of a snail crawling over a plate of blancmange. A couple of the team ran out of energy, and every time we stopped for a short breather, they collapsed exhausted in a bed of snow. It seemed impossible we could climb any more slowly, but finally we reached the tiny north summit, just 600m above ABC, nine hours after setting out. The main summit lay a short distance away along a narrow ridge, but the fresh snow rendered it too dangerous to cross without triggering an avalanche. My altimeter read 7,005m and I was satisfied: I had reached 7,000m for the very first time.

It took us another four hours to return. Our footprints had been obliterated by the fresh snow, and we had to break trail all the way down again, but gradually the clouds evaporated and the North Col reappeared. Darkness was falling as we stumbled into camp. Years later Phil Crampton, who was leading another expedition on the north side of Everest that year and will play an important part later in this story, told me he remembered watching our two rope teams vanish into the clouds from ABC. It was a day when everyone else in camp had not the slightest inclination to leave their tents, and by the time we reappeared just before dusk several people were thinking about sending out a rescue party.

It wasn't necessary; all we needed was drink. Howard Somervell had seventeen mugs of tea when he returned to ABC from his summit attempt in 1922. My pee bottle wasn't big enough to handle binge drinking on that scale just before I hit my sleeping bag, but I managed several mugfuls nonetheless.

We were a bedraggled lot during our rest day after the ascent. Despite having smeared on enough suncream to impregnate a wild boar, I woke up with a sunburned nose, mouth and chin, and my face was oozing a mysterious waxy substance which was impervious to wet wipes.

The weather was improving and several teams at ABC were preparing for their summit attempts. Petr went over to his daughter Klara's camp to wish her good luck, but not everyone was treating Everest with the respect it deserved. One climber, a Dutchman known as *The Iceman*, was aiming to become the first person to climb Everest in shorts. He had run a half marathon north of the Arctic Circle barefoot, bare-chested and clad in just his shorts, and was able to lie in a bath of ice for more than an hour without visible signs of suffering, although I imagine parts of his anatomy were difficult to find afterwards. We learned that someone else was planning to do a full traverse from north to south using a jet pack, and there was an intriguing tent pitched further up the moraine with a banner outside it advertising the *Korean Fly Jump Expedition*. We weren't sure what this meant, but the mind boggled.

With Everest becoming increasingly accessible to ordinary folk, climbers eager for sponsorship and publicity were arriving there each year announcing increasingly obscure firsts. Among the many outstanding climbs which deserve their place in mountaineering history are the first ascent by Hillary and Tenzing in 1953, the first traverse by Hornbein and Unsoeld in 1963, the first ascent without bottled oxygen by Messner and Habeler in 1978, and the first solo ascent by Messner in 1980 – but the first ascent by an amputee, first cancer survivor, first blind person, and first teen with Down's syndrome, are all obscure Everest records which have been claimed over the years. Every year someone announces they are the first from their country, the first woman, the oldest, or the youngest of a small subset of the world's population.

While these are undoubtedly great achievements on a personal level, so is every successful ascent of Everest for someone who has never climbed it before. The media attention paid to these obscure firsts is often disproportionate, and leads some people to believe, quite erroneously, that climbing Everest is easy. As for people claiming to be the first to take a bike up there, make a phone call left-handed, or have sex on the summit ... they are in danger of having their life's great achievement ranked alongside outlandish curiosities like the world's longest moustache, the most watermelons smashed with a single punch, or the fastest 100m sprint by a woman in high heels.

In 2013 the Nepalese government even announced they would be stationing a lookout at base camp, and one of their duties would be to 'constrain bizarre records'. They felt such publicity stunts tarnished the reputation of the world's highest mountain. It's difficult to argue with the sentiment, even if the provision seems as likely to succeed as a man playing a banjo on the summit without getting frostbite.

As I staggered up the moraine above ABC, gasping for breath and doubtful I had recovered after our ascent of Lhakpa Ri two days earlier, the prospect of becoming the first bald-headed Yorkshireman to drink a pint on top of Snowdon and go on to reach the North Col of Everest seemed unlikely. Petr turned round before we reached the far side of camp, and I was having doubts as I crossed the wide snow plateau beneath the North Col Wall. Up ahead I could see an apparently vertical wall of snow and ice leading up to the col. Fixed ropes zigzagged up it and disappeared out of sight, and the face was crawling with a mass of climbers looking like a very static army of ants. I gradually dropped behind the rest of the group. By the time I caught up with them and sprawled down in the snow at the foot of the wall I was completely overawed by what I saw ahead of me.

'How the hell am I supposed to get up that thing?' I asked Mic, panting with exhaustion.

I knew the slope ahead of us had been the scene of some legendary accidents. When descending it for the very first time in 1921, Mallory noticed their ascending track had triggered a small avalanche. The following year seven Sherpas were killed when a huge avalanche swept them over a fifty-foot ice cliff. In 1924 Mallory fell into a crevasse on the same slopes, saving himself by jamming his axe into its walls. Irvine described watching Norton glissade out of control during the same descent, and later in the expedition two more Sherpas slipped and were saved when Somervell drove his ice axe into the slope and hooked the rope over it. When descending just below the lip of the North Col in 1935, Eric Shipton was 'disconcerted'[46] to discover the entire surface of the wall had fallen a quarter of a mile in a two-metre slice, and crashed to the glacier below – the same glacier I was standing on at that very moment. What on Earth did I think I was doing?

Despite being the slowest across the glacier plateau, I was pushed to the front when we started moving again, and I clipped onto the fixed line behind Nima. To my amazement, as soon as we began climbing I found myself full of energy. The jumar helped. As I slid it up the rope I was able to pull on it and haul myself up by the arm. I had three limbs propelling me up the wall instead of two, and when we stopped for a few long breaths I could lean back in my harness and let the jumar take my weight.

Unlike on Lhakpa Ri when we were roped together, on the fixed lines we were able to climb at our own pace, and were held up only when we reached other climbers. One by one we overtook them when they stopped and let us by. The sun was beating down and a cold wind whipped spindrift across our faces, but Ian, Nima and I sped ahead of the others and kept up a steady pace all the way up the face. Although the wall appeared vertical from below, in reality it zigzagged between seracs and crevasses on slopes of around 45º. Just below the lip of the North Col it steepened significantly and became almost vertical. My ice-climbing training came in handy, but I was also able to drag myself up the rope with my jumar using a climbing technique as stylish as Noddy Holder's wardrobe.

I reached the top and flopped down in a heavenly sofa of soft snow I could easily have lost all of my worldly possessions down the back of. The wind had dropped and the sun tickled my face like a feather duster brushed soothingly across my cheeks. For a long while I had no inclination to move, but after half an hour, with no sign of the others, I stood up and plodded slowly through the North Col campsite to join Ian and Nima at the far end. Around a hundred tents were squeezed together in a narrow shelf beneath a tall ice cliff which provided shelter from southerly winds.

Ian and Nima were sitting in snow beside the path; in front of them was a huge drop to the glacier and an amazing view to the head of the East Rongbuk Valley. To the left ABC sprawled along the eastern foot of Changtse 600m below us, and Lhakpa Ri formed the horizon opposite.

My altimeter read 7,060m. I felt a great sense of achievement. Behind us the clouds parted briefly to reveal a sight that would return to my mind many times afterwards, and will continue to do so for a long time to come. The snow slopes of the North Ridge rose from the North Col up to the familiar profile of the North-East Ridge. Beneath it the black North Face of Everest fell for over 2,000m, and on its crown was the summit, the highest point on Earth. It seemed in touching distance, barely more than the height of Snowdon above our heads. In reality it was still 1,800m vertically and another three days of climbing, but ambition was beginning to stir.

As I returned through camp I passed Klara arriving on the col. She looked tired and was barely able to acknowledge me, but walking behind her was her guide Tashi Tenzing, grandson of Tenzing Norgay who made the first ascent of Everest in 1953. He was friendly, and stopped to shake my hand and congratulate me on getting this far. He said it was their fourth visit to the col, and they would be continuing to Camp 2 at 7,700m tomorrow, Camp 3 at 8,200m the following day, and the summit in three days' time. I was still in awe of Klara for what she was about to achieve (and achieve it she did), but I was starting to realise Everest summiteers don't have to be superhuman after all. She was a picture of good health when we saw her at base camp, but now she was as tired as we were, despite being much better acclimatised.

It was the moment I understood the summit of Everest was a realistic goal.

I descended confidently using my newly acquired ability with Prusik cords and my figure-of-eight abseil device. Despite the shorter day, I was much more exhausted when I staggered into ABC than I had been after our ascent of Lhakpa Ri.

The following morning my face was painful, and I examined it using the pocket mirror in my washbag. It wasn't a pretty sight at the best of times, but this time I gazed upon a purple leathery snout, cracked like a tortoise shell. My lips were badly blistered and turning white, and I had lost a small piece from the tip of my nose, which bulged bulbously like a proboscis monkey's. If a baboon was born looking like that, its mother would disown it.

At breakfast it was painful to eat. Although everyone had been affected by the weather to some degree, I was by far the worst off. Tim very kindly described my face as looking like a yak's arse. Although I had been applying suncream during the climb, it wasn't nearly enough. The Earth's atmosphere is very much thinner at extreme altitudes, and the wind that howled across the mountain scoured my face like sandpaper, making it drier still. Excessive and unnecessary sunburn after a climb is a classic sign of a novice mountaineer, and I had learned another lesson. As we returned to Kathmandu I left behind bits of my lips on tea mugs the length of the Friendship Highway.

More significantly I experienced exhaustion on a scale I

never believed possible. Three days later, after partying in a way only Mark Dickson knew, I woke up in Kathmandu troubled, and passed a morning in a strange mental state bordering on paranoia. For the next three days I spent much of my time feeling oddly lost and confused, as though I had woken from a coma and discovered the world had changed, rather like Woody Allen in the film *Sleeper* (although at that moment in time I was a good deal less handsome than the bespectacled New York screenwriter). I fell asleep anywhere and everywhere: in a bar in Thamel while talking to friends, sitting in a bean bag watching the FA Cup final at a house in Swayambhu, and sitting at a workstation in an internet café typing out an email. I wandered around Thamel, an area I knew well, feeling lost and bewildered.

The two Marks: Dickson (left) and Horrell (right) at Everest Base Camp (Photo: Jeremy Anson)

I had discovered how physically demanding big expeditions could be, but I wasn't discouraged. I had reached 7,000m for the first time, and the summit of Everest had become my ultimate ambition, one which I now believed to be possible.

I was ready for the next step, but to continue my journey I would need to find a way of earning a living which provided enough time off for expeditions. Mark and Ian had shown me that was possible too.

6 THE FIRST 8,000ER

I didn't know it yet, but I was becoming a mountaineer. I already had some of the skills of an alpine climber when Aconcagua introduced me to the siege tactics employed on large mountaineering expeditions. My climb to the North Col made me realise that Everest's summit was within reach, but there was still another important step. I needed to climb my first 8,000m peak, which meant crossing a significant boundary.

It was time for me to enter ... *The Death Zone* (cue evil laughter and dramatic organ chord).

The term *death zone*, or *todeszone* in its original German, was first coined by Edouard Wyss-Dunant, expedition leader of the 1952 Swiss Everest expedition which came within 250m of the summit a year before Hillary and Tenzing eventually reached it. In a paper on acclimatisation, published in the journal of the Swiss Foundation for Alpine Research, he described four zones a mountaineer passes through at extreme altitude. He used the term *todeszone* to describe altitudes where the body can no longer adapt and recovery is impossible, and placed the start of this zone at roughly 7,800m.

While the concept of the death zone is attractive to writers and mountaineers longing to make their climbs sound more exciting than they are, the term is somewhat theatrical. At the time Wyss-Dunant was writing, it was generally assumed the summit of Everest couldn't be reached without supplementary oxygen, but Reinhold Messner and Peter Habeler proved this theory wrong by making an oxygenless ascent in 1978. Many others have done it since then. Hundreds of people climb above 7,800m every year and come back safely, and while some people deteriorate, most who arrive back at high camp after their summit attempt wake up the following morning feeling better.

Of course, the higher you climb the less oxygen is available and the harder it gets, but there's no magic barrier at 7,800m where it suddenly feels like you've wandered into the smoking area at the World Tobacco Forum's Christmas party.

But I didn't know this at the time, and there was another dangerous phenomenon at that altitude which certainly did exist.

The jet stream is a narrow current of air that circulates the Earth between seven and twelve kilometres above its surface, frequently battering the summits of 8,000m peaks with winds of up to 200km/h. You can tell a peak is being clobbered by the jet stream when a strand of wispy ice crystals hangs off its summit like Peter Stringfellow's hair caught in a breeze. The summit of Everest often wears a distinctive plume of cloud which trails eastwards for as much as fifty kilometres. How on Earth would I be able to deal with such murderously high winds?

There was only one way to find out, and that was to get up to 8,000m and see.

It's not known who was the first person to notice there were only fourteen mountains over 8,000m. The British started measuring the heights of Himalayan peaks in the

19th century as part of the Great Trigonometrical Survey of India, a project to map Britain's Asian empire. The metre, on the other hand, was a French invention, first proposed as a universal measure of length by the French Academy of Sciences in 1791. Unsurprisingly, the Brits didn't adopt it straight away, any more than they asked their army to march to the Marseillaise, and all heights calculated by the Survey of India were measured in feet and inches. It's only been in the last thirty years the metre has become the preferred unit of measurement for altitude among British climbers. Americans still prefer to use feet.

In spite of this the fourteen peaks over 8,000m have enjoyed a special cachet, and the race to climb them defined the mountaineering history of the 20th century. The first man to attempt one was the British climber Albert Mummery, who in 1895 tried to climb 8,125m Nanga Parbat in what is now Pakistan. Nothing at all was known about climbing at that altitude, and Mummery had no appreciation of the enormous scale of Himalayan peaks, or how the reduced oxygen would affect his performance. He assumed he could use the same lightweight climbing methods which worked in the Alps, and assessed Nanga Parbat only in terms of objective climbing difficulties.

'I don't think there will be any serious mountaineering difficulties on Nanga,' he wrote in a letter to his wife, but later he told her 'the air is so baffling'.[47]

After being repelled by the 4,500m Rupal Face, a giant precipice which made Mont Blanc look like an amble up Primrose Hill with an umbrella, he decided to take a shortcut to another part of the mountain over a high, glaciated pass called the Diamir Gap – a name which in itself suggests an absence of something important. In Mummery's case this proved to be a dose of good mountaineering sense. He took two Gurkha soldiers with him, Ragobir Thapa and

Goman Singh, and was never seen again. It's likely all three died in an avalanche before they reached the pass.

Mummery, incidentally, is famous for describing three stages of *conquest* where mountains become easier with each new ascent.

All mountains appear doomed to pass through the three stages: An inaccessible peak – The most difficult ascent in the Alps – An easy day for a lady.[48]

Unusually for his day Mummery sometimes climbed with his wife, and perhaps even more surprisingly she never considered giving him a 'Joe Simpson' and cutting the rope while he hung over a crevasse.

If Mummery was a few spikes short of a crampon, he had nothing on the next man to attempt an 8,000er in 1902. Legendary occultist Aleister Crowley is better known for his self-proclaimed sobriquet *The Great Beast 666* than for mountaineering. His expedition to 8,611m K2 got off to an inauspicious start when he had an altercation with expedition leader Oscar Eckenstein (the man who invented the ten-point crampon) about whether they should hire a porter to carry his multi-volume occult library up the Baltoro Glacier. It descended into farce when he threatened teammate Guy Knowles with a revolver, causing Knowles to knee him in the groin in retaliation. In 1905 Crowley led an expedition to 8,598m Kangchenjunga, but his reputation as a mountaineer suffered irreparable damage when four of his companions were killed in an avalanche. He retreated into a world of black magic wizardry for the rest of his life. He was later immortalised by Iron Maiden in their song *Number of the Beast* and appeared on the cover of The Beatles' *Sergeant Pepper* album, and there aren't many mountaineers who can say that.

By now the race to climb an 8,000m peak was well under way. In 1909 Luigi Amedeo Giuseppe Maria Ferdinando Francesco di Savoia-Aosta (try saying that when you're suffering from altitude-induced hypoxia) organised an Italian expedition to K2. His name was a bit of a mouthful, but luckily he had another one, the Duke of Abruzzi. He was the grandson of King Victor Emmanuel II of Italy, and his father was briefly the king of Spain. Despite his royal upbringing he was an accomplished mountaineer. Unlike Mummery he wasn't going to make the mistake of treating K2 like a much smaller alpine peak. Although his team were never close to reaching the summit, they reconnoitred the eastern and western sides of the mountain, climbed to 6,300m on the Abruzzi Spur, and reached the 6,650m Savoia Saddle. As you can see, one of the benefits of having a ridiculously long name is that it provides a lot of scope for having places named after you.

The First World War caused a hiatus in Himalayan exploration. In 1921 the British returned for the first of three expeditions to Everest in quick succession, which ended with the disappearance of George Mallory and Sandy Irvine on the North-East Ridge in 1924. The 1930s brought a flurry of attempts on the 8,000ers. The Germans had a series of disastrous expeditions to Nanga Parbat, while the British made four more lame attempts on Everest. Americans twice tried to climb K2, with mixed results.

By 1939 none of the 8,000m peaks had been climbed, though many people had died trying. The Second World War intervened, and it would be 1950 before anyone made another attempt. Brits, Germans, Italians, Swiss and American climbers had all had a go, but there was one famous mountaineering nationality which had yet to try – a country which over the next fifty or sixty years would arguably cement its reputation as the one most likely to attempt crazy things on mountains, be it snowboarding off the top, skiing down impossible couloirs, or carrying paragliders to the summit and flying back down to base camp. I am, of course, talking about the French. The first Gallic team to attempt an 8,000m peak very much set the tone for those who followed.

Maurice Herzog was leader of the French expedition that set out for Nepal in 1950 with the specific aim of climbing an 8,000er. Three other members of the team were the guides Louis Lachenal, Lionel Terray and Gaston Rebuffat. When they left they weren't even sure which peak they were going to climb, and spent a month exploring the approaches to Dhaulagiri before dismissing it as impractical. They were running out of time before the arrival of the summer monsoon when they finally found a route to the northern foot of Annapurna.

Their progress thereafter was impressively quick. On the 2nd of June, barely more than two weeks after arriving, Herzog, Lachenal and one of the Sherpas, Angtharkay, were at their 7,400m high camp ready for a summit assault. Angtharkay was a legend among the Sherpas. He had been the mainstay of many of the Everest expeditions of the 1930s and had accompanied Eric Shipton and Bill Tilman on their many exploratory trips in the Himalayas. If anyone deserved to be the first man to stand on the summit of an 8,000m peak he was the one, and Herzog gallantly offered him the chance to accompany them the following day, but Angtharkay's response revealed a wisdom different to that of his leader.

'Thank you, sir, but my feet are freezing and I prefer to descend.'

The remark proved highly prescient. The team doctor had given Herzog the pill Maxiton, a stimulant that causes hyperactivity, to provide him with a bit of a buzz on summit day. Judging by the sense of euphoria he later described he may well have crunched a few funny mushrooms in his tent the night before as well. His attitude contrasted sharply with that of Lachenal, a Chamonix guide who made his living leading people up mountains and knew how costly a few missing digits would be to his career.

Halfway up, Lachenal realised he couldn't feel his feet, and if they continued to the summit he would probably lose toes to frostbite. Herzog was climbing confidently when Lachenal suddenly grabbed him.

'If I retreat, what will you do?' Lachenal asked.

But as far as Herzog was concerned, they were acting for the glory of France, and no sacrifice was too great. He sensed victory, and the thought of turning back revolted him. He was suffering from what these days we call *summit fever*: the excessive desire to reach the summit at all costs, with little thought for the repercussions of continuing. To him the summit was like the climax of a mystical experience, rather than a lump of rock covered in snow, albeit an extremely high one.

'I will continue by myself,' he said to Lachenal.

'Then I will follow,' Lachenal replied.

When they reached the top Lachenal wanted to descend right away, but Herzog was in no hurry. The rest of their expedition resembled the Light Brigade at Balaclava. Everything that possibly could go wrong did. Herzog took his gloves off, put them on the ground and watched them slither off the mountain. By the time they reached high camp the weather had become overcast; Lachenal missed the tents and fell into a crevasse. Herzog arrived to discover Terray and Rebuffat inside a tent, resting for their own summit attempt the following day. Terray was unable to shake Herzog's hand because it had turned into an icicle.

The four had little sleep that night as Terray and Rebuffat spent most of the dark hours massaging their compatriots' frozen digits. The following day they descended to Camp 4 but became lost in a whiteout. Terray and Rebuffat removed their sunglasses to try and see the way and ended up becoming snowblind. Respite came when Lachenal fell into another crevasse, which provided some shelter for an overnight bivouac.

The following day two invalids with frozen feet who could barely walk had to lead two blind men along a trail which had become covered in fresh snow. All that was needed to complete their misery was a hailstorm of biblical proportions and a plague of locusts, but luckily they were found by teammates and Sherpas who had come up to help. As they descended, Herzog and two of the Sherpas were caught in an avalanche and swept 150 metres, but miraculously they all survived and were able to continue.

The ordeal wasn't over when they reached base camp. Porters were recruited to carry Herzog and Lachenal back to civilisation on piggy-back across precarious log bridges. The hapless pair were subjected to a series of painful injections to save their hands and feet by team doctor Jacques Oudot. These were agonising, and both patients screamed aloud for hours as their teammates held them tight and tried to calm them. With their limbs safe from gangrene, Oudot began the amputations. To begin with he trimmed the dead skin away with a pair of scissors, but eventually he began chopping the digits off one by one. Several were left on a station platform as they returned across India. Herzog lost all his fingers and all his toes, while Lachenal just lost his toes.

It's possible to look at the 1950 French ascent of Annapurna in two ways. Very few people had ever explored the Kali Gandaki region of Nepal, and for much of the expedition the team was correcting errors on the British Survey of India maps. To do all this and return with the first ever successful ascent of an 8,000m peak under their belts was an exceptional achievement. It was undoubtedly a very bold climb, involving serious technical difficulties at an altitude few had ever climbed before. Their speed of progress once a route had been identified was astonishing, and would have been an extreme physical challenge. Their descent from the mountain and retreat across Nepal should not be forgotten either. It's a miracle nobody died, and this is thanks not just to the character of Herzog and Lachenal, but the outstanding support of the team below them. Taking all of these things into consideration the first ascent of Annapurna can be considered one of the greatest achievements in mountaineering history.

But there's another way to look at the expedition too: a team of mountaineers making a series of rash decisions, continually over-stretching themselves, returning with hideous injuries, and being lucky to escape with their lives. It was only due to the recklessness of Herzog they reached the summit, and wiser climbers would not have judged the prize worth the price he paid. Indeed, three wiser climbers were with him on the mountain: Lachenal, who wanted to abort his summit attempt to save his feet; and Terray and Rebuffat, who had no hesitation in calling off their own summit attempt to save their companions.

But we shouldn't judge the behaviour of the French team from the comfort of an armchair sixty years later. It's hard to imagine many people considering a holiday where you end up losing all your fingers and toes a roaring success, and today there would be few mountaineers who would look upon a climb that resulted in that degree of amputation as anything other than a failure. Personally I wouldn't sacrifice a single finger for a first ascent, however significant, any more than I would sacrifice my penis for a night with a supermodel. But these are the standards of our own times, not Herzog's. Exploration was a more dangerous business in those days; people took greater risks, and sometimes they paid the price.

Herzog never regretted the loss of his digits. He was acting for the glory of France, and whatever others may have done in his shoes on the 3rd of June 1950, as far as he was concerned he made the right decision. Today he would be evacuated from base camp in a helicopter and taken to hospital in little over an hour. His fingers may well have been saved.

It took fifty-five years between the first attempt on an 8,000er and the first ascent. After Herzog and Lachenal climbed Annapurna it took just fourteen years for the other thirteen to be polished off. Would my own crusade to climb an 8,000er follow a similar path? Before I could even consider climbing one I needed to make a lifestyle change.

Most expeditions last a minimum of six weeks to give climbers chance to acclimatise, establish camps and wait for a suitable weather window when deadly jet stream winds move away from the summit. The problem for me was that very few jobs came with six weeks' holiday allowance – and even fewer employers allowed their staff to take it all at once. I managed to scrounge the occasional three-week trip while in gainful employment, but my longer holidays all took place while I wasn't working. I quit jobs twice to go on extended periods of travelling, but that wasn't going to be sustainable in the long term. If I wanted to climb an 8,000m peak and then Everest I would need to do it twice more at least, and my CV was starting to look patchy. I went to lots of interviews for positions I was perfectly suited for, but was never offered a job. I expect employers thought I was as likely to stay at their company as George Best was to take a second coffee in Starbucks.

There had to be a way. Meeting Mark Dickson for a second time on our North Col expedition had been a revelation. He had travelled far more than I had since we were on Kilimanjaro together, and had found a way of working which enabled a more flexible lifestyle by going into partnership with two colleagues who didn't mind him taking six months off a year. Likewise Ian Cartwright had his own method of taking substantial holidays by completing short contracts on a boat, then coming ashore like an old sea dog with months to spare before his next job. If they could do it then it had to be possible for me, too.

On top of this was the cost. While I had no difficulty saving up $2,000 for a group trek, well-supported 8,000m peak expeditions were significantly more expensive. Many of them cost well into five figures, which meant it would be much harder to save the money on my fairly ordinary salary.

I discovered my solution quite by chance. After six months of trying to secure a permanent job I decided to book onto a Cho Oyu expedition anyway, a move which turned out to be my salvation. I told recruitment agencies I was no longer available for work, but unexpectedly, they didn't give up on me. Instead of putting my name forward for permanent jobs they offered me short-term contracts, of which there happened to be plenty in my line of work.

It wasn't long before I was offered a role as a project manager with an employer who was happy to hire me for just a few months before I went to Cho Oyu. Even better, because contract work didn't carry the same security, benefits or commitment for an employer, it paid considerably better than a so-called permanent position. Contract workers are typically hired to fill a gap for a short period of time, and then released as soon as the work is done. They have no pension or paid holiday entitlement, and can be made redundant at short notice, but that didn't matter to me because all I wanted was to save up money for Cho Oyu and then leave anyway. What mattered was that I was earning nearly twice what I was before, for doing roughly the same job. With one stroke I was able to save enough to climb an 8,000m peak and have plenty of time off at the end of the contract.

In the event, my expedition was cancelled and I stayed there for over a year. Perhaps I was lucky that I worked in digital communications, an industry that has expanded in ways I could never have foreseen when I started looking for work in the 1990s. After becoming a contractor I never had any difficulty finding work again – even after a series of expeditions.

While fate certainly played a part at key moments in my journey, factors which seemed like good fortune were actually influenced by choices I made. Many of you reading this may believe it's impossible to break out of the endless cycle, and for some of you it may be true. Some of you may not wish to make the choices I made, but for those who can, I believe there is a way if you look hard enough and take the opportunities when they come.

After securing a lifestyle that allowed me to go on two-month expeditions, my next tasks were to decide which 8,000m peak to climb and to find a suitable operator. Although I was gradually turning into a mountaineer, I still considered myself a hill walker rather than a climber. There was never any question of organising my own expedition to the Himalayas, any more than I would consider getting from London to Kathmandu by taking a few flying lessons and chartering a plane.

Since the first commercially guided Everest expedition took place in 1992, many mountaineering operators have become adept at organising expeditions to the 8,000m peaks.

I discovered near the start of my journey that I could explore the Himalayas by joining a commercially guided trek with like-minded people, and now that I had the necessary technical skills and experience at high altitude, joining an expedition to climb a big mountain was almost as easy. Experienced operators provided all the support I needed, including group equipment, comfortable base camp facilities, and Sherpa support to carry tents and food up the mountain and establish camps. There are mountaineering purists who regard this as cheating, but I didn't care about that. It was being there that mattered to me, and not the style. If George Mallory could employ Sherpas to carry food and equipment then I certainly wasn't going to say no.

In August 2007 I joined an expedition with Jagged Globe to climb Muztag Ata, a 7,546m peak in the Chinese Pamirs. It was my first meeting with elite high-altitude Sherpas. All three Sherpas on that expedition had climbed Everest a few months earlier, and I couldn't believe how strong they were. I was exhausted climbing 700m between camps, and invariably collapsed in a heap on arrival, unable to do anything more energetic than take off my boots – but these guys would regularly leapfrog two or more camps in a day, carrying huge loads of tents, food and other equipment.

Physical labour has never really been my forte. I spend most days sitting behind a desk, and the heaviest lifting involves carrying a mug of coffee from the kitchen to my workstation. While putting up a tent at sea level doesn't present too much of a problem, pitching one at 6,000m on the side of a mountain is a different proposition. A platform needs to be levelled in the snow, and at that altitude a shovel feels like an anchor.

A couple of times on Muztag Ata I arrived at a high camp, picked up a spade and started work, but two shovelfuls later my lungs would be rattling like a newlyweds' exhaust pipe. I never got very far before a Sherpa arrived, dumped his thirty-kilogram pack and effortlessly took over.

On our way down, they were packing away our high camp at 6,800m and I asked if there was anything I could help them to carry. Our sirdar Gyalzen looked around for a few seconds before selecting two foam mattresses. These gave my backpack a Sherpa-sized look when tied to the outside, but they weighed little more than the central part of a doughnut. Although I didn't know it at the time, this was typical Sherpa behaviour. It's a matter of pride for them to shoulder the lion's share of the burden, while helping their western clients feel good about themselves.

Muztag Ata was a memorable expedition for me. Although we experienced blizzards on two successive days during our summit push, we were able to climb through them, and our summit day was as good as could be, though bitterly cold. The ascent was a deep snow plod for almost the whole distance, with little in the way of interesting climbing, but I thoroughly enjoyed it. Several of us reached the summit, and it was another altitude record for me.

My expedition leader was a tall wiry Scot with a dry sense of humour called David Hamilton, who seemed to know as many Christmas-cracker jokes as I did. He had led dozens of expeditions to the Himalayas, and was a specialist in the Pakistan Karakoram. He was the ideal person to advise on the best 8,000m peak to tackle by someone of my experience.

He explained that around half the 8,000m peaks were what he unfavourably termed *suicide mountains*. These peaks are packed with what mountaineers call *objective danger* – danger that is beyond their control once they have made the decision to climb. On parts of these routes hazards like avalanches and serac collapse could happen any time; on some peaks there isn't even a safe place to camp.

On K2, for example, a section called the Bottleneck Couloir has to be negotiated on summit day. As its name implies, it's a narrow gully where queues of climbers can form. A giant serac of hanging ice looms over the couloir, and ever since it was first climbed in the 1930s, climbers have known the ice could collapse onto the route. In August 2008 it happened several times in a single night, severing the fixed ropes people had been using to climb. It was one of the few nights of the year when climbers were going for the summit, and eleven people were killed, either from collapsing ice or from falls.

The latter are what is known as *subjective*, rather than *objective*, danger. Or to put it another way, the level of danger is dependent on the skill of the climber rather than random factors. In considering which mountain to climb, I had to acknowledge that I was to climbing what Louis Armstrong was to singing. Peaks of great technical difficulty were likely to prove beyond me.

8,201m Cho Oyu, a short distance west of Everest on the border of Tibet and Nepal, is generally regarded as the technically easiest 8,000m peak. It was the obvious choice. Ian, who climbed with me to Everest's North Col, was also keen, and we signed up for Jagged Globe's 2008 expedition, but events took a peculiar twist. In March peaceful protests against the Chinese government in the Tibetan capital of Lhasa descended into violent rioting. The Olympics were being held in Beijing later that year, and the Chinese government organised an expedition to carry the Olympic torch to the summit of Everest.

Little is known about this attempt – the government closed the north side of the mountain to foreigners, and no information about it has been released outside China. To prevent westerners spoiling their party by turning up on the summit from the south side, waving Tibetan flags and wearing *Free Tibet* T-shirts, the Chinese government persuaded their counterparts in Nepal to allow the Chinese Army to police base camp on the south side of the mountain too. Climbers had their satellite phones confiscated, and armed soldiers patrolled Camp 2, stopping anyone from climbing any higher until the Chinese were finished on the north side.

By August, when I was due to leave for Cho Oyu, Tibet was still closed to foreigners and no climbing permits had been issued. With the political situation so uncertain many operators, including Jagged Globe, switched their expeditions to Manaslu, an 8,000m peak in Nepal which until then had received very few ascents and had never been considered a commercial peak. When I had a candid conversation with Simon Lowe about the chances of success, he accepted it was a step into the unknown for them.

I was intending to leave my job to climb Cho Oyu, but my employer offered to extend my contract. I wished Ian and Simon success on Manaslu and withdrew from the expedition, putting my plans to climb an 8,000er on hold for another year.

It was then that a new character entered my story.

While I was preparing for Cho Oyu somebody lent me a DVD about a team of commercial climbers attempting the mountain a few years earlier. One of the guides on the film was an Englishman called Phil Crampton, who sported a comical haircut which reminded me of King Charles I (who ruled England in the 17th century). Luckily his mountaineering pedigree demanded more respect than his hair. He moved to the United States in his early twenties and took up climbing, eventually becoming an instructor and guiding clients on peaks throughout North America. In the early 2000s he started working as a guide in the Himalayas for the mountaineering companies SummitClimb and Mountain Madness. By 2008 he had already guided over twenty 8,000m peak expeditions and summited Cho Oyu seven times. He helped to set up the Tibet Mountaineering Guide School in Lhasa, aimed at training local Tibetans to become the Tibetan equivalent of climbing Sherpas, and was an instructor there for many years.

Mark Dickson had been on Gasherbrum II in Pakistan with Phil. He introduced us in a bar in Kathmandu shortly after my Cho Oyu expedition had been cancelled. By coincidence Phil had just come off Manaslu, having switched his own expedition from Cho Oyu, and was in the process of organising an expedition to Gasherbrum I and II the following year with his company Altitude Junkies.

I liked him immediately. He shared my somewhat irreverent sense of humour, and while his expedition record spoke for itself, just as important for me was that he seemed a decent chap, who spoke fairly of the people he climbed with, while being self-deprecating about his own achievements. Beneath his slightly clownish exterior I sensed someone with integrity, and as I came to know him better this impression strengthened. As empty bottles of Tuborg beer collected on our table that afternoon, Mark and Phil convinced me to switch my 8,000m peak objective from Cho Oyu to Gasherbrum II.

Gasherbrum II was first climbed in 1956 by an Austrian team led by Fritz Moravec, and is one of the more remote 8,000m peaks. It took Moravec's team nearly four weeks to hike there from the trailhead at Skardu, with an army of 238 Balti porters who had a tendency to go on strike more frequently than London Underground staff. At Paiyu, a tiny oasis near the snout of the Baltoro Glacier, Moravec was approached by the Balti headman with a demand for 150 pairs of boots, a quantity most people don't tend to carry with them. A day later at Urdukas – the last place where anything grows before the trail rises into the barren rock citadels of the high Karakoram – the porters demanded a paid rest day, a large gift of money and some special chapatis. Another strike ensued when a goat was slaughtered in a manner not considered halal.

They arrived at Gasherbrum Base Camp at the end of May, and it was another two weeks before they found a route through the tumbling icefall of the South Gasherbrum Glacier to establish Camp 1 at 5,900m. Then a two-week snow storm drove them back to base camp, and when they returned they found Camp 1 buried under a ten-metre layer of compressed snow beyond their capabilities to dig out. With much of their equipment irretrievable, including tents, ropes, carabiners and high-altitude provisions, they had to reconsider their tactics. Until then most expeditions to 8,000m peaks had been conducted expedition style, as I had used on Aconcagua, with a series of camps established in advance of a final summit push. They now had to consider the radical approach of climbing a huge 8,000m peak alpine style.

In order for porters to carry heavy loads up to the higher reaches of the mountain, the Austrians had planned to follow the usual method of fixing ropes to hold on to. Although they were no longer able to do this, by cutting a staircase of steps they could get their porters up a steep ice spur known as the Banana Ridge. The brave porters managed to lug their eighteen-kilogram loads all the way up to 7,150m roped to the Austrians, but above this the slope became too steep and the technical difficulties too great.

Four Europeans, Sepp Larch, Richard Reinagl, Hans

Willenpart and Moravec himself, considered their options. To have any chance of reaching the summit they would have to make an alpine-style dash, carrying minimal equipment and enduring an overnight bivouac somewhere higher up the mountain. Until then no 8,000m summit had ever been stormed from an open camp, and for Reinagl it was too great a risk.

'I wish you three success on the summit, but I am taking the porters back to Camp 2,' he told his companions.

The standard route on Gasherbrum traverses underneath a perfect rock triangle before doubling back up it on the summit ridge. The three spent a cold night cowering underneath a bivouac sack, and when they started for the summit at 5.30am Moravec and Larch already had frostbitten digits. Moravec estimated the traverse beneath the pyramid took them only 200m higher in three and a half hours. By the time they reached the corner and turned up the pyramid onto the exposed summit ridge, they were so exhausted they were taking up to twenty breaths with every step. They travelled apart on a ridge where they would have roped together on any other mountain, but they were beyond caring. They reached the summit, marked by two small rocky teeth, eight hours after setting out.

'The toil and hardship are simply unimaginable, but still, this is the finest moment of my life,' Moravec later wrote.

But in contrast to Herzog's feeling after reaching the summit of Annapurna, he didn't view it as a triumph of conquest.

I shall never try to represent the ascent of Gasherbrum II as a victory over the mountain! If one may use the word victory at all when climbing an eight-thousander, then surely only in the sense that it is a victory of comradeship.[49]

When they met their porters back at Camp 2 on the way down, the Balti men clapped their hands and banged an empty fuel can like a drum while one of them danced. They were as pleased as if they had climbed the mountain themselves. Back in Skardu, Moravec sent a cable to the Austrian Embassy in Karachi to provide news of their success, but he deliberately left his, Larch's and Willenpart's names out of it, saying only that three expedition members had reached the summit. He recognised it as a victory of teamwork, and knew the porters were to thank every bit as much as his Austrian teammates.

In June 2009 I joined Phil and Altitude Junkies on their expedition to climb Gasherbrum II and its slightly higher neighbour Gasherbrum I, or G2 and G1 as they are affectionately known. Unfortunately Mark, the man who introduced me to Phil, wasn't able to come with us. He broke his ankle in a fall while racing for the teahouse after our ascent of Island Peak a month earlier.

I had climbed with him a few times in Nepal and was used to his occasional injuries, some of which his doctor may describe as 'alcohol related'. On one memorable occasion he flew out of the front of a rickshaw after it went too fast over a speed bump. Our driver turned round to apologise, but was unable to make himself heard over the sound of my laughter. Twice Mark came to breakfast at our hotel in Kathmandu bearing a mysterious scar on his forehead that nobody could account for. It was only on the third occasion, when he woke up on the bathroom floor in a pool of his own blood, that he realised there was an inch-high step in the doorway that he had tripped over on the way in, smashing his head on the toilet bowl as he fell.

His accident on the way down from Island Peak was more catastrophic. Back home in Britain he had his ankle X-rayed, and the doctor confirmed it required an operation. He had carried an old sporting injury in his other ankle for years, so he asked the doctor to X-ray that one as well out of curiosity. The doctor told him it was in an even worse state, and they might as well do both.

With not one but two broken ankles, Mark's Gasherbrum dreams were over; but Ian came with us, as did another friend of Mark's called Michael Odell. As we trekked along the Baltoro Glacier to base camp our porters had a habit of going on strike, as they had with Moravec. We were stuck at one of our camps for two nights when they thought better of walking in snow. Michael wasn't with us during the trek, and joined us later at base camp. He was a distant relative of Noel Odell, a famous British mountaineer who made the first ascent of Nanda Devi with Bill Tilman in 1936, and is best known for being the last eyewitness to the fate of George Mallory and Sandy Irvine as they disappeared into the mist on Everest's North-East Ridge in 1924. This relationship might have caused Michael to be treated with respect had he not arrived in base camp a few days after us wearing a *shalwar kameez* – a loose-fitting unisex garment combination popular in Pakistan, which may have helped him to blend in with locals during the trek, but invited ridicule from his climbing partners when he arrived.

I read many stories about Gasherbrum II before the expedition. One that captured my imagination more than any other involved Jean-Marc Boivin, a French extreme sportsman who planned to paraglide off the summit in 1985. It was to be a paragliding altitude record. He carried his seventeen-kilogram paraglider all the way to the summit on the 8th of July, only to find it too windy to fly, so he dumped the glider and returned to base camp. Six days later he climbed the mountain for a second time and found the glider buried under several metres of fresh snow. For me, digging a tent platform at 6,000m had been a struggle, but Boivin was 2,000m higher, and had to be careful to dig out his paraglider without damaging it. It took him four painstaking hours, during which time he became the world's highest gardener – another record that seems to have gone unreported.

His exertions proved worthwhile, and may have aroused a pang of envy from his countryman Maurice Herzog, who during his descent from Annapurna endured days of torture, hours of painful injections, and a few seconds of extreme pain while the team doctor lopped his digits off. For Boivin things were a little easier. Having dusted the snow off his paraglider, he launched into the air and was back in base camp twenty minutes later.

Extreme sportsmen certainly lead heroic lives, but they don't lead very long ones. Five years after his two ascents of Gasherbrum II, at the age of only 38, Boivin died trying to parachute off the Angel Falls in Venezuela.

I expected there to be many elite climbers like Boivin on my first 8,000m peak, but I found it wasn't like that at all. Inexperienced as I was, I hadn't considered climbing the mountain in any other way than by joining a full-service commercial expedition, but I discovered many of the so-called independent climbers weren't any more accomplished than I was. Most of the teams at base camp were collections of individuals on group climbing permits who happened to be sharing the same base camp services. They had no overall leader and members on the permit acted independently rather than as a team. Above base camp they generally followed the lead of the two commercial teams on the mountain, Altitude Junkies and Jagged Globe, who were the only ones supported by a full complement of Sherpas and

Pakistani high-altitude porters (HAPs). Our two teams did most of the rope fixing, and because we were paying for dedicated commercial weather forecasts we had better information about climbing conditions.

For most of the season there were only two truly elite climbers on the mountain: the *Swiss Machine* Ueli Steck, who was famous for record-breaking speed ascents in the Alps, and was planning to climb G2 solo; and the Finn Veikka Gustafsson, for whom G1 would be his fourteenth and final 8,000m summit. As things turned out they were two of only a handful of people to climb either mountain all season.

The expedition was something of a baptism of ice for me. We never came close to reaching the summits, but I returned richer in experience than perhaps any expedition I had completed until then. Both G1 and G2 have routes which are particularly susceptible to avalanches after a dump of fresh snow, and much of the time we were waiting for the snow to consolidate after a storm. When it wasn't snowing, we watched the summits spew forth plumes of cloud as they were battered by the jet stream. This was a frustrating experience. Often we would sit in beautiful weather at base camp, surrounded by a theatre of breathtaking peaks and itching for some exercise, but fully aware conditions were impossible three kilometres above us.

Base camp was at 5,000m, and separated from Camp 1 for both mountains by an enormous icefall of towering seracs and deep crevasses. The route through the icefall was hazardous and intricate; we made six return trips, and towards the end knew every inch of the tumbling ice like our journeys to work in another life. Camp 1 lay in a vast snowy amphitheatre at 5,900m, surrounded by the six Gasherbrums, all of them jaw-dropping pinnacles of towering rock and fluted columns of ice. We spent many days there and I never tired of it. It's one of the most beautiful places I have ever been, but so inaccessible that very few people have been lucky enough to stand there.

We concentrated on G2 to begin with, the easier of the two mountains, and made three attempts to climb it. On two of these attempts we climbed no higher than Camp 2 at 6,400m on a shelf above the Banana Ridge. On the second occasion we retreated in a blizzard with my crampons balling up with fresh snow. I fell on the 60° slope three times and would have fallen a long way had I not been attached to the fixed line.

Climbing the Banana Ridge on Gasherbrum II, with the summit triangle high above to the right

On the third occasion we spent three nights in a storm at Camp 1 while a drama unfolded around us. A Spanish climber had gone missing very close to the summit of G2 and was presumed to be dead. But in the darkness of early evening a flashing light appeared more than 1,500m above us on the traverse beneath the summit pyramid. It could only be the Spanish climber signalling for help.

There were dozens of people at Camp 1. They congregated around our tents while they discussed a plan for an immediate rescue, because they knew our superhuman Sherpas were the only people with a realistic chance of carrying it out. I didn't volunteer to help myself, because I knew what condition I would be in after climbing 1,500m very quickly at extreme altitude. At 1,000m higher than I had been on the expedition so far, and at severe risk of altitude sickness, I would be in no fit state to help with carrying down an injured climber. I may not be a very good climber, but as I listened to the proposals I realised I understood the issues much better than the bolder climbers around me who were discussing their options.

It was Phil who took control of the situation and explained that nobody was going to risk their lives climbing 1,500m in the dark with no idea whether the casualty was in a position to be rescued. He sent two of the volunteers down to base camp to arrange a helicopter fly-by at first light the following morning, to assess the situation and air-drop supplies if necessary. The clouds closed in and the storm resumed. By morning it was clear no helicopter could fly up there, and had a rescue been launched there would have been more climbers trapped in a storm on avalanche-laden slopes. If the Spaniard was still alive, he was beyond help.

The tragedy stayed in our minds, but as the days passed with no sign of better weather we become increasingly lethargic. We had climbed no higher than Camp 2 on G2, and spent an awfully long time at base camp. I had hoped to swap books with people, but the choice of reading material was limited to trashy thrillers picked up hurriedly in airport terminals. They were so bad that *Angels and Demons* by Dan Brown was one of the better ones. I even read it. I played so many games of cards that I was in danger of turning into a jack of hearts. On one occasion I woke up inside my tent in a cold sweat after dreaming my highest card was a four of clubs. As time passed, the ice around our tents melted and the tents began to rise up on platforms. Michael noticed that Phil's dome tent was beginning to look like a giant mushroom. To amuse himself, he spent several hours one afternoon while Phil was away excavating around it to make the mushroom even taller. When Phil returned, he needed to stand on a chair to reach the entrance.

Eventually we decided to launch a desperate last-gasp attempt on G1. The weather forecast wasn't promising, but we were bored and running out of time. Nobody had climbed high enough on G1 to fix ropes on the higher sections, which were known to be especially steep. This, combined with my experience on the Banana Ridge, the death of the Spanish climber, and the unpromising weather forecast, led me to have misgivings about the attempt from the start. I wanted to climb an 8,000m peak, but more than anything I wanted to return home safely and climb another day.

Phil, who was as strong as a Sherpa, persuaded us we were sufficiently well acclimatised to climb from base camp to Camp 2 in a single push. A bearded Canadian named Gordon and I were certainly well acclimatised after playing cards for two months at 5,000m, but we were far from strong enough, and we struggled into Camp 2 at eight o'clock in the evening like a pair of old men. We had run out of water climbing steeply on snowfields in the heat of the afternoon sun. One of our Sherpas, Gombu, had to pull a stove from his rucksack and melt some snow to quench our desperate thirst.

We were in no condition to tackle the steep 600m gully of the Japanese Couloir the following morning, and horrified when we watched an avalanche tumble down it during our rest day.

'I'm not going up that mother tomorrow,' said Gordon.

Had he been better-looking and washed himself at least once in the preceding two months, I might have kissed him.

I didn't need any more excuses. Gombu and Tarke, the two older Sherpas, immediately volunteered to return to base camp with us, and it was a joyous if exhausting retreat.

Spending two months on a remote glacier in Pakistan was an enlightening and enriching experience. I returned home a wiser mountaineer – but I hadn't climbed very high. If not by my own, then by most people's reckoning my expedition had been a failure, and my desire to climb an 8,000er remained unfulfilled.

But I didn't have to wait long for my next opportunity. I was working for the UK government in May 2010 when a general election brought a new regime to power. The project I had been working on was abruptly terminated and I was out of work again.

If this sort of life event is traumatic for many people, I had long since realised career setbacks presented an opportunity and should be welcomed. Jagged Globe had a spare place on their autumn expedition to Cho Oyu, so I booked it.

Ever since I first took an interest in the 8,000m peaks, Cho Oyu had stood out as the one people like me climbed. It was arguably the first 8,000er to be climbed by a fully commercial team in 1987, when the Austrian Marcus Schmuck, who made the first ascent of 8,047m Broad Peak in

1957, led an international expedition which put thirteen climbers on the summit. By 2010 it had seen over 2,000 ascents – ten times as many as most of the other 8,000ers. Only Everest had more.

Cho Oyu also saw one of the quirkiest first ascents, completed almost in alpine style by a team of rank amateurs. In autumn 1954 the Austrian geologist Herbert Tichy set out with his two friends Sepp Jöchler and Helmut Heuberger, and seven Sherpas led by sirdar Pasang Dawa Lama, who had nearly reached the summit of K2 with an American expedition in 1939.

Several days into their expedition Tichy was retreating frostbitten from an early attempt when a Swiss team arrived unexpectedly at base camp. He found himself in a race to reach the summit first. They were climbing the Tibetan side of the mountain and Pasang, their star performer, was across the border in Nepal procuring fresh supplies. He caught up with them at their 7,000m camp, which Tichy, Jöchler and Pasang left at six o'clock on the 19th of October. They reached the top at three o'clock that afternoon, finding a summit plateau big enough to play football on.

Pasang had ascended over 4,000m in three days, but it wasn't until they crossed the Nangpa La pass into Nepal and reached the Sherpa capital of Namche Bazaar, that the Austrians found out why he had been so determined to reach the summit. A few days earlier his father-in-law-to-be promised to waive his bride's dowry if he climbed Cho Oyu. This came as a surprise to the Austrians. Pasang was already a happily married man, but in those days polygamy wasn't uncommon among Sherpas.

The celebrations that accompanied Pasang's wedding had an unexpected side effect, which frankly I'm surprised no mountaineer has cottoned on to in the years since. When Herzog and Lachenal arrived back at high camp on

Annapurna four years before Tichy's ascent of Cho Oyu, Rebuffat and Terray immediately started battering their frostbitten digits with a bit of rope in an attempt to get some feeling back into them. It's rather like trying to cure a blackened fingernail by smashing it with a hammer, but at the time it was believed to be a legitimate way of treating frostbite. Nowadays we know the rope treatment and vigorous massage only aggravates frostbite and makes amputation more likely. Standard treatment now is to gradually thaw out frozen body parts by placing them in warm water, or warming them against a teammate's chest, armpit, or even crotch (though this last method can only be done for short periods to prevent the arguably more serious condition of frostbitten penis).

Why are Sherpas able to withstand severe cold much better than western climbers? This has not been studied, but Tichy discovered the probable reason entirely by chance in the days that followed their ascent of Cho Oyu. He was so sure he would lose fingers that when Indian customs officers inspected his baggage at the border on the way home and found it to be missing 180 pairs of socks which were on his inventory when he left, they thought he must have sold them and tried to charge him duty. With black humour Tichy held up his frostbitten hands and asked if they wanted to charge duty on his fingers as well.

But when he presented himself for treatment at a clinic back home in Vienna he was in for a surprise. His doctor examined his hands, and then looked at the photographs that had been taken of them in the Himalayas. He was astounded.

'You should by rights have lost one or two fingers,' he said, 'but I don't think we shall have to operate. Did you use any particular preparation?'

'Yes,' Tichy admitted, 'on the way down we were either

tipsy or completely sozzled for two whole weeks.'

'Well, that's what saved your hands,' the doctor said. 'Alcohol dilates the blood vessels and stimulates the circulation.'

The festivities in Pasang's honour had lasted for two weeks, and the *chang* (millet beer) that everyone consumed was paid for out of expedition funds. According to Tichy the Austrians were obliged to 'comport ourselves according to the laws of hospitality'.[50] Mountaineering teetotallers may like to take note.

It wasn't alcohol that was to be an abiding memory of my expedition to Cho Oyu in 2010, but food. Jagged Globe had discovered a gourmet chef, Gavin Melgaard, working in Antarctica providing meals for dozens of climbers as they jumped off a plane in Patriot Hills on their way to climb Vinson Massif, the highest mountain on the frozen southern continent. They were so impressed with his cuisine they invited him to be base camp cook on their 8,000m peak expeditions, and his food turned out to be not just the best I had eaten on any expedition, but by some margin. Lamb shanks in mint sauce was an example. The highlight for me was his steak and kidney pie with Yorkshire pudding, which tasted so good it could have been produced in a gastro-pub in Yorkshire accompanied by a mouth-watering pint of real ale, and not in a makeshift kitchen on a glacier in Tibet, assembled from a fraying marquee tent and a drystone wall made out of moraine slabs.

Even before I discovered Gavin's cooking I was feeling confident about my Cho Oyu expedition. Although the weather was the principal reason for our defeat on Gasherbrum in 2009, I had gone there inexperienced and had been out of my depth at times. While a successful ascent of Gasherbrum II may have been feasible in better conditions, I struggled during our retreat from the Banana Ridge in a blizzard, and could have been in serious difficulty had it not been for the fixed ropes. By 2010 I was a better climber, having improved my technique in Ecuador by making successful ascents of the glaciated volcanoes Cotopaxi and Antisana.

Nevertheless, Jagged Globe were determined to make me feel like a bumbling incompetent by assembling a formidable team for Cho Oyu, which included a former Welsh rugby international Richard Parks, double Olympic champion rower Steve Williams, and veteran mountaineer Ron Rutland, who led a 1979 expedition which made the first ascent of the South Face of Annapurna III (though he didn't let on it was actually his wife who reached the summit). One of our guides, Tomaz Jakofcic, had climbed a new route on 7,952m Gyachung Kang, and our leader was Robert Anderson, who led the international expedition which climbed a new route on the Kangshung Face of Everest in 1988. On that occasion Stephen Venables became the first Briton to climb Everest without supplementary oxygen. Two other team members had run 120 marathons between them.

I was relieved to be reunited with Geoff, a bald-headed English teacher who had been my tent-mate on Muztag Ata, and possessed a wardrobe which had been assembled at random from the bazaars of Central Asia. Often he carried his mountaineering equipment in a plastic carrier bag, as though he were on a shopping trip, rather than in a backpack like any normal climber. While lacking some of his eccentricities, in Geoff I knew I had a kindred spirit who enjoyed struggling up mountains without taking the ascent too seriously.

Despite these impressive resumés, I discovered Jagged Globe's 8,000m peak expeditions were pitched at a different level to Altitude Junkies'. Phil Crampton saw himself as more of a facilitator than a mountain guide, and he preferred to sign up clients who were experienced climbers, able to look after themselves (how I managed to slip through the net on Gasherbrum was a mystery). While he provided me with a lot of good advice when I needed it, most of the time we climbed unguided between camps and he assumed we all knew what we were doing. I remember one of his rare lectures came the night before our first summit push on G2. The weather forecast was far from perfect; strong winds were expected and there was a high risk of frostbite.

'If you want to go to the bathroom while you're up there,' he said, 'don't undo your down pants and pee normally, or your dick's gone. Instead, piss inside your down suit – you can always clean it later.'

Thankfully it was advice I never needed. By contrast Jagged Globe were happy to sign up less experienced clients and offer them a bit more hand-holding. Aware that many of the team hadn't been on big expeditions, Robert correctly gave a lot more advice. Twenty-minute lectures were frequent. These were sometimes pitched at a beginner's level, providing instruction on basic mountaineering sense and how to conduct ourselves with crampons and ice axe. While the lectures were helpful for some people, I found them less useful, and often lost concentration.

The climb to 6,400m on Cho Oyu was much easier than it had been on Gasherbrum II. Base camp was 700m higher, and there was no technical climbing to compare with the intricate maze of seracs and crevasses in the South Gasherbrum Icefall, or the steep haul up the Banana Ridge. On Cho Oyu we had to cross a knee-jarring boulder field to the foot of the mountain, then slog up a 400m scree slope where the snowline began at Camp 1 on the West Ridge.

It was pleasant climbing above Camp 1, as the broad ridge rose in a series of snowy terraces before reaching a wall of ice. On commercial 8,000m peaks technical sections like this are overcome using fixed ropes, which allow hill walkers like me to climb by sliding a jumar up the rope. Even with my jumar I found the ice wall exhausting, mainly because of the giant rower Steve Williams attached to the rope behind me. As I tried to climb to the right the force of Steve's body on the rope dragged me back to the left, and it was a hard physical battle to stay in the footmarks above me. When I finally flopped into the snow at the top of the wall I felt like I'd been playing tug of war with a horse, and it took a few moments to get my breath back.

View from Camp 1 on Cho Oyu, of the West Ridge and summit behind

Above the ice wall the terrain became more gentle, but for me the climbing didn't get any easier. We crossed a short plateau, and then had a relentless slog up steep snow slopes to Camp 2 at 7,150m. By then Steve was ahead of me. I watched his man-sized pack disappear over the horizon above me as I wheezed my way upwards, stopping every six steps for a few deep breaths.

Although I had been to 7,546m on Muztag Ata and 7,060m on the North Col of Everest, this was to be the first time I had slept above 7,000m, and I wasn't sure how I would cope. I arrived dehydrated and spent the rest of the afternoon melting snow to drink, but food and water heats very slowly at that altitude, and by the time I turned in for some sleep I was still feeling thirsty. I slept anxiously in five-minute snatches and drank two litres of water. By morning I was still very tired and dehydrated. I had trouble lighting the stove, and when we left to descend to base camp, I had only a few mouthfuls in my water bottle to last me all the way down.

I need not have worried. Once we started descending my anxieties vanished. We left in a white out, and I watched some of my teammates struggle with the conditions like I had done in similar circumstances on the Banana Ridge a year earlier, sliding in the fresh unconsolidated snow and taking almighty pendulum swings on the fixed rope. My technique was much better this time, and I remained on my feet, even when someone clattered into me from behind. I descended rapidly, and didn't need my water. I had slept restlessly at Camp 2 because of worries about the altitude, but next time I slept above 7,000m I would know better.

I also gained more experience of failure. Like on Gasherbrum, the weather was against us the whole season. For most of the first three weeks it snowed every day. The mornings started clear, but eventually it clouded over, bringing snow. As the days progressed the early morning window of good weather became narrower, until after three weeks at base camp it was snowing more or less continuously all day. Despite the heavy snow, the rope-fixing team from the China Tibet Mountaineering Association continued to push the route higher up the mountain. On the 17th of September seven members of their team were fixing ropes high above Camp 3 when they were caught in an avalanche which swept them over the sheer cliffs of a rock band they had just ascended. Remarkably, they all survived, but most of them suffered serious injuries, including broken arms and ribs.

Our progress continued, and after spending our night at Camp 2 we began our summit push on the 27th of September. Half the team left for Camp 1 while the rest of us remained in base camp to leave the following day. We sat in the sun watching the rope-fixers above Camp 3 through binoculars. They moved quickly across the rock band and were heading towards the summit. Everything seemed to be falling into place when another avalanche struck, carrying them 400m down the mountain. They were only prevented from being swept over the rock band when the rope linking them caught around a rock. By a miracle everyone survived again, but it was another warning from the mountain gods. The many weeks of mild temperatures and heavy snow had amassed several feet of fine powder which hadn't glued together and consolidated. A sudden drop in temperature had caused a hard crust to form on top, creating prime avalanche conditions. The mountain had become a death trap, and with high winds forecast we realised we had run out of time. Four hundred people abandoned the mountain *en masse,* and Cho Oyu, supposedly the easiest 8,000m peak, had closed its gates. It was a season in a dozen, and I was becoming used to being thwarted by the weather.

By spring 2011, Mark, Ian and I had attempted eight 8,000m peaks between us, and hadn't reached the summit of any of them. Mark had been on expeditions to Cho Oyu, Gasherbrum II and Everest; Ian had been to Manaslu and Gasherbrum II; while I had attempted Gasherbrum II, Gasherbrum I and Cho Oyu. It seemed we had as much chance of getting up an 8,000er as Wayne Rooney had of winning Mastermind, and had even talked about adjusting our goal from reaching the summit of one, to reaching Camp 2 on all fourteen. But did we think of spending our next holiday lying on a beach in the south of France or clubbing in Ibiza? Did the Vikings ever knock before pillaging?

Once bitten by the mountaineering bug my holidays were becoming more extreme, not less. When Mark and Ian announced they would be climbing Manaslu with Phil and Altitude Junkies in autumn 2011, I was offered a contract extension to the project I was working on, managing the content migration for a law firm website. It was an agonising decision. Do I spend the next few months staring at spreadsheets and managing a team of people copying and pasting text from one system to another, or head to the Himalayas and try to climb the eighth highest mountain in the world? I expect Edmund Hillary faced a similar dilemma when offered the opportunity to climb Everest or tend his father's beehives.

Manaslu had been on my radar for three years, after my first Cho Oyu expedition was cancelled and I was offered it as an alternative. Ian ended up going on that expedition, but had no luck. He took a helicopter to the village of Samagaon in the heart of Buddhist country, and had to make an emergency landing in a wheat field half a day's walk away.

He lost much of his equipment when Camp 2 was buried in a snow storm, and after six weeks of little progress he had no alternative but to fly home and return to work.

Bill Tilman was the first climber to have a look at Manaslu when he explored the Annapurna region in 1950. He viewed its West Face from the Marsyangdi Valley on what is now the Annapurna Circuit trail, and concluded it was too difficult for his small party to attempt. A couple of years later a Japanese team had another look at both the west and east sides, crossing the Larkya La pass from the Marsyangdi Valley. They thought they could identify a reasonable route up to the summit plateau from Samagaon on the northern side.

The Japanese returned in 1953 for what was to be the first serious attempt to climb Manaslu. Following the route they identified the previous year, up to the North Col between Manaslu's north peak and main summit, they reached as high as 7,750m before turning back on their summit attempt because it was too late in the day to reach the top and return safely.

Their next attempt in 1954 was abandoned for a more unusual reason. Legend has it they were met at Samagaon by an angry mob armed with stones and knives, and had to retreat half-naked after being subjected to what in public schoolboy parlance is termed a *de-bagging*. The reason for this humiliation was because the local people believed the Japanese had upset the mountain gods the previous year; an avalanche had destroyed a nearby monastery shortly after they departed. On the plus side, it was probably the first Himalayan expedition in history to return not only summitless, but trouserless too.

By 1956 things had calmed down for the Japanese, and they managed to acquire new clothes. They returned for another attempt. On the 9th of May Toshio Imanishi and

Gyalzen Norbu Sherpa found themselves at their high camp in good shape for a summit attempt.

I have talked about acknowledging the assistance of teammates for most of my ascents, but it was equally true for these two mountaineering pioneers. While sleeping in Camp 5 at 7,200m their oxygen man, Dr Tatsunama, kept them replenished with life-giving gas throughout the night. He rigged up a system of oxygen generators powered by 'oxygen candles' which generated gas by electrical combustion. Rubber tubes led from the generators to the masks of sleeping climbers in the neighbouring tents. In order to keep the generators operating Dr Tatsunama had to stay up all night changing the candles whenever they burned out.

The following day Imanishi set out for Camp 6, and without the doctor's help he found his oxygen apparatus less effective.

Walking should have been easy, but actually it was painful and tore at one's vitals. [By which I think he meant his lungs rather than his crown jewels.] *I was breathing two litres of oxygen per minute, but perhaps that was because I was not used to the mask.*[51]

A team of five Sherpas led by Imanishi's teammate Junjiro Muraki established Camp 6 at the comparatively high altitude of 7,800m, just 363m below the summit. Here the six men left twenty-three oxygen cylinders, six of which Imanishi and Gyalzen used on their summit climb the following day, and descended back to Camp 5, their job done.

Imanishi and Gyalzen set off at eight o'clock the following morning. Although they had only 363 vertical metres to ascend, they didn't make it easy for themselves.

On their backs they carried twenty kilograms each, including three oxygen cylinders inside a wooden frame; a ridiculous load for such a short summit day, but such was the value placed on oxygen at high altitude in that era.

Although their summit photographs show clear skies, there was evidently poor visibility just beneath the summit, as Imanishi's description of his summit day is mystifying. They approached a rock pinnacle via a sharp snow ridge, but as they neared it the peak disappeared and they could see another one behind it. They had reached the first of three steep summits, the final one of which was the true summit. They cut steps up a narrow corniced ridge. At the top of this, another sharp triangular pinnacle appeared – the true summit. In Imanishi's photographs it appears as a shattered rock tower with two distinct stripes dividing the dark granite and light limestone alongside it. They dropped down a deep gully between the two, and up onto the knife-edge summit the other side.

Their description is mystifying because nobody in their right mind would go that way now. There is an easy snow traverse beneath the first two summits which the two men somehow failed to notice, and the shattered rock tower is buried under several metres of snow. There is no trace of it whatsoever, and the summit is virtually unrecognisable from Imanishi and Gyalzen's day.

*　*　*

I have fond memories of my Manaslu expedition. We began with an exhilarating six-day trek up the spectacular Budhi Gandaki gorge, starting from the town of Arughat in humid jungle at an altitude of just 600m. It was the end of August and the heart of the monsoon season in Nepal. I was expecting the trek to be very wet and misty, and although it rained every day we were usually safely in camp when the heavens opened late in the afternoon.

Instead, I suffered from moisture of a less pleasant kind. If you happen to be reading this while eating then I recommend you finish your mouthful before continuing. The trail wove above the river on a path that was at times hewn from a cliff face. We passed through rice fields and temperate jungle, crossing the river many times on narrow suspension bridges. Sometimes the gorge became so narrow that it felt like the cliffs on either side were reaching out to touch each other, but shade was rare and pleasant, and most of the time we walked in hot sun and sweated profusely. Every afternoon I arrived in camp dripping wet and had to put on dry clothes, but my walking gear never dried out, and the following morning I put my wet clothes back on to begin the next day's hike. By the fifth morning my perpetually damp underwear had deposited a lot of salt and was beginning to chafe. I've never tried sandpapering my genitals but I can imagine what it feels like. I had to walk in bandy-legged fashion, and frequently arrived in camp much later than the rest of the team.

My regular travelling companion in those early days of the expedition was an American motorcycle dealer called Robert, who was carrying a slight injury to his knee, and lagged behind like I did. He had attempted Everest a couple of years earlier, and reached as high as the Balcony at 8,400m on the South-East Ridge before making the difficult decision to turn around. He had brought a pair of skis to Manaslu with him and was hoping to ski from the summit. I'm not a skier myself, and I know there is room in this world for all types, but ski mountaineering on giant Himalayan peaks seemed a bit like riding a unicycle across a tightrope; I couldn't imagine it increased the enjoyment of either activity.

On the sixth day of the trek we reached the village of Samagaon, in a fabulous setting on a high plateau beneath the foot of Manaslu. Despite becoming the base for expeditions to the eighth highest mountain in the world, it seemed to be trapped in a time capsule, full of traditional mediaeval stone buildings with grass drying in courtyards at the front. The paths were a quagmire of mud, and the children were all very dirty, but I loved the place for all these reasons. We also had cause to be grateful. Unlike the Japanese team in 1954, we weren't attacked with sticks and stones, and nobody tried to relieve us of our clothing. I spent two days relaxing in a teahouse, generally taking it easy while I acclimatised.

By far the two fittest and most energetic members of our team were the two women, Anne-Mari and Mila. I don't think any of us men were remotely embarrassed about it. Mila had a strange predilection for taking a paddle in the coldest streams she could find, and while we rested in the teahouse, she climbed up to Birendra Tal, an ice-cold glacier lake on a shelf above the village, to take a dip. Anne-Mari, one of Finland's top marathon runners, found her ambitions of doing more exercise thwarted. Every morning she got up early to go for a run, but the trails around Samagaon were far too muddy to do anything other than sink. Usually she had to content herself with sitting in the teahouse like the rest of us.

Manaslu base camp was located 1,400m above the village on a rocky outcrop up a very muddy hillside. Unusually for an 8,000m peak's base camp, it was situated below the snowline at a comparatively moderate altitude of only 4,840m. This elevation happened to coincide with a thin layer of fog which seemed to hang in the air permanently. It rained almost continuously for three weeks, and I can confidently say it was one of the wettest places I have ever been. It was like camping underneath a waterfall, and I'm sure it would have been a very enjoyable experience for a salmon. Almost every morning I woke up to the relentless pounding of rain on the roof of my tent. I would stick my head out into a thick grey mist, and just be able to make out the yellow storage and dining tents of Russell Brice's Himex team about a hundred metres away, the largest commercial team on the mountain. Above them a few miserable ice blocks, the tongue of a glacier, extended into the clouds.

On a rare clear morning Manaslu's impressive and somewhat daunting East Pinnacle rose above the moraine of base camp. From its top a snow slope eased down to the North Col which divided it from Manaslu's smaller north peak. We knew the summit route went that way, but the main summit itself was hidden behind the East Pinnacle. I never had a proper view of it until I climbed up there a few weeks later.

Thankfully the wet weather we were experiencing was localised, and seemed to be confined to the band of cloud beneath 5,000m where our base camp was situated. On our fourth day we embarked on a load carry up to Camp 1. We didn't have far to climb before we found ourselves above the cloud and looking up a long glacier to the V-shaped horizon formed by the two peaks. Our route to the summit was obvious – up to the col and then along the ridgeline below the East Pinnacle. Beneath the col was a giant snow slope that looked like an easy plod to get up, but would become a serious avalanche hazard after fresh snowfall. The tricky part of the climb looked to be beneath this, where we would have to negotiate a route through a high band of seracs and ice cliffs.

Camp 1 was located at the bottom of this section, and should have been a straightforward if tiring trudge up a gentle glacier. It was for most of us, but Ian managed to turn it into an ordeal by dislocating his shoulder leaping across a crevasse. It might have been even more of an ordeal for him had Mark or I agreed to his request to shove the shoulder back into its socket for him. Happily we were able to visualise the likely outcome of his arm pinging from his shoulder like an excited thrill-seeker hanging from a bungee cord. We sent him back to base camp to let the doctor in the Himex team have a go instead.

Ian was blessed with many things. He was a strong and determined climber, and had an easygoing, forgiving personality which made him a good travelling companion. He was also gifted with an insatiable craving for heroism that raised its head above the parapet at moments like this. To put it another way, there were times when he demonstrated the wisdom of a man peeing from a boat in a crocodile-infested swamp.

I hadn't gone far when I glanced back and saw someone who looked suspiciously like Ian climbing behind me. I looked again, and saw that I wasn't imagining things. It was Ian. He didn't want to miss out on the load carry, so having been refused our own medical expertise he attempted to fix his own shoulder by leaning on it. He heard a loud click and thought it was back in its socket, but he hadn't done it properly. Now he was ascending with a heavy pack slung over a half-dangling shoulder, and judging by his grimace, he appreciated his home surgery no more than anyone else enjoyed his home brew.

It can sometimes be difficult to put yourself in somebody else's shoes. Ian was clearly in agony; even after taking Tramadol, a severe painkiller, at Camp 1, his descent was excruciating. Had the same thing happened to me then wild unicorns pulling a golden chariot wouldn't have carried me to Camp 1, and my only consideration would have been to get back down as quickly as possible so the doctor could fix my shoulder. But we're all different, and that's what makes human nature interesting.

One of the challenges on a big mountaineering expedition is staying active while you wait in base camp for a suitable weather window. Some base camps are better for this than others. On the Gasherbrums our base camp was located on a narrow finger of moraine between an icefall and a viciously jagged glacier. There weren't many places to go for a walk in safety without a teammate to rope up with in case we fell into a crevasse. On Cho Oyu we had a very enjoyable hike up to the Nangpa La to look down into Nepal and see the view Herbert Tichy must have had on his way to Pasang's wedding.

Manaslu had a good meaty exercise option in the form of Samagaon in the valley 1,400m below base camp. It was a pleasant – if muddy – two-hour descent from base camp, along a moraine ridge, then down through grassy moorland, juniper-clad hillsides and a short stretch of rhododendron wood, which ended along a boulder-laden river valley into the village. It usually took me three and a half hours to plod back up again, so with a couple of hours at the teahouse in the village it was pretty much a day trip, but it was great exercise.

The trip was not hazard free for a certain type of person. A few times our Sherpa crew disappeared from base camp during a rest day, and a radio call down to Samagaon located them safe in the teahouse nursing glasses of chang, their favourite tipple. Dusk fell at six o'clock and we had to remember to give ourselves enough time for the return journey. Mark and Ian were not good at this. On their own they were able to exercise temperance, but when they were together it became my responsibility to steer them on the path of prudence – a task as straightforward as exploring for oil with a spoon.

On one visit to Samagaon I stood up to leave shortly after lunch, but they were convinced they still had time for another drink. I climbed on my own through thick mist and didn't see another soul, but the path was obvious, and in daylight there was little danger of becoming lost on the way back to camp. Some of our Sherpas were down in Samagaon that day and I fully expected them to offer my two companions blankets to curl up in the teahouse for the night.

Mark Dickson and Ian Cartwright at Camp 3 on Manaslu, during some climbing

I was back at six o'clock in time for dinner, and was surprised to hear Mark's boisterous voice carrying across camp as I headed to my tent at 8.30 in pitch blackness. At about 4.30 someone had been sober enough to realise there were only a couple of hours' daylight left. Ian and Mark made it back with an escort of three Sherpas, having completed most of the climb in darkness with a single head torch between five of them. Dorje led the formation with the flashlight, while Mark and Ian staggered behind him. The hardest job was given to Kami and Gombu at the back, who walked with their hands held in front of them like a pair of slip fielders ready to take a catch – only in this scenario they had to catch something slightly heavier than a cricket ball.

Despite these self-inflicted setbacks we were making progress up the mountain. After our first load carry up to Camp 1 at 5,770m we returned to spend a night there before continuing to Camp 2 at 6,400m, where we slept the following night.

The day after we returned from our first visit to Samagaon, Phil gathered us in the dining tent and said there was a possible weather window at the end of September, and we should take advantage of it to make a summit attempt. I was nervous on the night before we left. It was still early in the expedition and I felt like I wasn't fully acclimatised. But Phil had a great deal of experience on 8,000m peaks, and although we weren't in our best shape yet, he knew this window might be our one and only chance. I was able to draw on my own experience from Gasherbrum, when we waited two months without a summit window. I doubted whether I would be strong enough, but if there was a chance then I knew we had to try.

I was relieved when we climbed to Camp 1 and woke the following morning to find ourselves in a snow storm. The seracs up to Camp 2 would be in a dangerous condition with overloaded snow, and we could hear avalanches roaring in the blankness above. The only sensible option was an immediate retreat.

I don't know where Phil got his weather report from, but I think it may have been Michael Fish, the BBC weather presenter who famously announced there wouldn't be a hurricane a few hours before the worst storm since 1703 hit south-east England. In fact, so many factors are at play it's amazing our mountain weather forecasts are as accurate as they are. Although they are based on weather systems using satellite data, there are often local factors forecasters are unaware of and can't possibly account for. On Manaslu this included the mysterious infinite rain cloud that hung around base camp. Altitude Junkies was one of the few teams paying for a specialist mountain forecast, and although it predicted a promising weather window, it also indicated the small chance of a storm arriving from the Bay of Bengal, which is what eventually happened.

I learned a bit more about glacier travel during our descent in a blizzard. Gombu led the way and somehow managed to find the buried trail, but I made the mistake of following behind Anne-Mari and Mila, whose lighter frames glided over the freshly hidden crevasses like swans across a lake. By contrast I was the corpulent doughnut who annoys everyone in a swimming pool by belly-flopping into the water. Twice, snow bridges collapsed as I was crossing – snow bridges which had held Anne-Mari and Mila easily – and I found myself buried to my waist. I was clipped into the fixed rope on both occasions, and the piles of fresh snow cushioned my fall before I needed its security, but I had learned a valuable lesson. Behind me the stocky ex-rugby player Mark complained that I was climbing out of the holes too quickly for him to take a photo. I realised the best approach in a snow storm is to follow behind the team roly-poly.

Before I describe our summit push I should put our climb into context. One morning at base camp, Phil interrupted me as I was reading in my tent.

'Hey, Horrell,' he said, 'my wife Trish has been reading

your blog, and she says you keep saying our Sherpas are drunk all the time.'

Trish may have been right, and I was determined to set the record straight next time I posted a dispatch. These tigers of Himalayan mountaineering certainly like to party, but they are also superstars without whom people like me would have little chance of climbing a mountain like Manaslu.

In the days that followed the storm, as the snow pounded on the roof of my tent in base camp, our Sherpas regularly went up to Camp 1 to dig out our tents and keep them from being buried. On the way they also dug up the fixed ropes that everyone, even the expert climbers, clipped into as they ascended. I knew that as we passed Camps 2, 3 and 4 on our summit push, our Sherpas would be going ahead of us to dig platforms and pitch the tents, a task I found exhausting at extreme altitude.

The day before we left on our first abortive summit push, Phil introduced me to a very important person: Chongba, the Sherpa who would be accompanying me on summit day and carrying my spare four-kilogram oxygen cylinder.

'He's the one with no neck, like Tarke,' Phil had said before I met him.

This wasn't particularly illuminating. Tarke had been with us on Gasherbrum. He was built like a bulldog and incredibly strong, but several of our Sherpas fitted this description. When we stood in a circle to be introduced and I called out Chongba's name, I was pleased when a cheerful older man stepped forward and shook my hand. All the Sherpas were strong and lifted heaven and earth to help us if they had to, but I found I bonded better with the older guys like Tarke and Gombu. Chongba's face radiated warmth as it crumpled into a broad smile. I sensed he was wise as well as tough, a very important quality on big mountains.

The days before our summit push were among the most relaxing I had ever experienced on an 8,000m peak. Although I was nervous beforehand, it was as if the abortive summit attempt was a turning point in my mountaineering career. The conditions and the acclimatisation had brought my confidence back. The day before we left I took my final bit of pre-summit exercise by wandering a short distance down the moraine ridge towards Samagaon with Mark and Ian. It was misty, and we stopped above the vegetation zone, where a clear mountain stream of glacial meltwater came across from the left before spilling down grassy slopes to our right. The noise was deafening, but all I could feel was excited anticipation washing through me.

We'd had our share of bad luck and disappointment upon the 8,000ers, but this time it felt different. The weather always lurks in the background on big mountains, like a caterpillar in a salad, ready to appear underneath a lettuce leaf and ruin your enjoyment; but although I knew anything could happen in the next six days, it felt like our time had finally come. We were as well prepared as we would ever be, and as long as we kept putting one foot in front of the other, the rest was in the lap of the mountain gods. I hoped that in a week's time all three of us would be celebrating in Samagaon with no eyes for the long slog back up to base camp.

It would be another four days before we were in position to strike for the summit, but I knew I had nothing to fear from those four days. Each involved only four or five hours of climbing and then a long rest inside a sleeping bag. If you put it like that then all your anxiety vanishes. I just needed to get up each morning and go through the motions like I've done countless times before.

I don't like to get too metaphysical about the process of mountaineering, but those few moments by a stream below

Manaslu base camp brought about a realisation that caused me to come of age as a mountaineer. Although I still had to reach the summit, I felt like I had become an 8,000m climber, and the rest would follow.

We set off from base camp after lunch on a cloudy day in early October. There was a narrow weather window of only a few days, and most of the teams were leaving on their summit push at around the same time. Mark and Ian were content to let me lead at my usual plodding high-altitude pace, designed to conserve energy. At the wide crevasse we had christened *Dislocation Crack* in Ian's honour we were delayed behind a team of inexperienced Japanese climbers.

Its early climbing history has made Manaslu an iconic mountain for the Japanese, and it attracts their climbers in much the same way that Memphis draws Elvis impersonators. We were only 300m above base camp and there were still another 3,000m of mountain above us, yet already these climbers were being short-roped by their Sherpas – a technique which involves being pulled along on a two or three metre line of cord. It's used more frequently to help exhausted climbers descend when they may have difficulty getting down on their own. Among most western climbers the technique is frowned upon for ascent, and is regarded as cheating, but Japanese and Chinese climbers seem to be more accepting of it.

Personally I was comfortable with Sherpa support to carry some of our group kit. I was glad of the fixed ropes for the security they provided, and I considered it unlikely I would manage to reach the summit without bottled oxygen, but I drew the line at being short-roped. The technique of short-roping has led some critics to suggest commercial climbers get *dragged* up Everest by Sherpas, as though they are hauled along like a corpse. This is misleading. Cheating or not, the client still needs sufficient energy to walk, and I can think of few things more exhausting than being pulled along at a speed you're not comfortable with.

Whatever the rights and wrongs, it was clear these particular climbers had adopted a deliberate policy of short-roping right from the very start of their climb. We plodded slowly past them and continued on our way.

As we approached Camp 1, I looked behind me and saw Ian was right in my footsteps, but Mark had dropped a long way back. He arrived in camp half an hour behind us, complaining of running out of energy, but I took this remark as seriously as Andre Agassi's mullet. Thirty minutes is nothing on a 1,000m climb. Ian and I were in good shape, and Mark was fine, as far as I could see.

The following day I ended up as pace-setter again, but this time to Mila. This was a mistake on her part. She was much quicker than me, and the steep and broken terrain through Manaslu's infamous serac maze between Camps 1 and 2 enabled me to keep a constant steady pace as easily as a three-legged millipede. At one point we had to climb an ice chimney, where a fixed rope hung a metre away from the face as tightly as a fireman's pole. It was too far from the slope to be much use for climbing (except, perhaps, for Tarzan), but much too close to climb underneath with a pack on my back. I ended up having to unclip from the rope and climb up using my axe and front points of my crampons. This felt highly insecure. I clipped back in as soon as possible, but the rope was so tight I had to fight against it in order to progress up the slope. By the time I reached the top of the chimney and flopped on a snow ledge I was wheezing like a beached sperm whale.

Despite these difficulties our time at base camp had acclimatised us well, and we made it to Camp 2 much more quickly than on our previous visit. Mark arrived about an hour behind me this time, complaining that he was not as well acclimatised as me, and had now become the slowest person on the mountain. But it wasn't a race – and he was still a good deal quicker than the short-roped Japanese climbers.

The third day of our summit push involved a very short plod up the gigantic snow slope to Camp 3 just below the North Col. In September 2012, the year after we were there, a 600m chunk of ice broke off a serac high above this slope and triggered a huge avalanche. Eleven people sleeping in their tents at Camp 3 were swept to their deaths. Phil's Altitude Junkies team, including Mila, Tarke and Chongba, were at Camp 2 at the time. A large crevasse in front of the tents funnelled most of the avalanche away from them, but their tents were picked up and catapulted several metres while they lay inside. It's an incident that would have put many people off mountaineering for good, but most of the team retrieved their belongings and retreated to base camp, helping in any way they could amid the horror unfolding around them. A few days later, when they recovered from the shock and many teams had fled the mountain, they returned to the fray and reached the summit. A worldwide media storm accompanied the event. Many articles were written about how inexperienced climbers had caused the tragedy, but very few people who wrote those words understood either the contours of the mountain or the motivation of climbers.

A natural disaster on that scale was far from our minds as we climbed the gigantic slope in October 2011. It was clear the slope would be an avalanche waiting to happen after fresh snowfall, but with consolidated snow the slope was safe, and the seracs which caused the accident the following year were far from the line we were climbing. It would take something catastrophic to put us in any danger – an event so unlikely it was a risk we were prepared to take. Many people who are critical of adventurers like us will happily get behind the wheel of a car and embark on a journey where the risk of death is very much greater than ours had been as we plodded up to Camp 3. It was extraordinarily unlucky a serac that size collapsed at all, even more so that it happened on one of the handful of hours a year when people were camped nearby.

My main concern was not a calamitous avalanche, but that Mila had convinced Anne-Mari, the Flying Finn, that I was some kind of magic pace-setter. This time they both followed me. We were approaching 6,800m, and my slow plod had become little more than a drunken stagger. Actually it was a good deal less than a drunken stagger. Even after a good many pints a man can usually walk more than ten steps before having to stop and sit down. It took me two and a half hours to climb 300m. Our Sherpa team had time to take down our tents at Camp 2, overtake me on the way, and re-erect them at Camp 3 before I got there. Every time I stopped for a rest and gasped for breath I pleaded with Mila and Anne-Mari to keep going, but they were too polite.

If nothing else the climb confirmed to me that there is little use for testosterone in high-altitude mountaineering.

But my problems were minor compared to Mark's. We started the climb in clear skies, but it soon clouded over, and I was pleasantly surprised the featureless slog ended abruptly after two and half hours when the tents of Camp 3 emerged from the mist. It was only 9.30 in the morning; I had the remainder of the day to recuperate, rehydrate, and prepare for the longer days to follow. Everything was going well for me, but Mark was less happy, and arrived wearing down mitts. His hands were sensitive since getting frostbitten on Aconcagua a few years earlier, and the early starts were a problem for him. It was bitterly cold when we awoke at six o'clock. The worst time for our digits was the period prior to setting off, when we put on our harnesses, boots and crampons and laced them up tightly. This required a great deal of manual dexterity, and while the first two can be done inside the tent, the crampons can only be put on outdoors.

At that time in the morning it was inevitable we would be setting off with freezing hands, hoping they would warm up as we climbed. Usually this happened, and although the first few minutes were painful, I found if I swung my arms and wiggled my fingers I could get the circulation flowing and ease the pain. But Mark was unable to warm his hands that morning, and even with his down mitts they were as white as a corpse. While I dismissed his earlier complaints as trivial, this was serious. It was only going to get colder from now on. While he had plenty of tent time to warm up, it would be much harder on the longer climb to Camp 4 the following day.

In the meantime we were having a very lazy time of it at Camp 3. Chongba joined us in the tent and spent most of the day sitting by the stove in the vestibule melting snow to keep us hydrated. We talked about the mountains he had climbed: Everest twelve times, Kangchenjunga, Dhaulagiri, Cho Oyu – all 8,000ers. He hoped to add Manaslu to this list as well. We were in awe. In any other sport he would be an Olympic athlete, and Mark summed up the strangeness of the situation when Chongba went outside to refill the tent bag with snow.

'He's climbed Everest twelve times, and he's boiling fucking water for us!'

Sadly for Mark the climb ended at 7,000m the following day, on his way up the enormous 45º hill beyond Manaslu's North Col we christened the *endless snow slope*. It was a slope which could have been designed by the artist M.C. Escher.

No matter how much progress I thought I was making up it, every time I looked back I felt like I was still at the bottom.

Its gradient never changed; we could stop and sit down anywhere, but nowhere did we feel safe. About halfway up (or was it just ten percent of the way – I couldn't be sure?) Mark's hands had frozen like icicles, and he knew it was over.

'I'm not sacrificing a finger for this mountain,' he said as we passed him.

Ian and I were gutted. Between us we had made eight attempts to climb 8,000m peaks, and had our share of bad luck, but this year we thought it was going to work out. It was hard to describe how disappointed we felt for him.

He wasn't the only person having a hard time. A little higher up I walked past Robert with his naked foot inside Gombu's down jacket, warming it up against his chest. Had I witnessed this anywhere else in the world I might think I'd been drinking, but here it seemed normal.

It took seven hours to reach Camp 4. At the top of the endless snow slope a ramp led between the same band of seracs that would collapse the following year and trigger a catastrophic avalanche. The trail angled to the right above it, and another long and frustrating hill followed. I stared at the horizon ten metres above me for what seemed like an eternity, and every step brought me no closer. I felt like I was climbing the wrong way up an escalator, but after much effort Camp 4 finally appeared at the end of a wide shelf. We were at 7,450m and had a grandstand view of the Himalayas stretching as far as the eye could see to the north: mile after mile of snow-capped peaks, all far beneath us. I would like to tell you I stopped and admired it with a glow of satisfaction, but instead Tarke beckoned me over to our tent, where I flopped down and threw up in the vestibule.

There wasn't far to go now. We could see Manaslu's

summit crown rising up like a natural rock fortress. Between us was a gently rippled snow plateau with no obvious features barring our way. It would simply be an exercise in endurance from here; as long as I could put one foot in front of the other at a reasonable pace, and the weather remained fair, I felt sure I could reach the summit.

That night I shared a tent with Chongba and Tarke. On Cho Oyu I spent a night at 7,150m and slept restlessly all night. This time I was much more relaxed, and I slept soundly. Twice during the night Tarke sat up and barked a conversation with Sherpas in the neighbouring tents. The nylon was flapping violently in the wind and he decided it was too cold to leave.

At 5.45 I was resting comfortably when, without warning, he turned to me.

'Are you ready? We are going,' he said.

'Where?' I replied.

Now this might sound like the stupidest question in mountaineering since Reinhold Messner's outfitter asked if he needed oxygen, but luckily Tarke didn't think so. I was so accustomed to disappointment on 8,000m peaks that I genuinely wondered if the wind would be too strong for us to climb.

He pointed at the ceiling of the tent and spoke a single syllable: 'Up!'

It didn't take me long to get ready. I had prepared myself the evening before. I was wearing most of my clothes, and everything else I needed was either inside my pack or keeping warm inside my sleeping bag ready to put in the pockets of my down jacket. Outside the tent Chongba waited with my oxygen. Within twenty minutes of waking up we were heading for the summit.

The wind had sounded ominous inside the tent, but outside it was barely noticeable and it felt as good a summit day as we could have hoped for, with clear blue sky all the way to the summit fortress. It was bitterly cold though, and I set off with fingers and toes feeling like they were being bitten by a snake, anxiously hoping they would warm up soon.

The pain was far from my mind as I struggled with my oxygen mask. I had never worn one before, and I was expecting the oxygen to act like a magic elixir, powering me along much faster than the exhausting slog of the previous day. The reality was very different. I seemed to be no quicker, and to make matters worse the mask formed a suffocating seal against my face like a plunger glued to a plug hole. I peeled it away and breathed a sigh of relief, quite literally, as I felt ambient air filter in and reach my lungs.

Immediately above camp a long plateau led upwards for a few hundred metres at a very gentle angle. At the end it rose steeply in a bank of snow up to another plateau. It was almost flat, and yet I made my way across it at a painfully slow crawl. Other climbers left camp after me and overtook without difficulty, Ian among them. I was determined to continue onwards for as long as I could, but Chongba must have realised if we continued at this slow pace we'd never make it to the summit and back before dark. Halfway across the plateau he asked me stop. He fiddled with the regulator behind my neck, where the cylinder in my pack attached to the tube leading to my mask.

I don't know what he did, but when we started out again I was off like the clappers, overtaking Ian and all the other climbers who had passed me. We reached the snow bank at the end of the plateau and I ascended all 100m of it without any difficulty at all. I felt the blood return to my fingers and toes like a gentle rush of warmth massaging my skin, and it really seemed like reaching the summit would be easy now. I felt like I could do anything. Had Mike Tyson appeared and challenged me to a fight I might well have taken him on (I would need my ice axe, of course).

The second plateau sloped upwards a little more steeply than the first, and we were halfway across it when I realised I needed to stop for some water. I was still unfamiliar with the oxygen mask, and I asked Chongba to help me with it. When I put it back on again and continued walking the magic effect had worn off, and although I wasn't struggling as desperately as I had been when we left camp, from that moment on the climb became an exhausting slog again, just as every summit day should be.

At the time, I had no idea what happened. Some time later I spoke to Chongba about it, and I found out the reason for my changing fortunes. The regulator on the oxygen cylinder dispensed oxygen at variable rates. At the maximum of four litres per minute a cylinder lasted four hours, and at two litres per minute it lasted eight hours. Chongba wasn't climbing with oxygen himself, but he was carrying my spare cylinder in his pack. The intention was for me to climb on two litres per minute, providing sixteen hours of climbing with two bottles. This would be ample for me to reach the summit and get back to Camp 4 without running out.

After watching me struggle across the first plateau Chongba turned me up to four litres per minute. This gave me only eight hours of oxygen in total instead of sixteen. At the prodigious speed it set me moving, it was conceivable I could be at the summit and most of the way back before it ran out – but Chongba was climbing without oxygen. Strong as Sherpas are at high altitude, they are not so superhuman that they can keep up with a westerner climbing on four litres a minute. When I stopped for a drink, he turned my regulator back down to two without telling me, and nonchalantly strolled along behind me for the rest of the climb.

Our ascent of Manaslu was marked by a strange incident that played on my mind and dominated our conversation for a few days afterwards. By the time I was making my way up the mountain's final summit fortress, Ian had already overtaken me, and several climbers were passing us on their way back down. I reached the top of a steep gully and found myself on Manaslu's summit crown. Three small peaks stood in a line, and a trail traversed beneath the lower pair to the third and final peak barely more than a hundred metres away. These were the three peaks Imanishi had described climbing during the first ascent. Each was only a few metres in height, but the one at the back, reached by means of an exposed ridge, was clearly the highest of the three. It was the true summit, and I could see prayer flags fluttering from its top.

We were nearly there, but there was a complication. As I ascended the gully Ian beckoned to me frantically from the top, and when I reached the edge of the summit crown I could see he was holding his oxygen mask to the face of a bearded older man in a red down suit. We were so close to the summit there was no question of abandoning our ascent to help him down immediately. We had been here for several weeks, and my quest to reach the top of an 8,000er had been many years in the making. I didn't know how sick he was, but I felt he could wait a few minutes longer while I finished the job.

We persuaded Ian to come with us, and we crowded onto the tiny summit at 11.30 on the 5th of October 2011. Our late start meant we were nearly the last people to reach it that day, but the sun had already begun to warm its surface, and it was relatively mild given we were standing on top of the eighth highest mountain on Earth. In my summit photo I was gloveless, and held up a naked hand in celebration.

We stayed no more than five minutes, and left as soon as we had taken photographs. At the edge of the summit crown we met Anne-Mari completing her oxygenless ascent with two more of our Sherpa team, Pasang Ongchu and Kami. Fifty metres further down the bearded man was sitting in the snow beside one of the fixed ropes. Chongba descended past him, but he gave an anguished cry, and I knew we had to stop and help.

The trouble was, I had no idea how. We couldn't carry him; unless he chose to stand up and stagger we had no means of helping him down.

An 8,000er at last: Mark Horrell at 8,163m on the summit of Manaslu, in conditions mild enough to take the gloves off

Not everyone likes to be helped, and it soon became clear this man was one of them. But when you're struggling above 8,000m and there are only a handful of other people around, you don't have many options. As I fumbled with my high-altitude drug kit and tried to contact base camp on my radio, he was shouting at me impatiently in a language I could not understand. After a few moments of exasperated sign language I realised he was demanding I hand over my oxygen. I was flustered. I had never been at such a high altitude before, and if I gave away my oxygen I didn't know whether I would keel over and die. That's certainly what I'd been led to believe from books I'd read about Everest.

Ian had no such misgivings; being heroic came more naturally to him. He had already completed a load carry with a dislocated shoulder, and giving up his oxygen high above the clouds was no problem for him. Anne-Mari also helped when she arrived on her way back from the summit. She knew the steroid dexamethasone was the correct drug to administer in this situation. Pasang Ongchu and Kami turned the man over and held him while she injected it through the fabric of his down suit. This revived him partially, and with the help of Ian's oxygen they were able to assist him as far as the top of the second plateau, where one of his Sherpas had come to help.

It was only back at base camp that I learned he was the peak-bagger extraordinaire Juanito Oiarzabal. I had never heard of him, but he was very famous in his home country Spain. He was the sixth person to climb all fourteen 8,000ers, and only the third to climb them all without supplementary oxygen. He was aiming to become the first man to climb them all twice. When we found him high on Manaslu he was only two short of achieving his goal.

There was a time in the past when I would have been in awe of such a man, but the incident made me realise that no matter what our achievements in life we are all just human beings. Two days later, over a beer at the teahouse down in Samagaon, Russell Brice, the owner of Himex – the expedition team which had been responsible for most of the rope fixing on Manaslu – told us how four months earlier on Lhotse he had helped to coordinate a rescue of several members of Juanito's team. Juanito had needed assistance to descend through the Khumbu Icefall.

I was angry with him – not only because he seemed ungrateful, but because I felt that such an experienced climber should not have been putting himself in danger, and then demanding vital oxygen from less experienced climbers who were relying on it. But I later learned he suffered a pulmonary embolism, or blockage of the lung, on Lhotse, which he had not fully recovered from when we found him. I also understood that a climber's background isn't important in these situations. He had made a mistake, for sure, but we all do sometimes, and it wasn't our place to judge him for it. Whatever the circumstances, he had enjoyed a long and illustrious career, and being passed and assisted by a pair of high-altitude novices on Manaslu was probably a low point.

Illustrious certainly wasn't an adjective any of my teammates would apply to my own arrival at base camp. At some point during the ascent my oxygen cylinder had fallen over in my pack, which meant its life-giving tube could only reach the mask attached to my face if I hunched my shoulders. It must have felt natural to do this on the way up, because only when I started to descend and stood up straight did I find the mask being pulled from my face. I completed the whole of the descent to Camp 4 in this awkward posture before dispensing with my oxygen altogether.

I packed up my gear and continued to Camp 2 with a fresh problem: a rucksack which hung awkwardly to one side, causing me to stoop even more. By then my neck and shoulders were in considerable pain and my descent was alarmingly slow. Twice I slipped, and might have fallen off the mountain were it not for the fixed ropes. It had been dark for nearly two hours by the time I stumbled into Camp 2 at 7.30pm. Realising I had been left far behind, Pasang Ongchu stopped and waited for me; and Chongba, who had reached Camp 2 a couple of hours earlier, climbed back up to meet me with hot orange squash.

The following day was hell. There wasn't far to go, but my neck and shoulders were in agony and I was near the end of my tether. I knew the difficult seracs between Camp 2 and Camp 1 were potentially lethal for someone in my condition, and I took painstaking care while descending through them. It took me four hours to get back to base camp and I had to complete the journey in a series of hundred-metre bursts, stopping for a rest in between. As I crept along the final moraine ridge into camp my neck was so painful there was no comfortable position for me to hold it in. I massaged it as I walked, but the only semi-tolerable position was staring at my feet in the stooped posture I must have been adopting on summit day. I could barely stagger and I must have looked a hundred years old to the others watching me as I descended the final ramp of rock into camp.

I was the last of our team to return. A tin of juice was thrust into my hand and they gathered round as I flopped down on a wall someone had built next to the dining tent. The mood was congratulatory, but they looked concerned.

'It's at times like these you're glad you don't have to do that all over again,' I heard someone remark.

Phil was studying me closely. He had seen climbers of many levels of experience on his expeditions. Some had climbed multiple 8,000m peaks while others were attempting one for the first time. Some, like me, had been trying for a few years. There were those who revelled in the suffering and returned again and again, while others realised 8,000m peaks were not their cup of tea. Not everyone who made it to the top went back again. For many, a single summit was enough. It was the thrill of achievement that drove them on, not the enjoyment of being in the mountains.

Which one was I? I was certain of the answer myself; I had been aware of it for years, but Phil could not be sure. My welcoming party were waiting expectantly for a response.

'Yeah, but you know you will,' I replied, tired, relieved and satisfied.

How hard is it to climb an 8,000m peak? It's a question I get asked frequently now. *Climbing Everest is easy these days, isn't it?* This is a statement you will hear often in the media from people who have never tried climbing it. Emotive discussions regularly take place on blogs and online climbing forums about the relative difficulties of climbing a big commercial peak versus a technical rock climb. Some people have very strong opinions about it, but ultimately these discussions are as pointless as arguing about whether my shirt is sharper than yours, how hot a curry is, or whether jellyfish are nicer to eat than bananas.

As far as I'm aware (and I could be wrong about this) Reinhold Messner never did master the art of knitting a sweater, but it would have been hard for him to convince my grandmother, who – believe me – was a needle-clicking maniac, that it's more challenging than spending a night in a blizzard, as he did on many occasions. The point is, all things are relative. What's straightforward for one person may be a hard grind for another, and on another day their positions might be reversed.

Nothing illustrates this better than our ascent of Manaslu. For me it was an unforgiving physical challenge that almost proved beyond me. There were times I stretched myself so hard I was physically sick, and often my pace slowed to that of an overweight snail. The fixed ropes were my salvation more than once. An observer watching from afar may have concluded I worked them with all the grace of a fly tangled up in a spider's web. When I struggled back to base camp after the ascent I was on my last legs, hunched like an old man and barely able to walk. I looked like I had aged a hundred years, and my teammates, watching my approach from outside the dining tent, were shocked by my appearance.

Physically I was a wreck; that much was certain. Mentally, on the other hand, I felt much stronger. There were times I was frightened and I knew my life was in danger if I didn't concentrate. There were other moments when I didn't know if I would be strong enough to reach the summit, but that was OK. I felt in tune with the mountain; somehow everything would work out one way or another. Mark's summit push was in stark contrast. He was frequently stronger than me at high altitude, but this time he was beset with problems from the start, and I believe it got beneath his skin and affected his performance.

It would take time to sink in, but I had achieved something that would have been unthinkable a few years earlier. When I quit my first job to head for the mountains in 2002, the summit of Snowdon, a measly 1,085m above sea level, was the highest I had ever been. That year I climbed to 4,000m above Tengboche Monastery in the Khumbu region of Nepal, then above 5,000m on the Huayhuash Circuit in Peru. I finished the year with an altitude high of 5,895m on the summit of Kilimanjaro, but that wasn't enough. In 2004 I reached the 6,461m central summit of Mera Peak. In 2007 I reached 7,060m on the North Col of Everest, and a few months later I stood on the 7,546m summit of Muztag Ata in the far west of China. I waited four years to climb higher, but there were only seven mountains on Earth higher than 8,163m Manaslu, which I reached in October 2011. There was no question which one I was going to try next.

I no longer had any excuses. It was time for the Big One.

7 THE BIG ONE

Sometimes you get lucky in life, and everything seems to fall into place like pieces in a jigsaw puzzle. These times are rare – you need to soak them up and wallow in them, because they're not going to last for ever. The story of my arrival on Everest felt like just such a lucky streak. After trying for years to climb an 8,000m peak and suffering numerous setbacks along the way, I found myself on the final straight of a very long journey.

My excuse for not attempting Everest had always been because I wanted to climb one of the other 8,000ers first so that I knew what to expect. Until then I didn't have to think about it. The moment had come, but after Manaslu I still wasn't thinking about it. For a start, I was exhausted, and my brain was functioning as if I were still at 8,000m. It's difficult to think about *it* when thinking is itself a problem.

At base camp on Manaslu I listened to conversations between Mark, Ian and Phil about climbing Everest the following spring. Phil was leading an expedition to the north side, and my friends were determined to go with him whether they made it up Manaslu or not. But even though I'd bagged my elusive first 8,000er, I knew joining them on Everest only a few months later would be out of the question. Phil was charging US $40,000 for the climb, and I had already quit my job to join the expedition to Manaslu. While I had some savings, I still needed to earn more to pay for it, which meant getting a new job very quickly – one which enabled me to bugger off again a few months later. That sort of short-term contract is hard to come by.

I am often asked how on Earth I manage to pay for my expeditions, and many people assume I must be fabulously wealthy. How I wish this were true. I mentioned near the start of this book that I earned a percentage from the sale of a dot-com startup to finance my early travels. I spent most of this in the first two years, but I did save a small amount for the proverbial rainy day. I never allowed this contingency sum to drop to zero, and always looked for a job while there was still plenty of it left. This gave me the confidence to quit jobs and pursue the dream, safe in the knowledge there would be time for me to find another job when I returned. This is more a case of prudent management than fabulous wealth.

At the time of writing I would say you need to be able to save around $20,000 per year to support a lifestyle of contract work and the occasional 8,000m peak. Obviously Everest is more expensive and takes longer to save up for, and this is why I believe a ten-year plan to climb it is not only more enjoyable, but more realistic for most people.

My contracts varied in length depending on the project I was working on. On average I estimate that I managed to take six months off for every year I worked, and that it usually took three to four months to find another job after returning from an expedition. I did not plan expeditions very far in advance, and only booked my next one when I knew my contract was coming to an end. My choice of expedition was usually dictated by what was available at the time.

And in case you're wondering, I never considered

obtaining sponsorship to pay for my expeditions. This was because I already had a number of skills I could use to earn money, and telemarketing (a necessary routine for any professional adventurer) wasn't a change of career that appealed to me.

My lifestyle was perhaps more important than my salary and ability to find work. Apart from my mountaineering holidays I did not have expensive needs by most people's standards. I had no family to support, I lived in a one-bedroom box flat in Central London, and until recently I was still driving the second-hand Nissan Micra I bought for $4,000 from my sister-in-law ten years earlier.

By the time I returned from Manaslu, many of the friends I went to university with twenty years earlier had two or three children to support through school, four-bedroom houses with large gardens, spent $15,000 on a family holiday every year, and $50,000 on a new car every few years. This was wealth I could only dream of, but they had made different life choices, and it is not for any of us to judge which life is better. We were all equally happy with the choices we had made. I am yet to meet a parent who would swap one of their children for an Everest climb.

Five days after reaching the summit of Manaslu I was back in the UK. Just after getting off the plane, standing by the luggage carousel at Heathrow Airport, I read the following email on my phone.

Well done – grand job summiting!! Now get your arse back down here and get back to work! Your replacement has left. Come back, all is forgiven. If you want to pick things up (and it's all going well so no mess to sort out) let me know asap as I'm interviewing, but the role is yours if you want it.

It wasn't perhaps the politest job offer I've ever received, but if my former boss wanted to offer me my old job back I wasn't going to complain about the manner in which it was framed.

Everything was conspiring in one direction. The job offer was a six-month contract, and Phil's Everest expedition would be starting in five months' time, but I had a more immediate problem.

After reaching the summit of Manaslu I barely had a moment's rest. I was more exhausted than I had ever been when I collapsed into a tent at Camp 2 that evening, and the following morning I struggled through the intricate seracs above Camp 1 to return to base camp. When I got there I immediately spent three hours packing. The next day I descended to Samagaon and spent several hours in a teahouse trying to match Mark and Ian beer for beer (which, believe me, is nearly as taxing as climbing an 8,000m peak). No sooner had we returned to Kathmandu than we found ourselves in a bar, watching the Rugby World Cup. That afternoon I changed my ticket at the airline office, and the following day I boarded a four-hour flight from Kathmandu to Delhi, followed by a nine-hour connection from Delhi to London.

How I managed to remain active through those days I don't know. The moment I walked through the door of my flat in Central London at ten o'clock on Monday evening, my body decided it was payback time. Over the next four days I experienced a fatigue so severe it would have floored a bull elephant. I slept fourteen hours a day, and could only manage two to three hours of light activity at a stretch before needing a rest. I frequently woke up in the night with a feeling of acute anxiety bordering on paranoia, and found it so difficult to complete simple tasks it took me five days to unpack my luggage.

My concerns about my health were more intense because my neck was still in pain from the problems with my oxygen and backpack on summit day. I worried that I'd suffered a spinal injury. I spent some time Googling neck injuries and wasn't reassured to discover my severe fatigue could last for months or even years, depending on the extent of the damage. I spoke to my doctor, who wondered if I'd picked up an infectious disease. He recommended I take a blood test.

I wrote a short email to my boss which took about an hour to compose.

Thanks for the offer, and sorry to hear Martin is leaving already. My brain is frazzled and not much use to anyone at the moment (including myself) – combination of total exhaustion and then no time to rest and recuperate since summiting a week ago. Yes, I would be interested in picking things back up if it recovers sufficiently. Hopefully this will happen by the time you need me to start. Please don't stop interviewing for my sake in the meantime, however! Can I give you a buzz later in the week to discuss? Sorry to sound reticent, but if I spoke to you today you would get only utter gibberish.

In the end I need not have worried. The diagnosis was straightforward: I was suffering from extreme fatigue. By Friday I was beginning to recover, and the following Monday my jellied brain was lucid enough to handle a phone call.

'I'm ready to start if the job's still going,' I said to my boss. 'Can I do five months instead of six?'

'Why five months?'

'I want to climb Everest.'

He gave a nervous laugh. 'Oh, all right then.'

He must have thought I was joking, and truth be told, I probably didn't quite believe it myself.

〜〜〜

But I was becoming familiar with Everest. Standing on its summit no longer seemed as likely as the *Daily Mail* publishing an uplifting piece about refugees.

My first tantalising glimpse of its rocky pyramid jutting above the Nuptse ridge had been on that outcrop above Tengboche in 2002, when my trekking buddy John and I decided Kilimanjaro would be an achievable goal. I had a more elevated view of it from the summit of Mera Peak two years later, but I was too exhausted to take in the full breathtaking panorama until I returned home and looked at the photos. I returned to the summit of Mera in 2009 in much better physical condition, and was able to gaze on that great mountain panorama once again, containing five of the six highest mountains on Earth. I had an even better view as I explored the Gokyo Valley to the west, and spent a wonderful solitary hour gazing at its South-West Face from the summit of Gokyo Ri. In 2010 I had two more glimpses from different directions, including one as I departed from Cho Oyu.

But by far my closest look was in 2007, when I climbed all the way to the North Col at 7,060m on the mountain's Tibetan side – the saddle that divides Everest from its northern satellite peak, Changtse. I was just 1,800m beneath the roof of the world, among climbers who would be standing on the summit just three days later.

The North Col is a feature rich in mountaineering history. George Mallory knew it held the key to Everest's ascent. While I was first attracted to mountains by the scenery, the sense of space, and the feeling of peace and solitude they gave, I was fascinated by their history as well. People often think of mountains as wilderness places, far removed – if not completely isolated – from human activity. While such places exist, the reality is that rich traces of the early pioneers and those who followed can be found on most mountains. Far from diminishing these remote places, their human history only makes them more interesting.

Few mountains are as steeped in history as Everest, as the names of many of its features demonstrate: the Norton Couloir, the Hillary Step, and the Hornbein Couloir, to name just three. No one contributed more to its history than George Mallory. He named its outlying summits *Changtse*, *Lhotse* and *Nuptse* from the Tibetan for *North Peak*, *South Peak* and *West Peak*. He was the first to tread its slopes, the first to develop an obsession with climbing it, and when he died there in 1924, he left behind a legend and a puzzle that has never been solved.

He may even have been first to stand on its summit, a possibility still hotly debated. There is a subclass of Everest historians, the Mallory enthusiasts, some of whom have become so obsessed with his story they have lost all sense of proportion in their quest to dream up ever more elaborate scenarios to explain his fate. Some concoct mathematical formulae to calculate whether or not he reached the summit, using Mallory's climb rate, the hours of daylight left, the amount of oxygen he had remaining, the size of his feet – everything, it seems, except the elusive coefficient of mountaineering common sense.

As with many things in life, it was almost by chance that the destinies of Mallory and Everest became entwined. The story began much earlier, in 1852, when (as legend has it) an Indian surveyor called Radhanath Sikhdar rushed into the office of Sir Andrew Waugh, the Surveyor-General of India, waving a piece of paper containing calculations which proved he had discovered the highest mountain in the world. It's a nice anecdote, and there is no harm believing it if you have a romantic disposition. More certain is that someone in the Survey of India used observations from survey stations hundreds of kilometres away to calculate Peak XV of the Great Trigonometrical Survey to be 29,002ft high. These days it's more commonly quoted as 8,848m, or 29,029ft.

When announcing its discovery in 1865, Waugh claimed all efforts to find a local name for the mountain had been fruitless, so they chose to name it after his predecessor as Surveyor-General, Sir George Everest. Everest himself had introduced a policy of trying to find out the local names wherever possible, and there were local names for this particular peak: *Jomo Miyo Lang Sangma* and *Chomolungma*, both names derived from Tibetan deities. Later in the 20th century the government of Nepal complicated matters further by introducing a Sanskrit name, *Sagarmatha*.

Interest in actually climbing Everest began as early as 1885, when the English mountaineer Clinton Dent devoted part of his book, *Above the Snow Line,* to assessing the feasibility. Whether it was physically possible was irrelevant for many years. Both Tibet and Nepal, upon whose border Everest stands, were closed to foreigners, and then the First World War intervened. It wasn't until 1919 that the idea of climbing Everest resurfaced, when an army officer called John Noel gave a lecture to the Royal Geographical Society. Noel described an illicit journey into Tibet in 1913 which came within twenty-five kilometres of Everest, the closest any westerner had ever been. He was supported by prominent members of the Alpine Club and the Royal Geographical Society, two vanguards of British exploration established in the previous century.

The lecture reignited public interest and the Mount Everest Committee was set up in January 1921. It was chaired by Colonel Francis Younghusband, who had explored the Himalayas and the Karakoram as a young intelligence officer, and led an army to the Tibetan capital of Lhasa in 1904. It was also the only body anywhere in the world allowed to send expeditions to Everest until Nepal opened its doors to foreigners in the late 1940s. With two British establishment bodies in charge, this ruled out Everest for the vast majority of climbers, not only worldwide but in Britain too (if one wished to climb then it helped if one had been to the right university).

The Committee decided to send two expeditions to Everest. The first in 1921 would primarily be aimed at reconnaissance, mapping the surrounding area and identifying a practical route to the summit. The second in 1922 would actually aim to climb the mountain. It had taken the British years of international diplomacy to gain permission to enter Tibet, but now they had a very different problem. Between 1914 and 1918 over three million of Britain's younger generation had been killed or wounded in the First World War. With the pool of talent already limited to people (a) who could climb, and (b) could satisfy the Committee they were a good chap, there weren't many options available.

George Mallory ended up becoming Mr Everest almost by default. He was one of life's drifters – a school teacher with no real idea of what he wanted to do in life, but he had been to Winchester College and Cambridge University, where he had fallen in with the Mountaineering Club and made friends with Geoffrey Winthrop Young. Young was an influential member of the Alpine Club, and was probably the man who recommended Mallory to the Committee. But if Mallory became a part of Everest's enduring legacy, it was because he was not only the right man for the job, but also because – as J.R.R. Tolkien might have said – he saw the Ice Axe of Destiny and grasped it.

Surprisingly for a mountaineer, Mallory was somewhat absent-minded and accident prone. Several weeks into the expedition he and teammate Guy Bullock left the village of Shegar ahead of the rest of the party, intending to scan for possible routes up Everest from a nearby peak. They became lost, fell in a river and went round in a big circle in an attempt to find their way back. After leaving Shegar five hours later, the rest of the team spotted them soaking wet on the opposite side of the river, still trying to find their peak.

Later in the expedition Mallory lost a waistcoat while looking for a high pass and had to dispatch a Sherpa to go back and find it. He was given a camera to take photos of Everest's North Face and surrounding features while he and Bullock were exploring the higher reaches of the Rongbuk Glacier. He took enormous trouble composing shots at sunrise and sunset in places no human being had ever been, only to find that he'd inserted the plates back-to-front, ruining every single photo. Perhaps his most famous blunder was failing to spot the route up the East Rongbuk Glacier, as we discussed in Chapter 5.

Mallory and Bullock eventually made it to the North Col by descending into the East Rongbuk Valley from the Lhakpa La and climbing up the North Col Wall. Here, at 7,060m, with frostbitten companions and the monsoon season closing in, the expedition came to an end. From a climbing point of view it had achieved its objective of finding a practical route up Everest, but the real stars of the expedition were the surveyors. Between them they had mapped 30,000 square kilometres of completely unexplored territory (as well as making Mallory look a fool). One of the surveyors, Oliver Wheeler, even made it to the North Col with Mallory.

But the geologist Alexander Heron did blot the copy book. Some Tibetans saw him digging several feet into the ground, looking for rocks. When a scarlet fever epidemic swept through Tibet several months later, he was accused of disturbing demons deep in the earth, who voiced their disapproval by visiting disease upon the people. When the British political officer Charles Bell received a letter from the Tibetan prime minister explaining the situation, it was agreed the 1922 expedition would concentrate on climbing rather than exploration.

Led by General Charles Bruce, who had been Albert Mummery's transport officer when he died on Nanga Parbat in 1895, the 1922 expedition included more suitable climbers to partner Mallory. The expedition photographer was John Noel, the man who rekindled interest in Everest with his speech to the Royal Geographical Society.

A controversial aspect of the expedition was the use of supplementary oxygen. Scientists knew the air pressure at 8,848m meant there was only a third of the amount of oxygen available at sea level, and Scottish physiologist Alexander Kellas had trialled oxygen cylinders in the Indian Himalayas in 1920. One member of the 1922 Everest team, the scientist George Finch, was keen to experiment. He had the brains to tinker with the notoriously unreliable apparatus, and was also a gifted climber. But he encountered fierce opposition from people who thought climbing with oxygen was cheating. General Bruce considered it unsporting, Mallory felt it was a 'damnable heresy', and secretary of the Everest Committee Arthur Hinks even went as far as saying anyone who climbed with supplementary oxygen was a 'rotter'.[52]

There was no clear understanding of the rules of the game, or even the overall aim of the expedition. Finch felt particularly strongly about it: he believed those who refused to consider oxygen changed it from being an attempt to reach the summit to an attempt to reach as high as possible without oxygen.

The debate still rages today. While a huge number of technical innovations have been made to equipment in the decades since Mallory and Finch strode Everest's slopes, most of which climbers are perfectly happy to make use of, many still see the use of oxygen as unethical. Some climbing purists even liken it to athletes doping.

Back in 1924 a prominent member of the Alpine Club, Douglas Freshfield, made the same point to doubters.

So long as the summit of Everest is reached who cares whether it is with or without oxygen. One might as well claim merit for going up the Matterhorn without a rope or ice axe, in dress shoes or in shirtsleeves.[53]

The day someone reaches the summit barefoot wearing only their underpants I will happily concede Everest has been climbed in a pure fashion, but until then it's a point of semantics.

Cynics may not be surprised to learn that ethics went out of the window when Finch demonstrated the efficacy of the oxygen apparatus, but to begin with it was mocked and despised by other members of the team. He conducted regular oxygen drills during the long boat journey to India, so they would be familiar with the apparatus when they needed it; but by the time they reached base camp only three out of ten sets were working, and Finch confessed he was the only member of the team with any enthusiasm for using it.

With the knowledge gained from the reconnaissance the year before, they headed straight up the East Rongbuk Glacier. On the 13th of May, Mallory, Howard Somervell, and one of their Sherpas, Dasno, opened the route up the North Col Wall. The movement of the ice meant it had changed a lot since the previous year, and they found an ice chimney just beneath the col, where they fixed a length of rope for laden Sherpas to use as a handrail. While fixed ropes are common on Himalayan peaks now, particularly those involving guided expeditions, in 1922 they were an innovation. They didn't have the magic jumars I used on my 8,000m peaks, and the Sherpas had only their gloved hands to grasp the rope.

Over the next few days a cook house was erected out of boulders and canvas at Camp 3, at the top end of the East Rongbuk Glacier. They established a rudimentary base camp where Advanced Base Camp (ABC) is situated for modern expeditions, and a semi-permanent camp cook was appointed, a local Tibetan called Poo, whose meals thankfully did not live up to his name.

Gradually they ferried supplies up to the North Col. On the 20th of May, Mallory, Somervell, Edward Norton, Henry Morshead and four Sherpas set out on Everest's very first summit push. The plan was for the Sherpas to help establish a camp at 7,900m on the North Ridge, and the four Britons to leave for the summit the following day. It was an ambitious plan that had little hope of success, though they didn't know it at the time.

The summit of Everest appears tantalisingly close from the North Col – a steep climb leads up the snow slopes of the North Ridge to black slabs beneath the North-East Shoulder, the place where it joins the main North-East Ridge. From here the ridge appears to slope gently up to the summit, but although the height gain is only about 800m, there are two full kilometres of horizontal distance to traverse at an altitude more suitable for aircraft.

Two prominent cliffs could be seen clearly on the

ridgeline before it sloped more steeply up to the summit. They named these features the First Step and the Second Step, and they didn't know how formidable these obstacles would prove to be; nor did they recognise a third smaller cliff just below the summit pyramid, which is known today as the Third Step. If the Steps proved insurmountable, it might prove possible to bypass them by climbing below the ridge on the fearsome North Face. This wall of black rock dominated the view from the North Col, falling over 2,000m to the main Rongbuk Glacier. For much of its upper reaches it slants at a 45º angle in a series of treacherous sloping slabs like tiles of a roof, dusted with snow.

The phenomenal effort required, and the cold wind lashing them with every step, meant they had only reached 7,600m, some distance below the North-East Shoulder, when they had to stop and pitch camp. They found two suitable ledges sheltered from the wind and settled in for the night. Most were suffering from mild frostbite in their extremities, and Norton's right ear had ballooned like a cauliflower.

The following morning they set out for the summit at eight o'clock, agreeing to turn around at 2.30pm, wherever they happened to be. Morshead turned back almost immediately, but the other three continued up the North Ridge for another six hours. By 2.15 they were still more than a hundred metres below the North-East Shoulder. The summit might just as well have been on Jupiter; they had no chance of reaching it. Mallory estimated their height to be 26,985ft, or 8,225m, an unfeasibly precise figure given they were using an aneroid barometer which calculates altitude by measuring the air pressure (a statistic that changes with the wind). They were back in camp by four o'clock, and continued to the North Col. In his exhausted state Morshead took a tumble, and could have dragged all four of them off the mountain had not an alert Mallory jammed his ice axe into the snow and looped the rope around it, saving all of them.

Three days later, Finch, Geoffrey Bruce and the Gurkha soldier Tejbir Bura left the North Col at 9.30am on the expedition's second summit push. Unlike Mallory's party they made full use of the controversial oxygen apparatus. A short way up the North Ridge they sailed past twelve Sherpas, who had left the col an hour and a half before them. At one o'clock it began snowing. Fearing a storm may be on the way they pitched camp among the jagged rocks of the upper North Ridge at 7,800m, slightly higher than Mallory. It was a wise decision. The wind rose to a fury and they were trapped there for two nights.

Finch the scientist had a theory that cigarettes were good for the respiration at high altitude because they replaced the carbon dioxide in the tent and stimulated the nerves. This is a bit like trying to cure a broken toe with a game of football, and they lay inside their sleeping bags in a fug of smoke. At six o'clock they were astonished to hear voices outside the tent, and four smiling Sherpa faces appeared at the door with flasks of piping hot tea and Bovril. As soon as the storm abated at one o'clock, Noel had sent them up from the North Col with supplies, and as soon as they deposited their welcome gifts they turned around and headed back down again. It was an unlikely location to expect room service, and the three climbers were doubtless scratching their heads in bemusement for a few minutes afterwards.

Finch had another idea – a genuinely good one this time, which may well have saved them from frostbite and revived them sufficiently to have a stab at the summit the following day. He inhaled from the oxygen cylinder and felt warmth flood back into his frozen fingers and toes. He had discovered an important benefit of oxygen frequently overlooked: the ability to guard against frostbite by pumping oxygen through the bloodstream. He gave some to Bruce and Tejbir, who were similarly revived, and rigged up the apparatus to allow them to inhale it while they slept.

They left for the summit at 6.30am, each carrying loads of around twenty kilograms. Tejbir was suffering badly. Only a short distance after setting out he fell flat on his face in the rocks of the North Ridge and could go no further. Finch and Bruce divided up his oxygen and continued onwards. The wind howled across their faces, and they took shelter by diverting off the North Ridge onto the slabs of the North Face. Modern climbers bypass the North-East Shoulder by taking a shortcut across the North Face to join the North-East Ridge higher up, but Finch and Bruce chose to traverse laterally some distance below the ridge. They were unroped, and although the slabs weren't technically difficult, a fall would have desperate consequences. Even if a climber survived, they were in a place where rescue was impossible. It was a courageous struggle for both of them, particularly Bruce, who had no mountaineering experience and wasn't supposed to be a member of the climbing team.

They reached an altitude of 8,320m by Finch's estimate – a little higher than Mallory's team, and nearly a kilometre closer to the summit horizontally – when Bruce had a problem with his oxygen apparatus, and they abandoned the climb. It was a heroic attempt and they had set an altitude record, but if this wasn't enough they then descended all the way to the North Col and down the North Col Wall, reaching advanced base at 5.30pm.

Most people would flop into their sleeping bags at this point, but the two oxygen-fuelled superheroes wolfed down four whole quails and nine sausages between them. Few mountaineers since have eaten even a single quail at that altitude. In eleven hours they had climbed 600m, and descended nearly 2,000. They had set an altitude record and eaten for England.

It should have been enough, but Mallory wanted more. Camp 3 was under half a metre of fresh snow when Mallory, Somervell and Ferdie Crawford left for the North Col again on the 7th of June with nine Sherpas, but clear weather the previous day persuaded them the slopes of the North Col Wall would be safe. They weren't. A huge avalanche swept down it, and although the three Britons managed to jump clear, the Sherpas were thrown into a crevasse as fresh snow poured down on top of them. Mallory and his teammates hurried to rescue them and managed to pull two out alive, but the other seven had breathed their last.

The Britons were to blame, and Somervell recorded his feelings in his diary.

Why, oh why could not one of us Britishers have shared their fate? I would gladly at that moment have been lying there dead in the snow, if only to give those fine chaps who had survived the feeling that we shared their loss, as we had indeed shared the risk.[54]

They were the first of many climbers to lose their lives on Everest – and they were Sherpas, putting their lives at risk to fulfil the dreams of westerners. It is a theme that continues to this day.

From a distance of ninety years the final act of Mallory's story has the inevitability of a Shakespearean tragedy. The British returned to Everest in 1924 with some familiar faces from 1922, and two new ones: Noel Odell and Sandy Irvine, both of whom would play a big part.

To say the 1924 expedition didn't quite go to plan would

be like saying Genghis Khan had a bit of a temper. General Bruce caught malaria during a tiger shoot in India just before the expedition set off from Darjeeling, and had only been in Tibet a couple of days before he was escorted back to recover.

Norton took the reins as overall leader, but his perfectly calculated plan for ferrying supplies up the East Rongbuk Glacier failed to provide a contingency for one great unknown: the weather. The plan relied on teams of porters leaving in relays, each vacating camp in time for the next team along to occupy it. When Mallory failed to move his team of twenty porters from Camp 2 to Camp 3 because of a snow storm, he returned to Camp 2 to find Norton and his team just settling in. Meanwhile the porters at Camp 3 were deprived of essential supplies Mallory's team were expected to bring up, and had to survive in -30ºC temperatures on raw barley and a single blanket each. The following day Geoffrey Bruce's team also arrived at Camp 2.

The blizzard raged for several days. By the time everyone returned to base camp, loads were strewn at random along the East Rongbuk Valley, dumped by retreating porters. A Gurkha officer suffered a blood clot to his brain, and a porter had frostbitten feet up to his ankles which were turning gangrenous. Both of them died.

Later in the expedition twelve Sherpas stayed overnight at the North Col under the supervision of another climber, the aptly named Jack Hazard. The team were stranded as the snow continued to fall. When Hazard ordered a retreat before the slopes of the North Col Wall became dangerous, four of the Sherpas were too nervous to follow, and Hazard abandoned them. The following day three of the big guns – Mallory, Somervell and Norton – had to climb up and rescue them.

It wasn't until the 1st of June, with the monsoon

imminent, that Mallory and Bruce left the North Col with eight Sherpas on the first summit push. That attempt fizzled out at 7,600m when the winds on the North Ridge became too fierce for the load-carrying Sherpas, and Mallory ordered a retreat to the North Col. Norton and Somervell had better luck on the second summit attempt, when three of the Sherpas, Narbu Yishé, Lhakpa Chédé and Semchumbi, helped to establish Camp 6 at nearly 8,200m close to the top of the North Ridge.

Norton and Somervell left on their summit attempt in near-perfect weather at 6.40am the following morning, the 4th of June. They chose to traverse the sloping tiles of the North Face below the ridge, as Finch and Bruce had in 1922, in order to avoid the Second Step by edging beneath it. Their progress was painfully slow. After five hours of climbing Somervell developed a sore throat and rasping cough in the dry air, and urged Norton to go on alone.

Norton continued along terrain which, while technically easy, was increasingly hazardous. He rounded a buttress which formed the lower end of the Second Step, and continued towards a huge gully in the face which has since been named the Norton Couloir in his honour. The tiles became narrower as he crossed the couloir, and he found himself sinking to his knees in powdery snow. At one o'clock he realised he had to turn around if he was to return safely. His altitude was subsequently fixed by theodolite from below at 28,126 feet, or 8,573m – another impossibly precise figure which nevertheless has remained unchallenged. It was an altitude record for the next twenty-eight years.

The stage was set for Mallory's last act. He decided there was time for one final attempt before the arrival of the monsoon, and he chose as his partner the strapping 22-year-old Oxford University rowing blue Sandy Irvine: a man with very little mountaineering experience but who was a whiz with the oxygen apparatus. Historians have since argued about why Irvine was chosen over the more experienced Noel Odell, but given Mallory was about as practical as a giraffe with a periscope, Irvine's mechanical aptitude seems a good enough explanation.

They left the North Col with eight porters and climbed to Camp 5 on the 6th of June, then to Camp 6 with four porters on the 7th of June. Meanwhile Odell climbed in support to Camp 5 a day behind them, and received two notes from one of Mallory's descending porters which have been the subject of furious speculation over the last ninety years. In the first, addressed to Odell, Mallory said they were intending to climb with two oxygen cylinders. He apologised for losing the stove at Camp 5, and asked Odell to bring the compass he had forgotten up to Camp 6. In the second, addressed to cameraman John Noel at Camp 4 on the North Col, Mallory said to look out for them 'either crossing the rock band under the pyramid or going up the skyline at 8pm [sic]'.[55] He was intending to climb along the North-East Ridge, rather than beneath it as Norton and Somervell had, but the rest of the note could have referred to any number of positions along it. It also contained a significant error: it would have been dark by 8pm, so unless Mallory's torchlight illuminated the rocks, Noel would only have been able to see him with the aid of an owl.

The next morning Odell set out from Camp 5 at 8am. At 12.50 he climbed a rock tower on the way up to Camp 6, and saw two figures climbing a feature on the ridge far in the distance. The first one climbed to the top of it, and the second came up behind. Were Mallory and Irvine on the First Step, the Second Step, or even the Third Step? We just don't know, and Odell was so unsure he kept changing his story. In his diary that evening he seemed quite precise:

At 12.50 saw M & I on ridge nearing base of final pyramid.[56]

A few days later he wrote a more formal dispatch giving a little more detail:

My eyes became fixed on one tiny black spot silhouetted on a small snow-crest beneath a rock-step in the ridge; the black spot moved. Another black spot became apparent and moved up the snow to join the other on the crest. The first then approached the great rock-step and shortly emerged at the top; the second did likewise ... The place on the ridge referred to is the prominent rock-step at a very short distance from the base of the final pyramid.[57]

By the time he came to write his contribution to the expedition book he seemed no more confident of his powers of recall than if he'd claimed to meet a yeti at Camp 6 smoking a cigarette.

I noticed far away on a snow slope leading up to what seemed to me to be the last step but one from the base of the final pyramid, a tiny object moving and approaching the rock step ... I could not be precisely certain at which of these two 'steps' they were, as in profile and from below they are very similar.[58]

A moment later mist enveloped the scene, and that was the last time anyone saw Mallory and Irvine alive. Odell continued to Camp 6 and found it resembling a teenager's bedroom, with equipment, oxygen cylinders and spare parts strewn both inside and out. At two o'clock a squally shower began which lasted for two hours. At the end of it the ridge cleared completely, but there was no sign of the two climbers, so Odell descended to the North Col to wait for them.

The following day he left with two Sherpas and climbed back up to Camp 5 in the teeth of another North Face wind. They spent a tough night there, and by the morning only Odell felt able to proceed. He strapped on an oxygen cylinder and continued to Camp 6, hoping against hope he would find Mallory and Irvine somewhere. He was going so well he soon discarded the oxygen, deciding he could climb as easily without it. He had been slow to acclimatise initially, but now he was climbing like a high-altitude super-yeti. He found Camp 6 in the same state he had left it two days earlier, so he struggled onwards in a howling gale for another two hours. But he knew he was only looking for bodies. They could be anywhere in that vast expanse of crags and broken slabs.

Sandy Irvine's ice axe was discovered in 1933, close to the ridge a short distance beneath the First Step. In 1999, George Mallory's body was discovered a few hundred metres below it. There was a hole in his skull and a broken rope around his waist. His sunglasses were in his pocket, suggesting it was dark when he fell to his death. He was below where Odell had seen them, so they must have been descending, but had they reached the summit first?

Nobody knows, and perhaps we never will, but in 2012 I was closer than ever to climbing all three steps and understanding the story a little better. It was time for me to attempt Everest myself, but I still had one key decision to make: which route?

Although I felt within touching distance of the summit when

I stood on the North Col in 2007, I always assumed that when I attempted Everest it would be from the southern Nepalese side. It was a decision I arrived at gradually by talking to other Everest climbers over the years, most notably David Hamilton from Jagged Globe and Phil Crampton from Altitude Junkies. They had each led commercial expeditions to both sides of the mountain, and understood how they compared from a paying client's point of view.

On the north side I could drive to base camp at 5,200m, but it lay in a harsh desert landscape with no escape unless I drove hundreds of kilometres to the Nepalese border and a lower altitude. By contrast, on the south side I needed to trek for several days from Lukla to base camp at 5,350m, through a landscape of forests and stunning mountain views. As a hill walker turned trekker, I regarded this as far preferable to driving – an enjoyable experience in itself and a valuable aid to acclimatisation. I could stay at teahouses along the way and enjoy a bed, a warm dining room and a menu. And if I became tired of base camp while I waited for a summit window, I could descend to a lower altitude and recharge.

On the other hand, it was much easier and safer immediately above base camp on the north side. Here I could trek up the moraine of the East Rongbuk Glacier and arrive in ABC at 6,400m after little more than a strenuous plod. Yaks could transport my equipment up there too. Above base camp on the south side was the infamous Khumbu Icefall, an intricate maze of towering seracs the size of skyscrapers and crevasses as deep as mine shafts. I would have to cross many of these on a series of aluminium ladders strapped together, either by crawling on all fours, or striding confidently in cramponed feet while staring into the abyss (no prizes for guessing which of these two options I would be likely to choose). Avalanches and collapsing seracs from the West Shoulder on one side and Nuptse on the other were ever-present dangers, and the Icefall was constantly shifting as snow bridges collapsed and ice towers toppled over. For more experienced climbers the Khumbu Icefall is the most dangerous section of either of the two standard routes because of the random element to the hazards, what is known in mountaineering as *objective danger*.

Summit day on the north side began from Camp 3 at 8,200m, while the South Col campsite was only at 7,950m. Camps at higher elevations on the north side increased the chances of altitude sickness, but they also meant summit day on the south involved a bigger and steeper climb.

Most of the time the southern route had more snow and was generally believed to be warmer. The North-East Ridge was more frequently battered by the wind, leaving it rocky and bare, and if I climbed when it was windy I risked being a great deal colder.

While the South-East Ridge had the Hillary Step, a twelve-metre section of rock, the North-East Ridge had the First, Second and Third Steps; thirty, forty and ten metres, respectively. The Second Step was known to be particularly steep and exposed, but since 1975 it was considerably easier to climb due to the presence of a ladder left by the Chinese team who summited that year.

So much for the geography. There were also two significant human factors I needed to take into consideration: the price and the crowds. Traditionally the permit fees for climbing Everest were higher in Nepal. This meant the north side attracted more of the maverick 'independent' climbers who wanted to get up Everest on the cheap. While some of these were strong and talented mountaineers, as I had seen on Gasherbrum many had little more experience than I had, and posed a hazard to others. In 2006 there were several controversial deaths on the North-

East Ridge which attracted widespread media attention. When I climbed to the North Col in 2007 the north side was still very popular, but over the next few years the fickle attitude of the Chinese government regarding fees and permission became a barrier for both the mavericks and the commercial operators, and many of them switched over to the south.

By 2011, when it was time for me to consider my options, the south side was marginally more expensive and a lot more crowded, but operators had become very experienced in Nepal, and summit success rates were higher.

And then I had my own personal reason for travelling to the south side: I hadn't been there, while the North Col was still fresh in my mind. Little by little I was drawn to the Khumbu Icefall, the Western Cwm and the South-East Ridge, a decision that was echoing mountaineering history.

The British kept away from Everest for a few years after Mallory and Irvine vanished into the mist in 1924, but in the 1930s they sent four expeditions to the north side with varying degrees of success, ranging from heroic failure to ignominious flop. Perhaps the most significant contribution any of them made to summit success came in 1935 when Eric Shipton selected Sherpas in Darjeeling. 'There was one Tibetan lad of nineteen, a newcomer, chosen largely because of his attractive grin,'[59] Shipton wrote in his autobiography. The attractive grin belonged to a certain Tenzing Norgay.

By the start of the Second World War the British had made seven expeditions to Everest. When Himalayan mountaineering resumed afterwards they discovered their monopoly on the world's highest mountain was over. In 1950 the Chinese invasion of Tibet ensured the route from the north side would be closed to westerners for many years. By contrast Nepal was ending its international isolation and opening its borders to foreigners. In that year Tilman and Charles Houston trekked into the Khumbu region and surveyed a route up the Khumbu Icefall, and perhaps more significantly Maurice Herzog's French team made their perilous ascent of Annapurna in a bold and determined manner that would have caused the grandees of the Mount Everest Committee to choke on their cucumber sandwiches.

A reconnaissance expedition led by Eric Shipton in 1951 succeeded in finding a route through the Khumbu Icefall. Equally significantly, Shipton and a New Zealand beekeeper called Edmund Hillary climbed some way up a mountain on the Tibetan border called Pumori, and from the top they could see a route up the West Face of Lhotse to the South Col.

The following year a Swiss team made a valiant attempt to climb Everest for the first time by the South-East Ridge, but fell just short. Raymond Lambert and Tenzing Norgay reached a record altitude of 8,600m, but were travelling so slowly they knew they couldn't reach the summit and return alive. A second post-monsoon attempt that year got no higher than the South Col. The stage was set for the British to make one final attempt to reach the summit in 1953 before Nepal's floodgates were opened to other nations.

It was a slicker British operation that arrived in Nepal that year. They had a new leader, John Hunt, a colonel in the British Army who was under no doubt the only purpose of the expedition was to reach the summit at all costs. Perhaps his most crucial decision was to appoint Tenzing Norgay as expedition sirdar. In those days Sherpas were generally still recruited as porters rather than climbers, but Tenzing was one of the first to break the mould. He was the strongest Sherpa, and uniquely he also nursed an ambition to reach the summit. He was a good organiser, and had become a great leader.

1953 would be his seventh Everest expedition since Shipton picked him out for his cheeky grin. One of these, in 1947, was an illicit attempt from Tibet with the Canadian Earl Denman. Denman had almost no money and no permit for Tibet, so they had to travel secretly. They had little chance of success, and risked being imprisoned, but Tenzing had become consumed by Everest like no man since Mallory.

He described his reasons for accepting.

Any man in his right mind would have said no. But I couldn't say no. For in my heart I needed to go, and the pull of Everest was stronger for me than any force on earth.[60]

As sirdar, Tenzing was the link between the Nepali support staff and their European employers. While he was always loyal, both sides had a tendency to think he was working for the other. He recruited the support team, ensured they were paid, and dealt with dissatisfaction. He encouraged and cajoled, and did his share of load carrying while at the same time sharing the responsibility of being one of the lead climbers. Despite carrying more than his employers and having to deal with the added mental stress, he was arguably the strongest climber too. It's not without reason he is a legend and a hero to both Sherpas and western climbers alike.

Early on in the expedition the fiercely competitive Hillary latched onto Tenzing as a climbing partner. He knew only the strongest would be given a chance at the summit, and although his usual New Zealand climbing partner George Lowe was on the expedition, Hillary thought it unlikely Hunt would want two Kiwis reaching the summit first on a

British expedition. He was probably right. The only thing less palatable to the Brits would have been if the men were Australian. Instead, Lowe formed an important part of the support team which took supplies up the Lhotse Face to the South Col.

On the 26th of May, Charles Evans and Tom Bourdillon made the first summit assault from the South Col using the closed-circuit oxygen apparatus Bourdillon had helped to design with his father, and tested on Snowdon. All was going well until 8,500m, when Evans changed his cylinder to a faulty one which dispensed carbon dioxide instead of oxygen. Remarkably, he was able to continue, but he could no longer maintain the pace they had been travelling previously.

At one in the afternoon they reached the South Summit, a small bump in the terrain at 8,750m where the ridge drops ten metres before rising steeply on a knife edge. They estimated it would take another three hours to reach the summit. Although Bourdillon wanted to continue, the older and wiser Evans, whose oxygen was failing in any case, knew that if they did, they would be unlikely to return alive. They debated for half an hour, but Evans's opinion won the day and they descended.

It was just as well. From the South Col, Hillary and Lowe watched two tired figures descending very gingerly at the top of a high snow gully. Briefly a cloud swept across their view; when it cleared the figures were at the bottom of the gully, still descending. Evans had slipped, and yanked Bourdillon off as he tumbled past him. The pair had taken the quick way down using a technique they called *yo-yo-ing*, but which is known less politely as a *buttock bobsleigh*.

There is a famous photograph of them slumped on a rock at the South Col after returning from their summit attempt. They are staring at their feet, totally dejected and exhausted, and it vividly conjures up the conversation which I imagine took place with photographer Alfred Gregory as all the winds of Asia howled past them.

'Smile, gentlemen,' Gregory said.

'Fuck off, we're knackered.'

Three days later, at 6.30am on the 29th of May, Hillary and Tenzing set off from their camp at 8,420m on the South-East Ridge. Two days of wind and snow had obliterated most of the tracks left by Evans and Bourdillon, and they found themselves wading through powder snow just below the South Summit. They feared the slopes would avalanche, but as Hillary recorded in his diary: 'This is Everest and you've got to take a few risks'.[61]

They passed over the South Summit at 9am, and were higher than anyone had ever been before. Ahead of them the ridge looked nasty. To their left, frightening rock slabs sloped down the South-West Face to the Western Cwm; and to their right, huge overhanging cornices were suspended above the Kangshung Face. The final serious obstacle was a twelve-metre rock step which now carries Hillary's name. He found a way to ascend it by leaning back on a cornice and walking vertically up the rock, praying the ice behind him didn't snap off.

At 11.30am they reached the summit. Hillary later stated that he felt no sense of elation, because he knew how precarious their situation was. He extended his arm to shake his partner's hand, but Tenzing wrapped him in a hearty man-hug. They took off their oxygen masks and were surprised to discover they did not immediately keel over and die.

Hillary took photos of the view, and three shots of Tenzing holding his ice axe aloft, but in a moment of forgetfulness that makes leaving the iron on when you go to work seem deliberately calculated, he didn't ask Tenzing to take one of him. More controversially he then slid his zip down and took a pee over Chomolungma's crown. People have claimed many bizarre records on Everest over the years, but Hillary was definitely the first to have a slash on the top. If you will excuse the pun, he was a relieved man when he returned to the South Col and discovered no signs of frostbite.

After eighteen minutes on the summit they left to descend. Four hours later they reached the South Col, where George Lowe greeted them with flasks of hot soup. When Neil Armstrong became the first man to walk on the moon in 1969, he marked this great moment in history with a statement of true profundity: 'one small step for a man, one giant leap for mankind.' Hillary was cut from a different cloth. As Lowe poured out the soup he unclipped his mask, sat down on the ice and grinned.

'Well, George,' he said, 'we knocked the bastard off.'[62]

I always assumed I would follow Hillary's footsteps up the South-East Ridge if I climbed Everest. Life's big decisions are often dictated by chance, and as we have seen, an important factor caused me to change my mind. Phil was taking his Altitude Junkies team to the north side, and Mark and Ian were going with him. If I joined the expedition then I knew I would be going with friends.

Things were falling into place. After climbing Manaslu I returned to my old job to earn the money to pay for the expedition. I started running again, and that Christmas I went to Colombia to do some high-altitude trekking and climb a 5,410m peak called Ritacuba Blanco. All that remained to be done was to ramp up my training in the months before I left for Tibet, and I would be well prepared.

You may be wondering why I haven't talked about my training much. For many people it's an integral part of the journey, and they take it very seriously indeed – calculating their maximum heart rate, visiting a doctor and employing a personal trainer to devise a tailor-made training programme. They set themselves goals each week for running, swimming and cycling, and record times and distances to monitor their progress. Some even have a special healthy meal plan for training days and rest days, including protein and mineral supplements.

Some people love all that, and enjoy the training every bit as much as the climbing. If you're one of those people then I respect you for it, and I even envy you. If I enjoyed training then I would certainly be a lot fitter than I am, and would perform a good deal better on the mountain. But the fact is, I don't. I would rather spend an evening at the ballet than run a marathon, and a chickpea and mixed-bean salad washed down by low-fat yogurt has as much appeal as having my nipples pierced.

But without wishing to sound too melodramatic, sometimes it's necessary to do unpleasant things for the greater good. Maintaining a good level of fitness was essential to climb the mountains I did, and for me it was something to be endured rather than enjoyed. To write about it extensively here would be like writing a book about a road journey that includes a chapter on vehicle maintenance.

However, occasionally the car breaks down and its engine becomes a part of the story, and so it happens when you have a creaking old body like mine that can't be replaced. My training was fairly straightforward. Every morning I ran four miles to work, using the amusingly-named *fartlek method*. This involves alternating aerobic jogging with anaerobic sprinting. Once a month during spring and summer I strapped on a fifteen-kilogram rucksack and spent a weekend backpacking in the hills, and I went for twenty-five kilometre walks pretty much every weekend. Walking, of course, was something I enjoyed, but it wasn't enough on its own to keep in shape for big mountains.

Throughout 2011 I found my training interrupted by little niggles. During one particularly vigorous sprint I tore a muscle in my thigh and had to rest for a couple of weeks. When I started running again after returning from Manaslu I suffered an inflamed metatarsal on the outside of my foot, which might sound like I had an amorous sea creature clinging to it, but trust me, it's a genuine medical condition that is much more annoying. It was probably caused by an old pair of running shoes whose cushioning had receded, so I bought some new shoes, but I had to take another break from running for a few weeks.

Then on returning from Colombia I picked up a more significant injury: Achilles tendinitis in my right ankle. While it wasn't a death blow to my chances of success on Everest, it severely reduced the amount of training I could do. It was a regular sporting injury I had suffered intermittently since rupturing an Achilles tendon playing football in 1995. Tendinitis is the result of scar tissue healing across tiny tears in the tendon, causing it to become inflamed. The tendon becomes tight and needs to be stretched regularly to keep it loose and comfortable. It heals naturally with rest, but the Achilles tendon at the back of the ankle bears a lot of body weight, and too much pressure causes more small tears and more scar tissue, and then you're back to square one. I've had plenty of physiotherapy advice over the years; usually my ankle gets better and I'm back running again after a couple of months. This time it was more persistent, partly because I had to keep training and wasn't able to rest it as much as I should have.

Running was out of the question, but cycling is non-weightbearing, and although it developed the wrong leg muscles for climbing I was still able to maintain my fitness levels. Every day I returned from work and got on the exercise bike, but I didn't enjoy it any more than running, so half an hour was enough.

I used various gadgets to try and speed the recovery of my tendon. I wore a night splint on my ankle to keep the foot at 90° to my leg while I slept. I took ibuprofen and wore an orthotic heel inside my shoes, a stiffened arch which prevents the foot from rolling and causing additional stress. I wore heel lifts to reduce pressure on the tendon by keeping my heels a centimetre higher off the ground. Strangest of all was a TENS machine, an electronic device with electrodes to attach to my ankle. These emit small electrical charges which help reduce pain and massage the tendon. While it may sound like some kind of portable torture device, I was told it might work and I was willing to try anything. Some of these gadgets may have helped, but I could never be sure. One thing I didn't use was a faith healer, but for all I know they could have been just as effective.

Despite this apparent disaster at precisely the wrong time, I never once thought of cancelling my expedition and climbing Everest another year. There are always uncertainties with the weather when climbing big mountains, and summits are never guaranteed. The injury was just one more uncertainty to add to the mix, but a lot of being able to cope at high altitude is psychological as much as physical.

And I had one huge element in my favour: I was *mountain fit*. This is a factor not to be underestimated. As with anything in life, the more you do something the better you become at it. I was going on mountaineering expeditions two or three times a year. Each time my body became accustomed to high altitude and I acclimatised more quickly. I was going to Everest having summited an 8,000m peak a few months earlier, and this put me in better shape than completing an Ironman.

Despite my fitness troubles, Phil Crampton was bullish when I arrived in Kathmandu in April 2012, still carrying my injury.

'It's not about what you do in the three *months* before Everest, but what you do in the three *years* before,' he said.

In any case, we wouldn't be doing anything strenuous to begin with, and I still had time to rest.

Our acclimatisation programme started at Nyalam in Tibet: a dismal town overlooking a deep gorge just an hour up from the Nepalese border. I had driven through it twice before, and remember it hanging in a damp mist. On this occasion the damp mist was accompanied by a few centimetres of snow and a fug of wood smoke drifting out of every house on the main street.

We found a bar up a wooden stepladder at the top end of town, and spent an afternoon there. Mark, Ian and I were joined by our new teammate, the New Zealander Grant 'Axe' Rawlinson, a former scrum-half who had played rugby at a semi-professional level before becoming a mountaineer. The rugby connection meant he and Mark hit it off from the start.

'So why do they call you *Axe*, Grant?' Mark said as he sipped at his bottle of Lhasa beer. 'Is it because of the size of your chopper?'

I say *sipped*, but Mark was taking his acclimatisation very seriously indeed. By the time Phil arrived there were sixteen empty bottles sitting on the table, and he congratulated us for keeping so well hydrated.

Axe's approach to training was very similar to ours, but the same could not be said of another member of our team. Margaret Watroba was a 62-year-old Australian who had already climbed Everest from the south side in 2011. She looked twenty years younger, and her achievements on high mountains had earned her the nickname *Supergran* from the Australian media. She was one of those people who enjoyed training, as Axe discovered one morning during our first walk up the East Rongbuk Valley. I had stopped to eat my sandwich on a rock when the two Antipodeans, who had become good friends, plodded past me up the moraine.

'Margaret just told me her training schedule,' Axe said as he paused for a breather.

'What's that?' I replied.

'She gets up at five o'clock in the morning and cycles to work. She gets there at six o'clock and goes to the gym for an hour, and then she goes and does her work for about nine hours. Then at the end of the day she cycles home, so it's a round trip of about fifty kilometres of cycling. Then she gets home and has a small rest for about twenty minutes and then gets on the treadmill.'

Margaret was throwing rocks at Axe, though neither of us noticed. I asked if she would carry my pack, but Axe wasn't finished.

'And then at the weekend she does 200 kilometres of cycling as well. So I said to her, *how many days per week do you train like this?* and she said *Oh, just seven.*'

There was a time when I might have been embarrassed at being outperformed by a 62-year-old grandmother, but I had learned enough to know that mountaineering is a contest against yourself, not the mountain, and certainly not anyone else. Margaret's training regime had as much appeal to me as a sneaky peek at McDonalds' secret burger recipe, and we must all walk our own paths through life.

The final non-Sherpa member of our team was Mila, who had been on Manaslu with us six months earlier. At 25 she was comfortably the youngest, but she also had by far the most recent experience. After Manaslu she climbed Ama Dablam and several other peaks in Nepal, accompanied by Phil's sirdar Dorje and his second-in-command Pasang Ongchu. Both were members of our team on Everest. Dorje achieved fame as a young Sherpa in 1996 when he helped to carry the filmmaker David Breashears's nineteen-kilogram camera to the summit for the IMAX Everest movie.

When we arrived at base camp on the 14th of April, Everest was wreathed in a swirl of lenticular cloud like a prisoner wrapped in chains, but all around it the sky was a brilliant canvas of blue. The place was much as I remembered it from 2007: a flat expanse of grey rubble the size of several football fields, hemmed in by towering brown hills whose sole purpose was to channel your gaze to the giant marble and limestone pyramid at the far end of the valley. It was much quieter than five years earlier, a ghost town compared to the thriving hub of activity we had experienced then. In his far-fetched novel *Paths of Glory*, Jeffrey Archer put a willow tree teeming with butterflies in this barren valley, but the only plant life that seemed appropriate here was a basket of tumbleweed drifting across camp.

During our first seven days at base camp Axe spent an afternoon networking, and completed an audit of all the climbers and climbing Sherpas in each team. There were around a hundred of each, in contrast to the 350 climbers and 400 climbing Sherpas estimated to be over on the south side of the mountain at the same time. Two hundred people may seem a lot, but in such a vast area base camp felt empty.

We spent much of our time in that early period getting

our expedition communications working. The BGAN-Inmarsat satellite system, which worked so well on Manaslu, didn't work at all here unless you climbed for twenty minutes up a frozen river to an area of hillside high above camp. At first we thought the Chinese government was blocking it, but this theory didn't tally with the obvious cellular mast at the back of camp that enabled 3G connectivity during daylight hours. We posted short messages to Facebook and Twitter with our smart phones, but blogging was an issue until Axe came to the rescue. He had brought a laptop with a China Mobile connection, which we could do pretty much anything with except access websites deemed inappropriate by the Chinese government. Axe didn't tell us whether he was able to browse his favourite porn sites, but his laptop became our means of downloading the daily weather reports from Michael Fagin of West Coast Weather in Seattle – a true unsung Everest hero whose accurate forecasts have enabled hundreds of climbers to reach the summit in relatively benign conditions.

His laptop meant I could not begrudge Axe his status as our team's star blogger. I could browse the internet with my Kindle, and we kept up to date with news from the south side by reading the regular reports by the popular Everest blogger Alan Arnette. Axe's posts were often featured as Alan's *Everest Blog of the Day*, although he did have stiff competition from a man called Dave who was rumoured to be tweeting his way through the Khumbu Icefall. I tried to imagine what he was tweeting about. *Ouch, just got hit by a block of ice, ROFL LMFAO*.

The magic of modern technology did have other benefits. In one of my own blog posts I mentioned I was unable to find the Mallory Memorial, and received a response from a man in Dubai with a link to a map. I clicked on the link and found myself on Axe's website, where there was an annotated photo of all the tents in base camp. I thought about sending him an email, but in the end I decided just to go over to his tent and ask him.

Times have changed. For long periods of my journey to being an Everest climber I revelled in the feeling of being cut off from the outside world for weeks at a time. It was a blissful and stress-free life. I felt no compulsion to keep in touch with anyone, and sometimes friends and family had no idea where I was or what I was doing. I came back from trips having missed important world events, and I didn't care.

My family had become used to my lifestyle and not hearing from me for weeks. For most of my journey nobody else cared either. But gradually people I didn't know started following my travels through my blog, and Everest had an appeal of its own. At base camp I felt an obligation to stay in touch, and I became frustrated if I couldn't blog. It was an aspect of the journey I did not expect.

Two regular visitors at base camp were the Australian climber Andrew Lock, and the author and expedition leader Jamie McGuinness. Andrew completed his journey to climb all fourteen 8,000m peaks in 2009, but Everest was the only one he hadn't done without oxygen, an omission he wanted to rectify. Phil liked to tell us the reason such illustrious company visited was because of his popularity among professional climbers, but the fact they seemed to arrive just as happy hour started and Phil's chef Da Pasang produced the red wine told a different story.

On one occasion I posted a dispatch to the Altitude Junkies website on Phil's behalf.

We were honoured by a visit from superstar Aussie climber and member of the 8,000 Club Andrew Lock, and multiple Everest summiteer Jamie McGuinness.

Phil was Jamie's former business partner, and he thought my dispatch sounded too enthusiastic.

'No need to blow smoke up McGuinness's ass,' he said to me the following day. 'We're all multiple Everest summiteers.'

The other notable event during our first week at base camp was the puja. It started in sedate fashion with three monks chanting inside one of our supply tents. We gathered round with our heads bowed, but one of the monks noticed a shoulder of meat hanging in the corner. This was considered inauspicious, and he said we needed to have the carcass blessed. One of the Sherpas, Ang Gelu, who was wearing a red 1980s shell suit, was called upon to raise the meat and swing a large carving knife around while they continued chanting.

We completed the formalities by going outside to raise the prayer flags from the flagpole on the puja platform the Sherpas had built two days earlier. We burned juniper twigs in a small furnace and threw tsampa flour into the air to be taken by the wind. This part of the ceremony got a bit messy. Some of the Sherpas had secured extra handfuls of flour to throw over each other, and it turned into a flour fight, which I was surprised to see the monks participate in as enthusiastically as everyone else.

The tempo of the puja changed after the monks left. Religious ceremonies in Tibet and Nepal are more light-hearted than those in the West. Sherpas seem to believe that mountain gods can be appeased by heavy drinking, and it wasn't our place to talk them out of it. Several crates of Tuborg beer, bottles of cooking rum, and a few kettles of home-made Nepali rakshi were produced, and the puja continued for many hours after the monks had gone.

On the 21st of April we left for the first of two rotations higher up the mountain. I had misgivings on account of my injury. In the week we spent resting at base camp I disappeared into one of the storage tents twice a day for my stretching exercises, aimed at strengthening my Achilles tendon. Ever since my injury had recurred three months earlier, moderate exercise like walking up steep hills made my ankle worse and set my recovery back by a week or more. It would have been inconceivable to ascend 1,200m over ground as rough as the moraine of the Magic Highway. It had been hard enough on Manaslu, but Everest was going to be a different proposition and I wasn't sure I would be fit enough. An even worse possibility was that I could get some distance up the East Rongbuk Glacier and find I had crippled myself. My expedition would be over during my first day of strenuous exercise, which would be a bit like Mo Farah tripping over his shoelaces at the start of the 10,000m and ending up in hospital.

*The complete Altitude Junkies team, including clients, climbing
Sherpas and kitchen crew, underneath the prayer flags at base camp*

During my North Col expedition with Mark and Ian it had taken us three days to trek from base camp to ABC, but this time we did it in two, stopping at an interim camp halfway up the East Rongbuk Valley. The place was affectionately known as Yakshit Camp because of its close resemblance to a farmer's paddock. Phil told us it was one of the dirtiest places he had ever stayed, with so much yak dung lying about that it floats in the air and gets into your lungs. He said someone always became ill there, but we arrived in damp mist and billowing snow after a six-hour hike, and aerial yak turds were nowhere to be seen. Instead I shared a tent with Axe, which I'm happy to say was in no way comparable.

I was encouraged to find that my ankle seemed to be bearing up, despite the rough terrain. Four days driving across Tibet from Kathmandu and seven sedentary days at base camp had provided just the remedy my Achilles tendon needed – eleven days of inactivity that hadn't been possible while I was working and training for the expedition.

The walk the following day was a six-hour ordeal. I had forgotten how heartbreakingly monotonous the Magic Highway was, climbing up to ABC in a series of ankle-twisting ridges. My pack was heavy with my overnight things, and although it was bright and sunny, a bitter wind whipped along the valley. I plodded wearily, acutely aware of the 6,000m altitude that made every step an exhausting struggle.

The flip side was that my frequent rest stops gave me plenty of opportunity to take in my surroundings. Beyond Yakshit Camp, Everest rose like a towering citadel above the dramatic shark fins of ice. From that angle it was a broad mountain formed of two parts. The North-East Ridge was a horizontal wall attached to a black pyramid of rock, and the distinctive gully of the Norton Couloir formed the boundary between the two.

By the time I reached ABC the mountain had been transformed into a tangled mass of jagged black rock. I reminded myself of the features I had studied when I stayed there five years earlier. The lower part of the North-East Ridge dominated the view, capped by the series of broken crags known as the Pinnacles. By contrast the North Ridge, a subsidiary spur branching from the top of them, formed a gentle snow slope dropping to the North Col. The summit pyramid had all but disappeared behind the Pinnacles, and our attention was drawn by the ice cliffs of the North Col Wall.

We rested for three days at ABC before tackling the wall. On the first I was struck down by tent lassitude, and could barely summon the energy to leave it for one moment. Everything took so much effort, from climbing out of my tent to use the toilet, to sorting out kit, to walking the few short feet to the dining tent for hot drinks. The smallest of tasks left me out of breath.

My lassitude wasn't helped by the wind, which thrashed at the nylon tent, frequently bending its poles by 45º. It was warm inside for much of the day, but after 3.30 the sun dropped behind Changtse and suddenly it became perishingly cold. I had to jump inside my down suit and tighten the straps around my neck. Throughout the days I heard expletives as people emerged from their tents and felt the icy blast against their bones. Assistant chef Pemba produced some lovely meals of yak steak and roast potatoes, but they were wasted on my failing appetite, and it was so cold inside the dining tent that within five minutes the food was the temperature of ice cream drizzled in liquid nitrogen.

Gradually I became more active. On the second day I wrapped up warmly and left my tent for a short walk around camp. It was much quieter than the sprawling village we had walked through in 2007. My stroll brought back memories as I watched some figures ice climbing on the folds of the East Rongbuk Glacier, like we had when we learned the skills we needed to climb to the North Col.

On the third day I did even better, and ascended 150m up the moraine to Crampon Point, the start of the ice plateau at the base of the North Col Wall. From there I could see about fifty figures crawling up the slope like tiny ants. I was glad I climbed the wall five years earlier and knew it wasn't as daunting as it looked.

Even so, I failed to reach the col when we climbed up there the following day. I discovered the route up the wall was much steeper than it had been in 2007. Back then there were steep passages at the top and bottom, but the fixed rope sections in between zigzagged at a gentler gradient. This time the bottom section was solid blue ice which made it harder to get a foothold. Above this the snow was softer underfoot, but there were more steep and exposed sections than there had been five years earlier.

On the other hand, I was also a better climber, and it wasn't the terrain which prevented me from reaching the col, but the weather. A cold wind blasted across the face. Concerned about his fingers and toes, Mark turned back to ABC while we were still crossing the plateau. For the most part I climbed with Mila, Dorje, Margaret and her Sherpa Chedar. Dorje took every opportunity to light a cigarette when we stopped for a rest, and this became a problem when Mila and I decided to continue while he was still smoking. With only two hands available, he had to choose between cigarette, jumar and ice axe. He slid the axe into his harness and followed along behind us.

The wind became fiercer as we approached the col. Each time we stopped I shook my arms to bring warmth back into my frigid fingers. With no particular reason to reach the

North Col that day other than a few extra metres of acclimatisation, the sensible option was to turn around and head back to ABC. On an exposed section at 6,900m I looked behind me and saw Mila, Dorje, Margaret and Chedar already descending. I was on my own, and guessed I was still another hour from the col. I knew the climb had done me some good, and saw no reason to continue my lonely ordeal.

I needed three abseils to get down the blue ice section at the base of the wall, and as I was waiting at the bottom I saw Ian skipping down it using a Sherpa-style arm wrap. He had been all the way to the col and back, and had still caught me up. As on Manaslu, he was much stronger than me, and I envied his easy confidence on big mountains. As I trudged slowly back to ABC the winds howled across the icy plateau, and I felt like I was towing a sledge across Antarctica.

ABC is right up there among the most picturesque campsites, but we weren't sorry to leave. It must be one of the harshest places in the world to live. Headaches plagued me for days and I picked at my food despite Pemba's tempting meals. The smallest of tasks were exhausting, and the crashing of the wind became unbearable at times.

But my ankle hadn't troubled me – and base camp felt like a palace when we returned. The dining tent was spotlessly clean, and it looked as though our head cook Da Pasang had vacuumed the carpet while we were away. For an hour the sun beat against the walls, and we basked in its cosy warmth sipping Tuborg beer, our week of suffering high above forgotten.

We were another step closer to our goal, and it was a wonderful feeling. In moments like these the stresses of the world are far away as you relax in the great experience that is expedition life.

I don't want you to assume everything was easy; far from it. One thing everyone gets used to in Tibet is the howling wind. Apart from the occasional brief hour of silence, I couldn't remember the last time I didn't have to listen to it roaring past in a variety of forms. Sometimes it would be tent nylon bashing against our ears for all hours of the day, impossible to dismiss, even with ear plugs. During the trek up to ABC sudden icy blasts sliced through windproof clothing and chilled us to the core. At ABC the flapping of tent fabric was constant, and time spent outside was unpleasant. During our climb up to the North Col the wind was more sinister, leading to cold fingers and spindrift thrashing our faces. Higher still the winds merged into the killer jet stream, approaching 150 km/h on the summit, making climbing impossible.

The wind is familiar to everyone who has climbed Everest. The very first line of Edmund Hillary's autobiography, *View from the Summit*, was an allusion to it: 'Tenzing called it the roar of a thousand tigers.'[63] We needed it to disappear if we were to have a hope of climbing the mountain, but everyone was confident it would: every year the monsoon arrives and pushes the jet stream away.

The wind was getting me down, but I didn't know about its unexpected side effect. I liked to keep my fitness levels up during expedition rest days with some light walking, but the biting cold wind prevented this. It increased the risk of catching a chill, and threw a film of silver dust into the air which penetrated our lungs and gave us hacking coughs. To escape this threat I stayed inside. The only exercise I took during the next six days at base camp was staggering from sleeping tent to dining tent and back again. The farthest I walked from camp was twenty metres downwind for a pee.

We had news the howling winds would briefly recede, and we made plans for a second foray up the mountain. All was calm for the first time in days when we set out on the morning of the 4th of May. Cloud thinly veiled the North Face, but otherwise the sky was clear and the moderate temperature made for pleasant walking. Although the sun was high, there was a chill in the air and I walked comfortably in fleece and Gore-Tex salopettes. A light dusting of snow gave the East Rongbuk Valley a picturesque quality, and I found it easy to fall into a rhythm as I watched Phil and Ian race past me. I didn't expect to see either of them until I reached ABC.

We made an early start because we intended to skip Yakshit Camp, ascending 1,200m and traversing seventeen kilometres in a single day. It had taken me two exhausting six-hour days of slow plodding the first time around, and although I hoped to be quicker I knew it would be a long day.

To my surprise I felt in good shape and built up a rhythm as I plodded slowly up the dusty pathways on the lower part of the East Rongbuk Valley. I reached Yakshit Camp in only three hours, and on the rougher terrain beyond I began to catch up with Ian. He was stopping every few paces and bending down like a drunk over a toilet bowl, coughing his guts up. He looked exhausted.

I stopped to offer him water, but he waved me on. A short while later I heard his coughing right behind me and realised he was trying to keep up.

'Take it easy, Ian. We're making good time,' I said.

'I think I might turn back,' he replied.

'That sounds like a good idea.'

But of course, he continued. The man who gave his oxygen away on the summit of Manaslu wasn't going to give up so easily. He soldiered on and reached ABC only fifteen minutes behind me. It took me just seven hours to get there, and I completed almost the entire journey without stopping.

Phil poked his head out of his tent as I arrived, and his first words suggested he was surprised to see me.

'Fucking hell,' he said.

I was ushered into the kitchen tent, where all the Sherpas were sitting on a bench assembled from rocks. They had just completed a carry up to the North Col and I felt like a bit of a pansy as I swallowed a few mouthfuls of tea and got my breath back. The remainder of the team arrived one by one as I rested in my tent, and they weren't far behind me.

'Fucking hell, everyone's on fire today,' I heard Phil say each time someone arrived.

We all felt good except Ian, whose coughing fits persisted as he tried to recover in his tent. He was the only one of us who had been taking regular exercise; I wondered how much dust he had swallowed in the fierce winds of base camp. My own performance bore no resemblance to the two-day ordeal which got me to ABC on our first rotation. How can you explain such an improvement – had I been taking drugs? Not unless Da Pasang put some in the red wine.

In contrast to the howling wind that had greeted us on the ice plateau first time around, the weather was benign when we set off for the North Col two days later. Ian still hadn't shaken off his cough, and before we reached the foot of the wall he turned back to ABC. As he crossed the ice plateau he passed the superstar Australian climber Andrew Lock, who had come to know us better than we thought.

'Why are you turning back already, Ian – isn't there any alcohol up there?' he said.

Mark also returned with Ian, citing cold fingers as his reason for stopping beneath the first fixed rope. I continued onwards in a group with Mila, Dorje, Margaret, Chedar and Axe. We climbed together, mainly because I was leading;

and although the slow plod up to ABC was to my liking, I was still more of a walker than a climber. The steeper sections tired me out more quickly.

The others didn't seem to mind as I hauled myself upwards in exhausted fashion. Mila was behind me. Her English was fluent and she earned her living as a translator, but some of the more colourful motivational phrases I used were new to her, and I'm not sure whether she has ever made use of them since.

I flopped down in a bed of snow close to the top. It had been unremittingly steep for a while, and a short traverse along a rib of snow led to a tricky ladder section over a crevasse, which I christened the *Ladder of Death* in a desperate act of hyperbole.

I knew climbers on the south side had to make their way through a maze of seracs and crevasses in the Khumbu Icefall, crossing as many as fifty or sixty ladders. Four or five were lashed together in places, sagging in the middle over yawning gaps that could have swallowed a family of humpback whales. Compared with what south-side climbers were going through, our ladder section was tame – but I didn't particularly care about that. Two five-metre ladders were tied together at a 60º angle over a deep crevasse. At the top was a wall of ice with a narrow gully of snow leading even more steeply off to the right. The gully appeared to be more of a problem than the ladder itself. A tangle of ropes was attached to the wall at the top of the ladder for climbers to pull on, and two of them continued up the gully to where it flattened out. Even without the yawning crevasse directly beneath it, the gully looked hideously exposed.

I bravely allowed Axe to go first. There was a rope tied to each side of the ladder, and when it was my turn I attached my safety carabiner to one and my jumar to the other. At the top of the ladder I switched them to the two ropes leading up the gully. There were some steps on this section, but my ice axe was packed away in my backpack, and I found the most secure way to climb was by pulling hard on one of the ropes with my jumar.

Climbing the North Col Wall

I made good progress.

Just at the top of the gully I chanced to glance down, and was sickened by the exposure. I could only imagine myself getting down again by abseiling, but the angle was awkward and the tangle of ropes above the ladder would be sure to cause a problem. I didn't look forward to descending, and wondered how I could possibly manage it on my way down from a summit attempt, in an exhausted state and carrying a heavy pack. But I might just as well have worried about what to say to the Queen when she presented me with my knighthood at Buckingham Palace. We still had a long way to go.

In some ways the North Col seemed unfamiliar. If it had

felt like the Glastonbury Festival campsite in 2007, this time it was more like a lonely beach on the Outer Hebrides, so quiet it was. Another important detail had changed. Five years earlier this place had been the culmination of our journey; now it was just a step along the way, albeit an important one.

Behind the tents the familiar shelf of ice rose several metres, sheltering the campsite from the west wind; on the other side a gigantic balcony overlooked ABC and the top end of the East Rongbuk Valley. But the mist denied us our view of the North Face rising up in touching distance.

Andrew had overtaken us on the way up, and Phil was helping him to pitch his tent. He was climbing Everest solo and unsupported, and would be continuing up the North Ridge the following day. We asked him to take a photo of us as we rested. Margaret was accused of being a groupie when she asked to have one taken with him.

Groupies come in all shapes and sizes. Earlier in the expedition we were sitting in the dining tent at base camp when a bearded Australian trekker poked his head through the door.

'G'day fellas, I'm looking for Andrew Lock,' he said.

'He's in a different team,' said Phil. 'Are you a friend of his?'

'Nah, I'm just a bit of a climbing groupie,' the trekker replied as he stroked his beard and hitched up his trousers.

Mountaineers don't get the same perks as rock stars.

After a short break it was time to steel my resolve and descend. My arm-wrapping technique was still rudimentary. It had saved me from a long fall on Manaslu when my arm became trapped in the rope, but it hadn't prevented me stumbling in the first place. On my way down the gully above the *Ladder of Death* Phil taught me a technique which provided the control my existing one lacked. Instead of circling my arm around the rope, I pulled the rope behind me with my upper hand and used it to guide me down the slope. I descended the gully easily, and even felt confident enough to stop halfway and switch my carabiner from one rope to another. I used the technique all the way down to the ice plateau, and didn't need to abseil.

Seven more days at base camp passed in much the same fashion, as we waited on a weather window for our summit push. The high point was a party thrown by the Russian 7 Summits Club team in their big dome tent at the far end of camp, to which everyone in camp was invited. There was food, drink, music, laughter, dancing, and a refreshing absence of the macho rivalry that often characterises expedition base camps. But with our sun-ravaged, wind-scoured and unshaven faces, rarely have I attended a party with so many ugly people.

I felt an inevitable nervous tension creep into my bones as our summit attempt loomed. This wasn't helped by Axe, who published a horror show of a blog post a few days before we were due to depart, listing all the ways he might die on summit day. He described how every moment spent in the death zone would slowly kill him, and how it's so cold up there that if he took his gloves off he might lose his fingers 'for ever' (implying there was a way of losing his fingers and growing them back again). And in case there were any members of his family reading who weren't sufficiently concerned about his safety he reminded them he could fall 2,000m down the North Face and die instantly.

I read the post to Mark in a deep voice you might hear in Hollywood movie trailers, embellishing it with manic laughter at appropriate moments. If I'd had an organ on me then I would have played a dramatic chord as well. He rescued me before I went completely insane as I described how the oxygen deprivation above 8,000m would give Axe the mind of a seven-year-old boy.

'But how does that work?' he said. 'How can a lack of oxygen make him more intelligent?'

I would be sharing a tent with Axe during our summit push, so I reminded myself he wasn't as pessimistic in real life as he presented himself on the page. I was confident we would be able to keep the conversation lighter as we whiled away the time at the higher camps.

But while we tapped away at keyboards, partied in subdued fashion, or more often than not simply dozed in tents while the sun gently warmed their surface, our Sherpas performed heroics high above. Andrew joined us for happy hour one afternoon and told us how they overtook him *on juice* while he did a load carry up to Camp 2 on the North Ridge. This was mountaineering parlance for breathing supplementary oxygen. Although our Sherpas liked to remind Phil they could climb without it, he was happy when they used it. He wanted his Sherpas to be treated well and we needed them to be strong for our summit push. While we rested at base camp they carried tents all the way to Camp 3 on the North Face at 8,200m, establishing Camps 1 and 2 on the way. As well as tents, the camps needed a cache of food, and oxygen cylinders for us to retrieve on the way. Each of us would be using six cylinders during our summit push. With six clients, eight Sherpas and Phil this amounted to ninety bottles, each weighing 3½kg, that needed to be deposited somewhere between Camps 1 and 3.

I couldn't imagine how exhausted I would be if I had to do all this extra load carrying. From my ascent of Manaslu I knew I would be climbing at the limits of my endurance just to reach the summit with my own personal kit. Having reached its 8,163m summit and descended safely, no force on Earth could have induced me to go back up again a couple of days later – but that was effectively what we needed our Sherpas to do on Everest. Their ability at high altitude is legendary and has been praised so many times by others, but this story would not be complete without mentioning it again. To put it simply, it was as likely for me to climb Everest without them as it was for England to win the World Cup on a penalty shoot out.

It looked like there would be a good summit window on the 19th and 20th of May, but the team from the China Tibet Mountaineering Association was not due to fix ropes on the summit ridge until the 18th. We feared a bottleneck with so many teams squeezed into such a narrow window. We opted for the 20th of May as our summit day because we thought it might be quieter, and this meant leaving base camp on the 15th if we wanted to spend a rest day at ABC on the way up. Our Sherpas only returned to base camp on the 12th, but they seemed to have no concerns about going back up so soon.

The sight of Chongba looking so confident and cheerful helped to ease my own nerves. Phil, however, was nervously pacing around camp on the 13th. He was waiting for a last-minute weather report from Michael Fagin in Seattle, but it didn't arrive until eight o'clock that evening when we were all tucked up in our sleeping bags. It brought bad news, predicting the return of high winds on the 20th of May and a summit window even shorter than originally forecast. Phil summoned us out of our tents for an emergency meeting in the kitchen.

Everyone else was already there when I arrived, clients and Sherpas alike, sitting in an ominous circle. Phil broke the bad news and asked for our thoughts. The 19th of May now looked like our one and only chance, but it meant that if we wanted to keep to the same schedule, with a rest day at ABC, we had to leave the following morning. Groans met this suggestion. We quickly agreed to stay in base camp the following day as planned, and push on through ABC without a rest day. This made things tougher, but we believed it was possible.

My biggest concern was a queue of people on the North-East Ridge. With the 19th the obvious summit day, wouldn't every climber be going at the same time? I had no idea how many climbers could be on the summit ridge at any one time before it became unsafe, so I asked those with more experience – our Sherpas. But I could have been speaking in Swahili for all the response I got. Only Chedar had summited from the north, and the rest would take whatever opportunity they could. Margaret had the final word, pointing out that a calm day with many climbers on Everest is very much safer than a day with high winds and no climbers. Weather posed our biggest danger, not people.

Our summit day would be the 19th of May, and we returned to our sleeping bags to enjoy the final pause before the toughest six days of our lives.

When we left base camp on the 15th my nervousness had been replaced by acceptance, verging on fatalism. I knew I would do my best, but there were so many factors out of my control, from my own fitness and skill, to the safety of the ropes which had not yet been fixed, random accidents, the presence of other climbers on the summit ridge, to the most decisive factor of all, the weather. Sherpas call these things the will of the mountain gods. I just had to trust they were smiling on me.

Unlike the south-side Everest climb, which begins with

the difficult and dangerous Khumbu Icefall, north-side climbers have a gentle start with the trek up the moraine of the East Rongbuk Valley. As I started out on my intimidating summit push I found it provided the perfect confidence boost. I was a hill walker rather than a climber, and as long as I could find a rhythm, I was able to walk all day.

I left early, soon after six, to give myself as much time as possible to rest at ABC. A light wind blew behind me, but the ankle-twisting debris of the Magic Highway had become familiar, and I plodded slowly with barely a break. An icy section of track beneath Changtse had melted a lot since our last rotation, forming ponds of water I needed to tiptoe around. This was a good sign. It meant the mountain had become warmer for our summit attempt.

Seven hours after setting out I was 1,200m higher. I had completed the trek to ABC ahead of the rest of the team, and I felt strong as I sat on a patch of wall inside the kitchen tent with a mug of milk tea. Even so, Phil's greeting was a little premature.

'Dude, it's in the bag!' he said.

'It's never in the bag till we've got up and down,' I replied.

But Phil's bullishness was infectious, and although I knew the easy bit was over I was happy everything was progressing smoothly.

In one respect his confidence was justified. He had talked to the Tibetan rope-fixing team, many of whom had been his students when he taught at the Tibet Mountaineering Guide School in Lhasa. They told him they intended to fix the summit ridge on the 17th, which might help reduce the bottleneck on the 19th by giving an extra day for climbers to summit. We knew some teams were sticking with the 20th for their summit day despite the change in forecast, and others were hoping for another window before the monsoon arrived, so perhaps our summit day would not be so crowded after all.

I set out with Mark and Mila shortly before ten o'clock the next day. We hadn't walked far when Mark realised he'd forgotten his ice axe. This was a bit like Lewis Hamilton jumping into his car at the front of the grid and realising he's left his keys on the hook behind the kitchen door. It was Mark's fifth attempt at an 8,000m peak, and he was still waiting for his first success. Avalanches, excessive vomiting and frostbite had all cut short previous attempts, and few of us gave him much chance of succeeding this time. So far on the expedition he had not been above the base of the North Col Wall and he was now intending to climb more than 2,000m higher. He would be poorly acclimatised compared to the rest of us, but his fingers were his biggest problem. Frostbite he had suffered in the past had left them very sensitive to cold. His Sherpa Ang Gelu had strict instructions to ensure Mark didn't take his gloves off during the summit push. This meant Ang Gelu would have to help with his harness, boots and crampons every morning, and on the fixed lines he would clip him in and out at every anchor. Luckily for both of them, Ang Gelu's duties didn't include helping Mark when it was time to make yellow snow.

Mila and I continued onwards as Mark went back for his axe. Though we were better acclimatised since our last rotation it was tougher with the extra kit we carried for the summit push, which included sleeping bag, sleeping mat and down suit for the colder temperatures high above. Nevertheless we made slow but steady progress across the ice plateau and up the zigzag ropes of the wall as it wove between crevasses. Just before the angle of the wall steepened beneath the North Col we encountered our first bottleneck. Twenty or thirty people had caught up with a very slow Chinese climber who had overtaken us at the foot of the wall. Now she had run out of steam and wasn't letting anyone past. On this exposed section nobody felt confident enough to unclip from the rope and stagger past her, as a slip would be likely to prove fatal.

There was one exception. A climber was ignoring the fixed ropes entirely and climbing alongside us using a pair of trekking poles rather than an ice axe. This meant he would be unable to arrest if he fell, and would slam into other climbers in his tumble. The slope was so steep he had to clutch his poles near the base of the shaft, and he looked about as safe as an elephant riding a penny-farthing. The climbers below him looked very nervous.

'What's that prick doing with his sticks?' Phil said. 'He's going to cause an accident.'

Thankfully he remained on his feet and we proceeded slowly onwards. At the ladder we had to wait again when a large group of Indian climbers and their Sherpas came down just as our long queue reached the bottom. Ian, Mark and Axe arrived behind us as the sun dropped behind the col and the cold air rustled against my skin.

The sun was no longer warming the tents when we reached Camp 1 on the North Col at four o'clock, but Axe and I were able to lie in our sleeping bags and recover our strength as Chongba joined us and boiled water. My appetite was already fading but I tried to force down soup and noodles. By contrast Axe seemed to be coming into form at exactly the right time and even managed chicken noodles for breakfast.

The 17th of May was a fine morning. We couldn't have been in a more beautiful setting, high above the glacial basin of the East Rongbuk Glacier with its ring of high mountains, but I knew it was going to be a long day. We had more than 700m of ascent up the North Ridge on a band of snow that stretched upwards into the far distance. The snow petered out somewhere high above and Camp 2 sprawled vertically for 200m over wind-blasted rock. The lowest tents were pitched right above the top of the snow band, but I had been told the Sherpas had erected ours at the top end of camp to give us a shorter day tomorrow before we left for the summit.

I was one of the last to leave camp. Dozens of figures crept up the snow band above me like motionless ants, getting smaller as they vanished up the slope. The ones at the top were no more than tiny dots, betraying the demoralising scale of the ascent.

I did have one joker in my pack. Balanced at the top was an oxygen cylinder and mask, and I planned to start using them from an altitude of 7,200m. I would remain on oxygen until we returned to the North Col in three or four days' time, and I had enough to climb on a flow rate of two litres per minute, sleeping on half a litre. I would not use it as I rested in the tent, but during the night it would help me to sleep.

Soon after leaving Camp 1 at eight o'clock I emerged from under the ice cliff which sheltered our North Col camp. Suddenly I found myself gazing south towards Nepal over a landscape I had imagined after reading Mallory's account from 1922 in my tent earlier in the expedition. Mallory was not averse to writing the odd bit of purple prose, and when he described the view from the North Col he excelled himself.

A world exciting, strange, unearthly, fantastic as the
skyscrapers in New York City, and at the same time
possessing the dignity of what is enduring and immense,
for no end was visible or even conceivable to this kingdom
of adventure.[64]

Or to put it another way, there were mountains as far as the eye could see. I had expected to look across the curtain of the West Ridge and West Shoulder and recognise the mountains surrounding base camp on the south side, but it was hard to identify them in the tangle of peaks before me. Most were far below me. I recognised the desperate pyramid of Pumori, and the two giant peaks of Cho Oyu and Gyachung Kang in the middle distance, which still loomed nearly 1,000m above me. The skyscrapers of New York City would have appeared insignificant in this landscape.

Wonderful as this view was, it was just a distraction compared to the one straight ahead of me up the North Ridge and across the North Face to Everest's summit. The black rock of the summit ridge and pyramid was a daunting sight, but it was also inspiring. The highest point in the world was only 1,800m above me. For the first time in my life it seemed within my grasp. If all went well I would be standing there in three days, and a ten-year journey would reach its climax.

I looked up at the smooth snow slope rising 500m above me, with dozens of figures crawling up it on a fixed rope. It looked depressingly steep, but slopes always do when you look at them head-on. Above that finger of snow the mountain was mostly black rock with a few dapples of white. The face was so steep and so frequently battered by jet stream winds that little snow was able to lie there.

I cast the view from my mind and plodded slowly onwards, focusing on the mindless drudgery of putting one foot in front of the other. After about an hour, as the ridge gradually steepened, I caught up with Mark and Ian sitting down to rest on the relentless slope.

'How are you feeling?' I asked.

'Fucking fucked,' Mark said. He was rarely a man who needed time to choose his words.

'This is Everest – you're supposed to be,' I replied, still not quite believing the summit was so close. What more motivation did we need?

'You're not thinking of turning around are you?'

'Fuck, no,' he grunted.

I didn't ask about his cold fingers. We all remembered a similar slope to this one on Manaslu where he abandoned the climb.

Figures on the North Ridge above Camp 1, with the North-East Ridge and the summit pyramid high above

We walked together when we continued, with Mark in the lead. Halfway up the snow slope, at 7,300m, one of our Sherpas, Pasang Nima, was waiting to help with our oxygen apparatus. I was noticeably quicker when I set off again, but this feeling of supernatural energy only lasted a few minutes before the numbing reality took over again.

When we reached the end of the snow band and scrambled through the loose rocks of the upper North Ridge the terrain was more varied, and I found the going easier. The tents of Camp 2 huddled together on whatever tiny platforms people had been able to find. A line of pink rope marked the trail, and space was so limited in the lower parts of camp that many climbers had dumped their kit clumsily across the path. I tramped carefully through, trying not to pierce anything with my crampons. Higher up there was more space, and tents were no longer crammed onto every shelf.

I reached the very top of camp at three o'clock. I was so exhausted that as soon as I flopped down beside Axe and Chongba in the tent, I had to stick my head into the vestibule and dry retch on the ground.

'That's a fine way to greet your tent mates,' Axe remarked.

We were at 7,815m, in literally the highest tent of the whole campsite, just where the trail left the tumble of jagged boulders on the North Ridge and diverted onto the North Face. I felt like I was in the luxury villa on the hillside, looking out over the slum housing in the lower part of camp. We had so much space I could relieve myself in comfort and privacy, though it was a little breezy as privies go. We could see all the way down to the North Col more than 700m below us. Beyond it a narrow corniced ridge led dramatically up to the 7,543m summit of Changtse, but this was now some distance below us too. At some point during the day we had climbed far above it.

I felt like I had made good time, but Axe had arrived two hours earlier and was in the shape of his life. While he wolfed down a whole packet of dehydrated rice and chicken in a matter of minutes, I could only manage half a dozen mouthfuls before I felt nauseous, and I had to stop eating to let it settle. I could eat only fun-sized Snickers bars after that, which at that altitude were about as much fun as dog biscuits at a business meeting, but I did drink copious quantities of tea and juice.

I slept abysmally with an oxygen mask strapped to my face which didn't seem to be helping me. Meanwhile Axe slept like a stoned koala, and in the morning he noticed the regulator on my oxygen cylinder was reading the same as it had the previous afternoon. Somehow I'd not even breathed half a cheek of supplementary oxygen. I might as well have been sleeping in a gimp mask.

We left Camp 2 at nine o'clock on a good trail slanting across the North Face. In 1924 Mallory pitched his high camp near the top of the North Ridge, but more recently climbers have diverted across the North Face to join the North-East Ridge much higher up, pitching their high camp some way below the ridge on a flatter part of the face. We took this diversion now, and it wasn't long before Axe became a dot on the rocky slope ahead of me. My own progress was more laboured. I could barely imagine a more barren, desolate place than this. All around me was dull grey rock stripped of snow by the bleak Tibetan winds, and a line of figures toiled up the trail clipped to the fixed line, pausing for breath with almost every step.

But on the horizon was the holy grail we all sought. The summit pyramid was the only feature clad in white on that bare wasteland, rising like a lost city in the desert. I don't know what we hoped to find there, but it didn't matter – it drew us onwards like pilgrims to an oasis. It was a place I had dreamed about for so long, and now I was almost there.

I scrambled over rocks and up snowfields at a pace that would have pleased a tortoise. On a steeper section I found myself trapped on a rope between Sherpas who were moving more rapidly, and I was embarrassed into rushing. Elegant climbing was out of the question; I hauled on my jumar in a manner that would make climbing purists wince, levering myself over the rocks with barely a breath in my body.

After Edmund Hillary climbed what became known as the Hillary Step on the South-East Ridge of Everest in 1953, he described how Tenzing Norgay followed him up and collapsed exhausted on the top, 'like a giant fish that had just been hauled out of the sea after a terrible struggle'.[65] Tenzing took great exception to this description, because he believed it made him look like a clumsy oaf who needed to be dragged up, rather than a competent climber and equal partner of Hillary.

In my case such a description would have been flattering. Unlike Tenzing, I can happily say I reached the top of this section and collapsed above it like an ungainly walrus who has flopped down at the top of a beach after an exhausting struggle with sand. I looked up and saw Chongba and Kami perched on the rock next to me, smiling happily and taking a breather with their huge packs lying next to them. Neither had summited Everest from the north side before, and I expect they were looking forward to tomorrow much more than I was.

I struggled onwards alone as the weather closed in, and I found myself ascending another snowfield in a white-out. I caught up with Mark, and a few minutes later we saw the tents of Camp 3 emerge through the mist ahead of us.

We had made it to the world's highest campsite, on sloping, featureless, snow-dusted rubble just beneath the North-East Ridge. We were at 8,210m, the highest either of us had been in our lives.

I squeezed in between Axe and Chongba in what was easily our least comfortable pitch on the expedition. Our legs were sloping downwards at a considerable angle and a large rock was wedged beneath my shoulder blades. As soon as I lay down I slid to the bottom of the tent. Axe helped me inflate my Thermarest and suggested I put my boots underneath it to raise the level of the lower part of my body. This made for an even more irregular surface to lie on, but it worked, and kept me in place without sliding downwards.

Despite feeling as comfortable as a cucumber in a sandwich, I was tempted to spend the rest of the afternoon lying there – but that would have been a wasted opportunity. Our setting high on a mountainside, with the entire world beneath us blanketed in cloud, was hard to ignore. As for the world above – all 638m of it – the slanting slope of rubble partly doused in snow might have been innocuous but for what lay in its upper reaches. The steep summit pyramid was even closer now, but the route to its base looked more intimidating with the First and Second Steps rising prominently above the North-East Ridge. I summoned the energy to step outside and take photographs. It was exciting to be there, but also frightening, and only the mountain gods knew what tomorrow would bring.

Although it was a step into the unknown for me, it wasn't for everyone. Chongba had never reached the top from the north before, but he had summited twelve times from the south and had a good idea what to expect. We were following a well-trodden path using methods expedition outfitters like Phil had been perfecting for a few years, from the Sherpa support to the oxygen and the fixed ropes we would be following to the summit.

When Mallory and Irvine set off for the same patch of snow eighty-eight years earlier, they had no such experience to draw on. The number of people who had been higher could be counted on one hand, and they had all traversed the North Face some distance below the North-East Ridge, stopping far from the summit. Mallory and Irvine intended to climb along the ridge. Among many other unknowns they would be making the first ever attempt on the Second Step.

They had no idea whether it could be climbed.

I differed from them in another important respect. My ten-year journey had taught me that I enjoyed just being in the mountains, regardless of whether I reached the summit or not. Although I had invested a great deal in the last few weeks, I knew I could always come back again if I wanted to, as long as I survived. I was determined to reach the summit, but it was much more important to come back alive.

I don't know whether Mallory and Irvine had the same attitude, but it's likely they did not. Mallory knew it was his last chance, and the prize was much greater – the first ascent of the highest mountain on Earth. It was a different era, when life was much less certain and people took bigger risks. He had somehow survived a war which had taken much of his generation. I believe when he and Irvine set off for the summit that night they were prepared to sacrifice their lives for an objective that would be theirs and theirs alone.

I was in a state of nervous anticipation that afternoon. I tried not to dry retch as I watched Axe stuff his face with food, and continued my enforced starvation diet while keeping hydrated with a bath of mint tea. I discovered the hydration sleeve in my backpack was the perfect shape and size for an oxygen cylinder, which meant I could keep it standing up inside my empty pack and avoid the stooping problem I encountered on my Manaslu summit day. I did have something in common with Mallory that afternoon. We know he was forgetful and left his tent in a bit of mess for Odell when he came sweeping up behind. He probably fussed with his equipment before he left for the summit just as much as I did.

A series of radio calls between our tents informed us that the rope-fixing team from the China Tibet Mountaineering Association was keen to stagger start times to alleviate bottlenecks on summit day. We were given the 11.30pm slot, which made us the very last team to depart. (We were running on Kathmandu time, which was much more convenient for the hours of daylight; these are the times I have been quoting in this chapter. 11.30pm would be 1.45am China time.)

As I lay back on my bed of rocks, I tried to grab what sleep I could and think of less pleasant things than the exhausting night and day ahead. These included attending a business meeting and listening to someone drone on about 'finding synergies', and sitting in front of a computer staring at an Excel spreadsheet. Nothing seemed to work. My mind was relentlessly drawn back to the summit ridge and an oxygen mask over my face. It didn't help that a very noisy and restless group were camped next to us, talking for hours as they carried out their final summit preparations. Briefly I nodded off, but all too quickly it was 10.30 and time to start preparing myself.

Axe was already gone by the time Chongba and I left at 11.30. Almost immediately my oxygen mask gagged against my face like it had on Manaslu. I felt like I was climbing with an orange in my mouth and I stopped to make adjustments while Chongba waited patiently. I had no clue what the problem was, but I was relieved when we moved off again and I could breathe normally.

The trail was much harder than the previous day as we climbed up to the North-East Ridge. By the light of my headlamp I saw boots above me pausing to step up high ledges, and I knew today there was proper climbing to be done – not just the slow plod we had experienced until now. I hoped I would be able to overcome the obstacles at this altitude. Features I'd read about in books would be my struggles for the day, and I felt a surge of excitement and trepidation.

We climbed slowly. I had no concept of time. For one hour, maybe two, I zigzagged steeply up rock steps in the darkness, with Chongba a few short paces behind me. Usually I could proceed with my feet alone, but once in a while I needed my hands to steady myself. By ordinary standards it was easy scrambling, but there was nothing ordinary about our situation.

Presently we reached a more significant series of rock scrambles. In my giant boots and crampons I took the least exhausting option, and hauled on the fixed line with my jumar. These were the Exit Cracks which led onto the North-East Ridge, and I wasn't prepared for them. I was aware of three technical sections to climb today – the First, Second and Third Steps – but nothing had warned me about these, and as I flopped down in a bed of snow at the top I wondered if I had climbed the First Step already.

A short snow ramp led up to the ridge. Suddenly there was nothing beyond it but a 3,000m drop down the Kangshung Face. I was standing on top of a giant limestone wall that had been our horizon for the last five weeks, and my exhaustion vanished as I proceeded along a broad snow-lined ridge. Relatively flat terrain above the Exit Cracks gave me an opportunity to get my breath back and appreciate my surroundings. Ahead of me a few dozen pinpricks of light illuminated the ridge, like lanterns on a promenade – the headlamps of climbers who were already well on their way to the summit. There were not so many, and Chongba and I climbed alone for now.

I felt exhilarated, but I didn't know that for the next sixteen hours I would be treading a slender tightrope between life and death.

We dropped below the ridge on its right-hand side, and the snow-dusted slabs beneath our feet began to slope more steeply towards the Rongbuk Glacier. Somewhere along that section Sandy Irvine's ice axe had been found in 1933, and 150m below us George Mallory's body lay still. None of this crossed my mind as I approached a thread of vertical lights ahead of me belonging to climbers struggling up a more difficult feature. It was the First Step, strung with figures edging up slowly and pausing with every stride. It was thirty metres high and comprised three main sections: a short slope of about 45°, thick with snow a metre deep; a short vertical section with intermittent ledges; and a diagonal rightward traverse to get back under the ridge.

I was relieved to see it didn't look too daunting, and I strode up deep footsteps to the base of the vertical section, feeling more confident. Here we stood precariously with our feet in awkward positions while we waited for the climbers above to move on. I climbed most of it by lifting my leg as high as I could onto the boulder above me, then hauling myself up with my jumar. Each boulder was just big enough to stand on with both feet as I waited for the people above to make their next move.

I tackled the traverse without resting. It was easy scrambling by sea-level standards, but the exposure and altitude meant I relied on the fixed ropes more than I otherwise would have. It was still dark, and I wasn't conscious of the 2,400m drop below me, but I knew this section would be terrifying on the way down, and its sideways traversing nature would make it hazardous to descend.

I rushed across quickly, keen to keep on the heels of the climbers in front. But I didn't realise how steeply the traverse rose upwards over the grey limestone of the North-East Ridge. When I reached the top I was wheezing badly and felt myself about to retch. I slumped down on the first safe rock and fumbled for my mask. It seemed more trouble than it was worth to wrench it off, but throwing up into it and plastering a mouthful of vomit to my face would kindle unpleasant memories of my student days. I took a few deep breaths, calmed my stomach, and gradually slowed my breathing until I was ready to move again.

By now the climbers ahead of me had disappeared along the ridge and Chongba may have been wondering if I was ready to give up. Despite my physical frailty, mentally I was in good shape and had no thought of turning back. I didn't know the most frightening part of the ascent was just ahead.

I loosely registered the bundle of colourful material a few feet below the line of fixed rope without thinking about why it was there. Somebody had pitched a tent, perhaps. It didn't really matter; the important thing was to concentrate on putting one foot in front of the other in such a way that I didn't plummet down the slabs. OK, I was clipped into a rope, but a twisted ankle or a broken limb here would be a death sentence.

I caught up with some other climbers at an anchor point in the slabs, took off my mitts and tucked them under my arm while I clipped in to the next section of line. When I put them back on again and looked up, I gasped.

A man was lying on his back a few metres below me on a sloping slab, with the crown of his head pointing down towards the Rongbuk Glacier. Snow had partially drifted across his body, but his face, arms, boots and parts of his torso were still clearly visible. His red Mountain Hardwear down suit had faded to pink and his hair was bleached white by the sun. One arm rested behind his head like a pillow, while the other stretched to one side, bare hand frozen into a claw. His mummified face had been tanned black and he stared into space through frozen pupils.

A rope and carabiner emerged from the snow beside his feet and it was easy to imagine how he died. A simple slip as he stumbled down from the summit at the limits of his endurance sent him crashing onto his back. He was clipped into the rope, so the fall hadn't necessarily been fatal, but he was so exhausted that he was unable to rise from the position he landed in. He probably tried a few times, but there was no one there to help him, and each time he struggled he slipped closer to the brink. Finally he put his hand behind his head and drifted comfortingly into a sleep from which he never woke.

One of the things that shocks and surprises people the most when I tell them about my Everest climb is that I walked past dead bodies on my summit day. Why have they not been removed and sent home for burial? Upsetting as it may be, the simple fact is that it's logistically impractical. Helicopters cannot operate so high, and on the north side they are banned from flying. To carry the bodies down would take several strong climbers whose first priority must be to get themselves down safely. A dedicated expedition to climb the mountain and bring down a corpse would cost a family tens of thousands of dollars, putting other lives at risk in the process – and insurance policies don't cover such an expense. Some who died in falls have landed in inaccessible locations, and others have been frozen in place. When a research team found George Mallory's body in 1999, it took five strong climbers over an hour on dangerously steep terrain to chip away the frozen gravel and rock that encased him, and another forty-five minutes to gather enough rocks to give him a decent burial.

In many cases climbers and their families are coming around to the feeling that it's better to leave bodies where they lie, high above the clouds. Those on the trail are often rolled down the face to move them out of view. Clearly that hadn't happened with this particular climber, and it didn't occur to me to remedy the situation.

It was a stark warning. This was no picnic, and every step took me closer to the same boundary he had breached. Whatever I achieved today, the most important priority for me was to ensure I had enough energy to get myself back to camp.

We moved on, and gradually I came to my senses. It was 4.30am Nepal time, dawn was breaking over Tibet and I began to understand where I was and how slender was my grip on the world.

The route was a series of ledges barely big enough for a boot, some horizontal and others sloping at an angle of 30° to 40°. A light dusting of snow glazed their surface, and half a dozen strands of old rope from previous years lay at ground level for me to snag my crampons on if I lost concentration for a single moment. We were just below the ridge. A wall of rock provided security to my left, but I could safely say the 2,400m drop to my right was the biggest, most unimaginable void I had ever seen. Ahead of me the Second Step loomed like a three-headed beast guarding the Gates of Hell (well, OK, maybe not, but you get the idea).

Suddenly a light bulb fizzed into life inside my brain, and letters of flashing red neon appeared in the sky above me.

'What in the name of Satan's dumplings are you doing here?' they read.

It wasn't the last time the thought would cross my mind that day (though maybe not in quite the same words).

I had no logical answer, so I continued onwards in a state of disbelief. For five weeks I had stared up at the summit ridge, a distant skyline I could scarcely comprehend reaching, and now I was here, a yak's bellow short of the stratosphere, and only vaguely capable of appreciating it. Until that moment the darkness had kept reality at bay. Now the dawn brought a measure of understanding, but only just. It still felt like a dream.

I started mumbling the mantra that kept me going throughout my summit day, and may just have saved my life: *must get down safely, must get down safely.*

The other climbers were much quicker than me through that section, and by the time I reached the sanctuary of the Second Step I looked up and saw no one. Behind me, Mark and Ian were catching up, accompanied by their Sherpas Ang Gelu and Kami.

I was relieved to reach the ledges of the Second Step, which felt safer than those sloping slabs. Its lower section involved climbing a short ladder into a small alcove. To its right was a large diagonally sloping boulder with a crack broad enough for a boot down its left side. Several ropes, old and new, ran down the crack in a tangle of nylon. The boulder itself was several feet high with very few cracks for crampons. Somehow I had to get my right leg on top of it then haul myself up using the ropes. I couldn't ignore the sickening 2,400m drop down the North Face that I knew was waiting for me at the top of the boulder, and this knowledge shredded my confidence.

I tried three times, but I knew I wasn't trying hard enough. I was a long way outside my comfort zone and the mantra kept returning. Was I up to this climb or had I over-reached myself?

Chongba had joined me in the alcove, and I turned to him.

'I don't think I can do it, Chongba, I'm sorry.'

He looked very sad, but before we could think about our predicament Ang Gelu joined us and took control. Mark was standing at the bottom of the ladder waiting to come up, and there wasn't space in the alcove for any more of us. Turning round was no longer an option.

'OK. I climb up the rock and pull you up,' Ang Gelu said.

I watched him effortlessly complete the manoeuvre I had tried in vain, and then turn around to proffer his hand. Before I knew it I had joined him on the rock. The die was now cast; Chongba joined me, and we continued onwards.

After a short step onto another rock which led towards the ridge, we climbed an easy snow ramp angled ten metres up to a ladder. This was the Second Step's most famous feature, left by a Chinese team in 1975. It was about five metres high, and to its left was a broad vertical crack which the climbers Conrad Anker and Leo Houlding free-climbed in 2007, hoping to understand whether George Mallory could have done so in 1924.

When the Chinese and Tibetan quartet of Wang Fu-chou, Chu Yin-hua, Liu Lien-man and Konbu climbed this feature in 1960, it took them three hours. Liu made four attempts to free-climb it, but kept falling. Chu took his boots and socks off to have a go, but also fell. They eventually got up when Liu used his expertise as a fireman, crouching down to let his teammates stand on his shoulders, then hoicking them up as he stood. The effort exhausted him so much that he couldn't go on, but his three companions continued to the summit and made the first acknowledged ascent of Everest from the north side. Their achievement was greeted with scepticism in the west when it was first announced, mainly because of the ludicrous Communist propaganda in their account. It is now generally accepted by all but a handful of doubters, who wouldn't be convinced if a bust of Chairman Mao were discovered on the summit and carbon dated.

The Englishman Houlding graded the top section of the Second Step an HVS, or Hard Very Severe (which means *extremely hard* in plain English). He believed it was highly unlikely Mallory had climbed it – but you don't need to be much of a climber to use the shoulder method employed by

Liu, which was in common use in the 1920s. The American Anker rated it 5.10, which is a climbing grade, and not its height in feet and inches.

At that moment I could have LOL'd at these abbreviations. There was a ladder, and I was fine with ladders.

The Chinese ladder on the Second Step. From the height of the figure standing nearby it's possible to imagine Mallory climbing the crack on the left by standing on Irvine's shoulders (Photo: Grant Rawlinson).

Within moments I climbed a feature they had spent three hours struggling with in 1960. Was I cheating? I didn't care. After another two metres of scrambling through a tangle of old ropes I was standing on top of Everest's most feared summit-day feature.

In front of me the ridge widened and I found myself looking up a relatively gentle incline to the Third Step. Beyond that was the much steeper snow slope of the summit pyramid, but it didn't look massive. If Mallory did climb the Second Step then he probably had much the same thought as I did when he looked up.

'You know what, I can climb this thing.'

The summit may have seemed within my grasp for the first time, but distances are deceptive on the roof of the world. I was now on a broad, safe ridge. It was the straightforward (if strenuous) snow plod I'd hoped and expected my summit day would be like, instead of the rock scramble which had been demanding every gram of my concentration. But I felt sapped of energy, and could not walk far before I needed to rest. We were in a safe place for the first time since leaving camp hours earlier. Chongba took the opportunity to change my oxygen cylinder.

I stopped again at the top of the broad ridge beneath the Third Step. Mark and Ian overtook with Ang Gelu and Kami while I sat down to rest beside another corpse. This one was curled up in a foetal position beside the trail, and I was no longer shocked, like I had been when I saw the first one. Many climbers had fallen to their deaths and now lay below on the rocks of the North Face, but here on the North-East Ridge I was quickly learning the most common cause of death was exhaustion. This man, whoever he was, had simply curled up for a sleep, as though the soft snow beneath him were a comfortable mattress. It was probably a blissful way to die, though traumatic for his family. It was only a summit, and I was determined not to end it that way.

The Third Step turned out to be just a couple of shoulder-high boulders to scramble over – simple but exhausting. At the top I slumped among rocks for another rest, and saw Chongba surreptitiously adjust my flow rate. I was climbing so slowly he was worried about my oxygen running out before we returned to camp. I'd started on two litres a minute, and now he turned me down to just one – barely enough to counter the weight of the cylinder. But I trusted him. It didn't occur to me I might just as well have been climbing without it.

I was now having serious doubts about continuing, but two things kept me focused. One was Chongba, who had worked so tirelessly. Although he had climbed Everest twelve times, he had never done it from the north and looked absolutely determined to carry on. And then I watched the two figures ascending the steep snow slope of the summit pyramid. I would be gutted if Mark and Ian made it to the summit and I didn't. As long as they were ahead of me, I would keep going.

The summit looked so close it would be agonising to turn around. I didn't know that, behind me, Margaret was wrestling with that very decision. She had been struggling with a throat infection throughout her summit push, and just below the Third Step she decided she was going too slowly to reach the summit and descend safely. Two years earlier, in May 2010, she had made a similar decision on the south side when she looked up the South-East Ridge from the South Summit and concluded it was too much. She returned and summited from the south the following year, and now here she was again. It wasn't for nothing they called her Supergran.

Meanwhile, Mark and Ang Gelu broke clear of Ian and Kami when they became stuck behind traffic. Phil was descending from the summit when he spotted a figure in a yellow down suit struggling up the summit rocks. He thought it was me, but when he remembered I was wearing a red suit, he assumed it must be Ian. Little did he suspect it was Mark, who we agreed had as much chance of reaching the summit as George Mallory appearing above the Third Step on horseback.

'What the fuck are you doing here?' he said when he recognised him.

Mark was a little taken aback by his leader's display of confidence, but he had no time to show it. At that very moment Phil noticed the air intake valve on Mark's oxygen mask had iced up, and he puckered his lips to blow on it. I've often shaken hands with Mark on the summit of a mountain, and once or twice he may have indulged in a man-hug with a climbing partner, but that was definitely the first time anyone had given him a big juicy kiss (albeit through an oxygen mask).

Step by agonising step, I laboured up the steep snow of the summit pyramid, stopping to gulp down many breaths as I plodded upwards. Frequently I waited as climbers descending from the summit unclipped and clipped around me. There were lots of them, and it was an encouraging sign. I reached a rock wall at the top of the slope where the fixed line diverted to the right. It passed along a narrow rocky ledge only a few centimetres wide, teetering over the North Face.

Suddenly I recognised Axe and Pasang Nima coming towards me. They were the first of our team to summit, and Phil was right behind them. Ice had clogged my mask too, and he subjected me to the same intimate procedure he had given Mark. I was disconcerted, but it eased my breathing and I wasn't in a position to worry about whether any passers-by thought we were tongue-kissing.

'Everyone's done amazing, dude,' he said as he squeezed past me. 'It's just five minutes to the summit from here.'

This was what's known as a white lie. Phil knew

perfectly well it would take much longer, but we were so close, and he knew it would spur me on.

It took another hour. I shuffled along the ledge, pausing frequently and breathing in while more climbers slipped past me. We reached a break in the wall where the fixed line doubled back to the left up a rocky gully. I scrambled up it, and recognised Mila and Pasang Ongchu on their way down. I congratulated them and continued onwards.

After about fifty metres the gully broke out onto a snowfield and I was on the summit ridge. I turned right and plodded up a brow. Beyond it I saw another brow, but beyond that was a tangle of prayer flags, colourful against the white and blue glare of the mountain. There were figures; at last I could see the summit. I struggled on.

Mark, Ian, Ang Gelu and Kami were sitting down in the shelter of a snow bank just below the summit. They had been on top already and Mark wanted me to stop for a photo, but he was asking too much. I had only one goal in mind. Nothing would divert me from it. I shook hands with them and plodded onwards, eyeing a convenient seat in the snow just below the prayer flags. In a few moments' time I would be able to flop down on the roof of the world.

But no. Just as I arrived some other sod appeared over the other side and pinched my seat. Looking down the South-East Ridge, I saw many figures coming up from the Hillary Step. Several were on the summit with me, but it didn't matter. I had done it!

I turned round and gave Chongba a hug. He looked happy, but I didn't feel elated. It was ten o'clock Nepali time exactly, and it had taken me ten and a half hours to get here, concentrating on every step. It could take almost as long to get down again, and I knew the descent would not be easy. We were lucky with the weather; I had only liner gloves on and my camera worked without having to warm up the batteries. I gazed around me, and it was like looking out of the window of an aircraft. Everything was so far below me the world looked very much flatter than I imagined. I noticed the view down the South-East Ridge as soon as I walked onto the summit, with its smooth surface sloping to the right, and heavily corniced overhangs on the left. A rough black triangle beyond its far end was Lhotse, the fourth highest mountain in the world. It was latticed with narrow snow couloirs, and looked innocuous down below us.

The view on the north side into Tibet was more familiar, as we had been looking at it for much of the climb. The once impressive pyramid of Changtse was now just an intersection of three narrow ridges far beneath us, dividing the two arms of the Rongbuk Glacier which disappeared into drab brownness far beyond. The most distinctive peak from Everest's summit was Makalu – a dark mass of rock rising out of clouds just a short distance away to the south-east. It's the peak climbers most frequently position in their photos to prove where they are, but I wasn't paying attention as I stood on the summit and my mind was on other things. I didn't even notice the peak, but luckily Chongba was a bit more aware. We took photos of each other, and Makalu was in several, including one Chongba took of me.

Hillary noticed Makalu when he stood on the very same spot fifty-nine years earlier, and he liked what he saw so much that he vowed to climb it. He also looked around for traces to prove that Mallory had been there too, but he said there were none.

Of course there weren't. Twenty-nine years of brutal Himalayan storms had battered the world's highest place in the intervening years. Mallory could have left a gold-plated statue of King George V on the summit and chances were high it would no longer have been there.

I no longer harboured any doubt Mallory had been there before both of us. I didn't need to insert his vital statistics into a set of Newtonian formulae and calculate his climb rate. I knew the contours of the mountain, and now I had a very good idea of where he and Irvine had last been sighted. I knew enough about his character to be absolutely sure he would have pressed on – a decision he would not live to regret.

But if Mallory and Irvine first summited Everest that in no way diminishes the achievement of Hillary and Tenzing, who were the first to reach that spot and return alive. Nor does it diminish the achievement of all of us who followed. By the time I reached the top, over 3,500 other people had been there before me. For Tenzing it had been the culmination of a life's quest, but Chongba was standing there for the thirteenth time. I was the 318th Brit, and I hadn't even arrived before Mark. As I stood on top, many more were streaming up the South-East Ridge, and over 200 would make it that very day. In fact, more people reached the summit of Everest on the 19th of May 2012 than on any day previously. The summit had become a monument of prayer flags to the mountain gods who had kindly allowed us to reach it safely. In my own summit photo somebody is standing behind me taking a selfie with their phone.

Times have changed, but reaching the roof of the world will still be a special moment in all our lives.

We had no need to discuss how long to stay on the summit. The North-East Ridge was reasonably sheltered, but a chill wind struck us as soon as we arrived at the top. It was not a wind that tempted us to linger, and within five minutes of arriving we were on our way back down. I didn't think about whether I would ever be there again.

We paused below the summit in the same place Mark and Ian had, perfectly sheltered from the wind in a peaceful spot looking down the North Face to Changtse. That was when I realised we were the last to reach the summit from the north, and were entirely alone on the world's highest balcony. In any other context it would have been a time and a place to relax and contemplate our existence on this amazing planet of natural wonders.

But in our precarious position between life and death that was impossible. I knew our descent to Camp 3 would demand every gram of strength and mental stamina I could muster, and even then it might not be enough. I also knew I owed it to Chongba to avoid turning it into an epic. We had the safety margin of radios and a team below to help us, but they would be as exhausted as we were and it would be foolish to rely on their assistance. I had to get off the mountain on my own if I still had it in me, and I was determined to succeed.

At the bottom of the Third Step I was surprised to see another climber waiting to ascend. We had not seen a soul since leaving the summit, and I was sure we were the last people on the mountain. The climber was all by himself, and it was much too late to continue to the summit and descend to Camp 3 before nightfall. I was too absorbed in my own struggle for survival to pay much attention, so we continued onwards.

I had no difficulty descending the Second Step, but the same could not be said for everyone. As I stood on top of the giant boulder which had given me so much trouble on the way up, two climbers were in the alcove below, and one of them was struggling. I saw the first get down safely and continue along the slabs without waiting for the other. By then I was beyond fear, and much more confident than the man in dark clothing beneath me. At the bottom of the step he dithered with the ladders, moving them, adjusting the ropes and refusing to let me pass. He seemed lucid and polite, but none of my entreaties persuaded him to step aside and let us proceed. Most likely he was concentrating on his own battle for survival and didn't even think about Chongba and me. We managed to overtake him at the first anchor point beyond the end of the step, when he finally listened to my pleas and stopped still, allowing us to clip around him and edge past on the narrow slabs. Time passes differently up there, but I believe he delayed us by a precious hour.

I was overcome with exhaustion, and had never been more aware of the tightrope I was treading between life and death. Relieved to be past him, it didn't occur to me whether he would make it down safely too.

A short while later one of my crampons slipped on a patch of snow which turned out to be a thin veneer on the surface of the rock. Before I could think about my situation I had fallen two metres and was lying on my chest in thick snow. I managed to dig my axe firmly in, but the fixed rope was taut at my waist, and almost certainly saved me from falling any further.

I heaved myself wearily out of the snow and climbed back onto the path, sucking in deep breaths while Chongba watched impassively. He didn't try to help me up, and I appreciated that. We both knew it was up to me to get myself down. His reassuring presence was all the help I needed.

As we continued, I noticed I had fallen only a few metres from the corpse which had given me such a shock earlier in the day. Our slips may have been similar, but our stories were very different. He had landed more awkwardly, was too tired to get back up, and there had been no one there to help him. My safety margins were wider than I realised.

A huge surge of relief washed over me when I reached the bottom of the First Step. I had been terrified about descending it, and since leaving the summit I pictured it as the crux of the descent. I managed to get down through a combination of careful hand-wrapping and an abseil, and now I believed my chances of survival were good.

As we walked along the easier slabs below the First Step, I spied a convenient nook in the wall to our right to stop for a rest, but when we reached it I saw it was occupied by another dead body. It was the corpse now known as Green Boots, although he was once Tsewang Paljor, an Indian climber who had stopped for a rest on his way back from the summit in 1996. He never woke up.

Were it not for his presence, the alcove would be an inviting place for an exhausted climber to stop and lie down. In 2006 a British climber called David Sharp did just that. Many people passed him as he lay dying. Some thought he was Green Boots and others were engaged in their own fight for survival. Some stopped to help, but he was too far gone. At 8,500m on the North-East Ridge, unless a climber is capable of walking they are beyond help. But when the media heard about the incident, headlines cried out about selfish climbers stepping over dead bodies in their pursuit of summit glory.

Glory wasn't on my mind at that moment, only survival. I understood how David Sharp had met his fate, and I didn't have it in me to judge the people who passed him and survived. He chose to climb solo without a team, and no one was looking out for him as he staggered to the point of total collapse. He was treated with kindness in the end. His body no longer lies beside the trail, unlike Green Boots.

I shuddered as I passed that place, and like so many before me, I walked on.

I had forgotten about the Exit Cracks, and was approaching complete exhaustion as I descended them. Twice I felt myself drifting into a sleep that could so easily last for eternity. I managed to snap out of it just in time, and shocked myself into movement.

Axe's voice came over the radio in Chongba's pocket. We were taking so long he was worried about us, and when we hobbled into Camp 3 at 5.30pm I understood why. We had been gone for eighteen hours. I had eaten nothing and drunk just a single litre of water. My throat was drier than sandpaper, and my first act on reaching the tent was to dry retch into the vestibule (again). A little piece of flesh at the back of my gullet felt like it was about to snap off, and when I tried to have a pee the few drops I managed to squeeze out were dark brown. They had the consistency of real ale, and thirsty as I was I recoiled from the temptation of drinking it.

Axe was lying on one side of the tent. He'd been there since midday, and must have felt very lonely as the hours ticked away and Chongba and I did not return.

The next morning, as we made our way down the remaining 1,800m to the safety of ABC, the full horror of what happened on our summit day slowly filtered through to us.

I left Camp 3 in a gale and struggled down to the North Ridge in a snow storm. I emerged from cloud near to where our Camp 2 tents had been. The view across to Changtse was magnificent, but it took me a further two hours to pass through the sprawl of Camp 2, a mass of jagged rocks through which the line of fixed ropes had become as frayed as my summit-day nerves. I carefully arm-wrapped down the snow slope beneath it for another hour, and was surprised and grateful to find the majority of my teammates sunbathing at the North Col campsite. The gale at Camp 3 had blossomed into a pleasant summer's day, and I spent a blissful hour lying in the sun, resting my weary limbs and starting the long process of rehydrating.

Unless I was going to be mauled by a yak on the trek down to base camp, the only dangerous obstacle remaining was the North Col Wall. Many days earlier I had found the steep ice gully leading to two bulging ladders over a yawning crevasse so terrifying I christened that section the *Ladder of Death*. But after scrambling down the North-East Ridge the previous day this name now seemed like outrageous hyperbole. The gully looked positively tame, with bucket-sized steps, and I skipped down it easily.

Only when I reached the ice plateau at the bottom of the wall, and started trudging down to ABC, did I understand for certain that I had survived. My emotions had been ripped to shreds and my senses were dull, but somewhere inside me a seed of happiness was beginning to grow. I staggered into camp like Oliver Reed returning home from a party, but the sense of relief was like no feeling I had ever experienced. For eighteen hours I had brushed with death, and boy how I knew it. It was the closest I had ever come to crossing the threshold. I felt like a prisoner who had been granted another chance. I was safe again, and profoundly relieved to be alive.

But as I rejoiced in my own success, terrible news reached us from elsewhere. It had been a relatively straightforward season on the north side, but it was very different on the south. Early on a Sherpa was killed by rockfall on the Lhotse Face, and the route had to be moved to a safer line further to the right. A hanging serac on the West Shoulder threatened the route through the Khumbu Icefall. One of the biggest operators, Russell Brice's Himex, decided conditions were too dangerous and pulled out altogether.

In a typical Everest season the mountain gods provided ten or more good days for summit windows, but in 2012 there were just four. With less than 200 climbers on the north side these numbers were manageable; we experienced few queues and very little waiting, but there were four times as many people on the south side, and the risk of bottlenecks was much higher.

With so many people pushing beyond their limits in such an inhospitable place, it was no surprise to learn there were fatalities. As I was basking in my own survival at ABC, Phil told me as many as six people who left for the summit on the same day as us never returned.

I was horrified. It was a number that made the 19th of May 2012 one of the dark days in Everest history, like the 7th of June 1922 when Mallory's seven Sherpas lost their lives on the North Col Wall, and the 11th of May 1996, when eight climbers died in a storm made famous by Jon Krakauer in his book *Into Thin Air*. It was not a single catastrophe, but a series of incidents resulting from human error.

Arguably all the deaths on the 19th of May 2012 were preventable had the victims exercised more caution. On the south side one died of cerebral edema near the South Summit; another fell on the Hillary Step while descending in a state of exhaustion; and another died of altitude sickness just below the Balcony at 8,400m. Most controversially, a climber with very little experience reportedly ignored her Sherpa's pleas to turn around, continued to the summit and died of exhaustion on the way down.

Because Chongba and I were the last to leave the summit that day and survive, the two who died on the north side hit me the hardest. One was almost certainly the figure we passed at the bottom of the Third Step. I met a guide in Kathmandu who summited the day after, and he told me he saw the body at a landmark below the Second Step called Mushroom Rock.

A disproportionate number of corpses lie near the Third Step. From there the summit looks so close, and it must be agonising to turn around. Margaret very wisely made that decision – this climber did not. Would he have done so had he known the summit was still two hours away? Possibly, but we will never know. Of course, I should have told him, but it was long after we passed him that it crossed my mind. By then he was alone on the North-East Ridge, and there was nothing anyone could do for him.

The death which haunted me the most was a climber who was widely reported to have died after breaking his leg at the Second Step. A dozen questions leapt to mind when I heard, and none of them tallied with what I had seen. Where exactly had he died? Was it at the Step, or had he descended a little further before dying? Did he make it back to Camp 3? I saw no one with a broken leg at the Second Step or anywhere further down, and apart from the lone climber struggling his way to the summit, we were the last two people on the mountain.

There was only one conclusion I could draw, but it wasn't consistent with the reports. He must have been the climber who delayed us on the Second Step, but we saw him descend it safely. If it was him, how did anyone even know the manner of his death? Was his body also found the following day, and had somebody examined the corpse and diagnosed a fracture? Such an investigation hardly seemed possible on those terrifying slabs between the First and Second Steps, where it's hard enough to focus on your own predicament.

A few days after I returned home I was contacted by a friend of the victim, who read my dispatches and wrote to ask if I could provide any information about his final hours.

By then I was convinced he was the climber we passed below the Second Step, and he had never made it back to Camp 3. I described to his friend what I had seen with as much detail as I could recall. He reassured me he didn't think either of the people I saw could have been his friend.

I was still unsure, so I contacted staff at the Himalayan Database, who keep the archive of Everest historian Elizabeth Hawley. Ms Hawley is famous for grilling Everest climbers about their ascents after their return to Kathmandu, and if anyone knew more about these fatalities, it would be her team. They told me the information they had was very sketchy. The climber with the broken leg was travelling alone without oxygen or Sherpa support. The other victim was accompanied to the summit by a Sherpa, who came down alone after his client refused to descend immediately.

Unless my memory deceived me I knew this couldn't possibly be true, but I felt like I was stirring up a hornet's nest. Some ghosts are best left undisturbed. Chomolungma has many secrets and these two should rest peacefully beside Mallory and Irvine. For whatever reason, both of them made a decision to climb alone, and by making that decision they paid the ultimate price.

All our actions have consequences. There is one thing I do know for sure: had I stopped to help the climber at the Second Step, the threads that joined me to life would have become more slender. I believe Chongba would have waited for me, putting his own life in greater danger. We would both be gambling with the happiness and welfare of his five children at home in Lukla, but none of these thoughts crossed my mind as I was driven by a primal instinct for survival.

In that extreme environment there's a fine line between heroism and martyrdom. Next time perhaps I will act differently, but I hope I will be spared that opportunity.

I had a day of complete rest at ABC while our superhuman Sherpa team returned to the North Col to dismantle Camp 1. The following day I walked slowly down the Magic Highway back to base camp. My main priority was to avoid being trampled to death by the yak teams coming up to retrieve our gear. That would be a silly way to go after all we had been through. I lived the day in slow motion, and took nearly seven hours to descend the 1,200m to base camp – exactly the same time it had taken to climb *up* on our summit push.

Phil produced champagne that evening and the others celebrated, but my body was reacting very differently to theirs. My brain was recovering from the supreme mental exhaustion I experienced on summit day by switching off my sense of humour. Nothing my teammates said that night could make me laugh.

The following day we rested. I sent out a very short blog post which a friend later described as *chilling*. The title of the post was *The world's most terrifying ridge walk*,[66] and it was a celebration of survival rather than success.

The last word went to Ian as we sat in the dining tent at base camp.

'I don't think I respected Everest enough before,' he said, 'but I do now.'

He shared much of the journey with me – a journey from the hills of Britain and the summit of Snowdon to the highest point on planet Earth. It was a journey that took ten years, with lifestyle changes I would never have imagined, but it produced some unbelievable highs and amazing memories. And yes, back in Kathmandu a few days later, we celebrated with a sense of satisfaction we had never felt before.

I hope many of you reading this will be inspired to follow your dreams to the greatest extent possible, because however far you go, every step will be worth it.

But I hope I have also shown you that the end result isn't so important: it's only a tiny moment which passes. The important part is the journey, and even if you travel only a short distance along your chosen route, you will have memorable stories to tell.

Good luck. I hope you enjoyed my journey, and I hope I have convinced you to find your own Everest and climb it with all your heart.

Mark Horrell on the summit of Everest, the 19th of May 2012

EPILOGUE: THE TARNISHED GODDESS

I returned from Everest feeling pleased with myself, proud and surprised by what I had accomplished. Although my journey took ten years and Everest had been in my thoughts for much of that time, it hadn't quite sunk in that I had really done it. All those years, the mountains, and all that training had enabled me to fulfil a dream. It was a dream that took me very close to the boundary between life and death – something I hadn't considered seriously beforehand – but somehow I managed to avoid stepping over it and came back alive.

Of course, in order to achieve it I needed a lot of help from other people and a number of mechanical devices like fixed ropes and bottled oxygen. I was approximately the 3,788th person to climb Everest (I haven't counted them all). I knew that didn't make me Reinhold Messner, or even Phil Crampton, but I had exceeded my own expectations, and that was my great achievement.

But if I thought everybody else would be as impressed as I was, it didn't take me long to discover the truth. Within days of arriving back in the UK the mainstream media launched an avalanche of Everest stories, none of them positive. A photograph of climbers queuing up the Lhotse Face, taken by German climber Ralf Dujmovits, went viral on the internet. Dujmovits obliged journalists by providing a few choice quotes about Everest's *hobby climbers* and the *human snake* he had witnessed.

Soon every major news publication jumped on the bandwagon with articles about how easy Everest had become to climb for people with no mountaineering experience. Queues of four hours were reported on the Hillary Step. Many of the fatalities were blamed on the traffic jams, as well as the lack of experience. I lost count of the number of stories about climbers callously stepping over dead bodies in their single-minded pursuit of summit glory, showing a complete lack of compassion and humanity in the process. Everest had become a *tourist attraction,* as if that were not only a surprise but also in some way wrong. Climbers were only interested in bagging the summit for their *bucket list*. It was now possible to be *dragged* to the top by teams of Sherpas following a *staircase* of fixed ropes.

'You literally have people showing up at base camp who have never strapped on crampons before,'[67] one journalist reported (while strapping on his crampons at base camp).

Another said that people 'trundle up and down the slopes like commuters on an escalator,'[68] (in much the same way cross-channel swimmers float across to France like toddlers in a paddling pool).

'You can basically pay your way up Everest these days,'[69] a tour operator was quoted as saying.

I have picked these three quotes at random, and I'm not singling them out. You can read any negative story about Everest that has been published by the mainstream media and you will find any number of statements like these.

Reading those stories after arriving home was a shock. It was my first experience of a phenomenon I politely refer to as *Everest bashing*. It was obvious journalists who wrote the articles had no idea what climbing Everest was like, and I was deeply upset. I responded angrily in a blog post that was shared widely.[70]

I've now become used to this phenomenon and I'm no longer so hurt by it, though I frequently respond to misinformation on my blog. Everest bashing is still common in the press and on some blogs and web discussion forums, but I have to say it's not something I have ever experienced face-to-face. On the contrary, at the time of writing I have yet to meet anyone who appeared to hold me in contempt after discovering I climbed Everest. There are plenty who are indifferent, and plenty more who don't quite believe it – *what, you went all the way to the top?* they ask in utter disbelief – but the vast majority are genuinely interested and impressed, and ply me with eager questions about what it was like. Strangers have even offered to buy me a beer with the words *I've never met someone who's climbed Everest before.*

I have addressed much of the misinformation elsewhere in this book. It appears to be endless, and is exacerbated by a seemingly infinite supply of meaningless announcements by the Nepalese government which are gold dust to the headline writers. Stationing police and army at base camp to keep the peace; barring helicopters from flying to base camp; placing ladders on the Hillary Step; compelling climbers to carry trash down from the higher camps, or sign in and sign out when making trips into the Khumbu Icefall – these are just some examples of announcements that have been made by the Nepalese government and reported widely as fact. None of them have ever been implemented.

At the time of writing the latest of these was a statement by the government that certain disabled people will be barred from climbing Everest in future.[71] As happened in all the previous examples, the officials were quoted verbatim in the media, and mountaineers were interviewed to provide quotes and lend credence to the announcement. But they might just as well have discussed whether Pope Francis would be making an attempt to get up Everest on a Harley-Davidson for all the likelihood it had of actually happening. It's not only past history that tells us this. As the media furore raged a disabled Japanese climber Nobukazu Kuriki made two valiant attempts to reach Everest's summit by the South-East Ridge but was turned back by deep snow. He was the only climber who had been granted a permit by the Nepalese government for the 2015 autumn season, and they had announced it to great fanfare. He had lost nine fingers to frostbite during an attempt on the West Ridge a few years earlier – a disability some might consider a drawback to safe mountaineering. But it was also his fifth attempt to climb Everest, a quality far more important than the number of his fingers.

As with all the earlier announcements, it is (thankfully) doubtful a ban on disabled climbers will ever happen. A more worthwhile proposal for climbers to have ascended another big peak before attempting Everest was announced at the same time, but you can be certain this was also fantasy. Nepal suffers from a moving conveyor belt of politicians who are not in office long enough to have an interest in the long-term development of mountain tourism.

One day a journalist who cares about his or her profession will become tired of being asked by their editor to parrot the words of government officials without examining if there is any substance to them – the media equivalent of arriving at base camp having not worn crampons before. Instead of blaming inexperienced climbers – who will come to Everest as long as there is no regulation and they think it's easy – they will ask why none of these announcements by the Nepalese government have been implemented, or why the millions they receive in permit fees every year have not been invested in the Everest infrastructure. Until that happens the announcements and the media hype will continue, more people will arrive on Everest believing it to be easy, and the story will continue to be a self-fulfilling prophecy.

I hope that having read this far you have a better understanding of what it takes to climb Everest with a commercial expedition, and can judge the media hyperbole for yourself.

***

While many of the stories are hype, there are important issues about the changing face of Everest. Since I climbed it in 2012, two major events have occurred that raise questions.

In 2014 I returned to Everest, this time to the south side. My objective was not to climb it for a second time, but to climb its south peak, Lhotse, the fourth highest mountain in the world at 8,516m. I was keen to sample the south-side experience and visit the places I had read so much about. I wanted to follow in the footsteps of Tenzing and Hillary, and climb through the tumbling seracs of the Khumbu Icefall. I also wanted to find out for myself how closely the negative media reporting – much of which focused on the south side – described the reality.

Lhotse shares a base camp with Everest, and follows the same climbing route through the Khumbu Icefall to the Western Cwm and all the way up to Camp 3 on the Lhotse Face. By attempting Lhotse I would learn more about Everest's south side while climbing a new 8,000er.

Or so I hoped, but once again Chomolungma produced something I was unprepared for.

At 6.45am on the 18th of April I walked with teammates through base camp on my first foray into the Khumbu Icefall when a large chunk of ice fell off one of the seracs on

Everest's West Shoulder. We looked up to see a huge avalanche sweep across the entire width of the icefall. We were very lucky; had we set off two hours earlier we may well have been swept away, but others weren't so fortunate. As many as a hundred people were picking their way through the Khumbu Icefall that morning. We didn't know how many were trapped by the avalanche, but it soon became clear a major tragedy was unfolding before our eyes.

In fact the catastrophe could hardly have happened at a worse time, or in a worse location. A ladder had fallen out of position at a steep section of the route through the icefall, causing a bottleneck. At that moment forty or fifty Sherpas were standing by the ladder in the path of the avalanche, waiting to use it. Sixteen people died that day. Although others were in the icefall – a team of western clients from International Mountain Guides (IMG) were just fifteen minutes away from the site of the tragedy – all the victims were Sherpas and other staff, as had been the case with George Mallory's team in 1922.

It was the worst single loss of life Everest had ever witnessed, and I never thought I would ever come to view it as a straightforward climbing accident, but a year later something happened to put it into perspective. Early in the afternoon of the 25th of April 2015, many of the team I had climbed Everest with in 2012, including Phil, Margaret, Dorje, Pasang Ongchu and Chongba, were at base camp on the Nepalese side of the mountain, when a 7.8-magnitude earthquake shook the ground and sent them scurrying for safety. The quake caused a huge chunk of ice to break off a shoulder of Pumori, one of the ring of mountains circling camp. It triggered an avalanche that gathered vast quantities of snow and rock as it fell, sweeping through the central part of base camp. The Altitude Junkies team were metres from the edge and escaped death by little more than the length of an ice axe. Eighteen people weren't so lucky and lost their lives. Meanwhile, in other parts of Nepal, thousands died, and many more had their homes destroyed.

The tragedies were different in many ways, including their outcome. The avalanche in 2014 triggered a labour dispute which a week later led to the mountain being closed for climbing. The incident also triggered another media storm, and this time the theme was selfish westerners mistreating Sherpas and sending them to their deaths. As had been the case in 2012, much of the coverage was tendentious and badly informed. One prominent outdoor magazine even produced statistics it claimed demonstrated Everest-climbing Sherpas were twelve times more likely to die at work than US soldiers fighting in Iraq, and although their data didn't stand up to close scrutiny, media eager to publish negative stories about Everest quickly latched onto their claims.[72]

I returned to Kathmandu bewildered by what had happened. The Sherpa strike was bad tempered, and we witnessed many incidents at base camp that left a bad taste in the mouth. We were torn between sympathy for the victims and their families, and a sense of grievance that we were being unfairly blamed for the tragedy. The events divided the Sherpa community. Many, including our own team, wanted to hold a puja and then keep climbing. They felt the strike would damage their reputation and harm the Sherpa economy.

It was only months later that I understood the dispute was not between workers and western climbers, or workers and expedition operators, but between workers and government. The profile of Everest was so high, and so important to the Nepalese economy, that disenfranchised minorities had used the aftermath of the avalanche as a bargaining chip in their dispute with government.

Nevertheless, the avalanche had confirmed one thing that we already knew. The Khumbu Icefall was a dangerous place, and the more people who climbed Everest, the more journeys Sherpas had to make through it, and the more likely these accidents would become.

A few things changed for the better afterwards. There was a great outpouring of goodwill from westerners who had travelled in Nepal and maintained affection for the country and its people, and a lot of money was raised to help the families of the victims. There had been valid scrutiny of insurance for mountain workers, and the amount they were insured for was raised. The quality of media reporting also improved, as journalists began to understand how important trekking and mountaineering is for Nepal's economy.

There can be no doubt that climbing through the Khumbu Icefall is a risky occupation. Sherpas choose to accept that risk to support their families and give their children better opportunities. After the 2014 avalanche, many media outlets presented them as an exploited underclass who are treated poorly by uncaring (and rich) westerners in pursuit of Everest glory. This overlooks the fact that mountaineering, and the trekking industry that grew from it, has provided Sherpas with greater opportunities and enabled them to become wealthy by Nepali standards.

In the 1920s and 1930s Sherpas from the Khumbu region emigrated to Darjeeling in search of work with mountaineering expeditions. When the closure of Tibet after the Chinese invasion of 1950 coincided with Nepal opening up, Sherpas moved back to their original homeland as the mountaineering centre switched from Darjeeling to Kathmandu. Far from being exploited, the Sherpas are extremely resourceful.

The Sherpas of our generation may be Everest guides, but

their children are the doctors, teachers and airline pilots of tomorrow. Many Sherpas are now teahouse owners or have their own trekking and climbing agencies. Many of the climbing Sherpas I speak to do not want their children to follow in their footsteps, but the wages they receive enable them to send their children to good schools and support not just themselves, but extended families. This is a decent standard of living by any measure. As more Sherpas find opportunities outside mountaineering, other ethnic groups, such as Tamangs and Gurungs, are starting to fill the vacancies left behind. This is progress, and it benefits everyone.

The earthquake of 2015 was a much more devastating event than the 2014 avalanche, the impact was more far-reaching and will last for longer, but in some ways there was a more positive outcome too. If climbers had been aggrieved by what happened in 2014, they showed no animosity the following year. Many stayed on in Nepal for a few days after they escaped from base camp, helping out charities and aid agencies in parts of the country affected by the earthquake.

The earthquake also gave the Nepalese an opportunity to show how resourceful and resilient they can be. I'm a trustee for an education charity that operates in Nepal, and I was linked up on Facebook with charity partners working there. This gave me an opportunity to see how the Nepalese were helping themselves. Every day my newsfeed was alive with posts. One partner was coordinating logistics for supply vehicles, and went out with a European search and rescue team supplying relief bags. Another sourced hospital information to locate children displaced by the earthquake, and then sent out youth volunteers with supplies. One, a school principal, got his hands dirty helping to dig toilet pits. Another set up a movement within two days of the earthquake to mobilise volunteers to help with the relief work. By the end of the week they calculated that eighty of their volunteers had reached nearly fifty areas, distributing 3,000 kilograms of food and benefiting around 25,000 people.

Nepal is a poor country going through difficult times, but I have no doubt its people have the resourcefulness to recover.

You may well be asking what any of this has to do with Everest, and why I'm banging on about Nepal when I climbed it from the north side in Tibet.

It's a good question, but if you have been following then you will understand this book is about a journey and not a tiny plot of land 8,848m above the sea. It's a journey that took me to four continents, but focused on the Himalayas, and in particular Nepal. During that journey I saw how modern tourism has affected places that were once remote – and not always for the best.

But I also saw how modern tourism has enabled people in poorer countries to develop, by bringing employment and progress from the outside world. Progress is unstoppable, but must be moulded, like a vase spinning on a potter's wheel, so that it doesn't produce an untidy mess of clay.

Everest is changing as night follows day and civilisations rise and fall. It will never return to the era of Mallory and Irvine any more than we'll see horse-drawn taxi carriages trundling across the streets of London as the smell of manure wafts from every corner. People may regret this, but they can't prevent it. This phenomenon isn't confined to Everest. America has lost much of its charm since Columbus first sighted it in 1492, or Lewis and Clark completed their great expedition across the continental divide in 1804. The South Pole is no longer like it was when Scott and

Amundsen raced there in 1911. There's now a research station. In fact, exploration has lost much of its magic now that you can zoom in to pretty much anywhere on Google Earth.

Everest is the jewel in Nepal's tourist crown. Climbing permit fees alone bring millions of dollars every year, before climbing Sherpas, cooks and other support staff have been paid, or the hundreds of porters who carry supplies up to base camp, or the teahouse owners who provide food and accommodation en route. And these are just for the people climbing Everest. Think of all the thousands more who trek to base camp every year, and those who are attracted to the country simply by the fact that it contains the world's highest mountain. Think of all the people who visit Nepal to see Everest, then fall in love with the country and return again and again. That's what happened to me.

So there's the clay – but how are we going to mould it on the potter's wheel? That's the tricky bit. I'm not much of a craftsman myself, but I do know that if we can make a pot then we can grow roses, so I'll give it a go.

Some people believe Everest should be closed permanently for climbing and be left as a memorial to the supremacy of the mountain gods and all those who have died climbing it, but when it means so much to so many people, this is not a move that would be in anyone's best interests. Nevertheless, after two major tragedies in successive years, and smaller incidents every season, it appears the mountain gods are not happy. Nepal was rocked by regular aftershocks following the earthquake, some nearly as strong as the main event, and it's likely these will continue for some time. The Khumbu Icefall is dangerous and unpredictable at the best of times, but ascending it amid earth tremors would be verging on suicidal, and more deaths are likely to follow.

Despite the tragedies, Everest continues to grow in popularity in an environment that remains largely unregulated. With so much money involved, and so many people willing to part with it in pursuit of a dream before gaining the necessary knowledge or experience, a great many sharks are operating. Eventually there will be a saturation point, and many people believe this has already happened. Now seems like a good time to pause the expeditions, take stock, and make changes.

Rules need to be introduced to improve the working conditions for Sherpas and mountaineering workers. There needs to be a minimum wage, a maximum load they are permitted to carry through the Khumbu Icefall, better insurance cover, and a trust fund to help those families whose principal earner has been injured or killed in the course of duty. There needs to be a minimum qualification or experience level for workers going above base camp, and operators should have a duty to provide training where necessary.

Climbers should serve their time before arriving on Everest. There needs to be a minimum qualification every climber should achieve before being granted a permit. I don't know what this is; perhaps another 8,000m peak or two 7,000ers. It will give them the opportunity to visit other beautiful places in Nepal, and spread the wealth they bring to other Nepalese outside the Sherpa community.

Operators need to be vetted and meet minimum standards before being granted a license to run expeditions. These standards should include the prices they charge, their environmental credentials, how they treat their staff, client safety, and a willingness to invest in Nepal.

Oh, and people should be obliged to use poo bags.

There is no lack of willingness on the part of clients, operators and Sherpas to see more regulation in place – and some of these recommendations are already being introduced on a voluntary basis – but the biggest barrier, and Nepal's biggest problem, is its politicians. Corruption is endemic, and there is a lack of motivation on the part of those in power to act for the common good. Nobody knows how much of the $11,000 permit fee every climber has to pay to climb Everest finds its way into the Everest infrastructure, or how much disappears into pockets. Very few teams ever see the liaison officer they are obliged to pay for, who is supposed to remain with them throughout the expedition, to help with any difficulties and ensure they follow the rules.

I'm not qualified to suggest a solution to Nepal's political problems, but in the many years I've been travelling there, and particularly in the wake of the earthquake, I've seen so many honest and capable people working hard to better their country, to be optimistic about its future – if and when they are able to cure themselves of their corrupt politicians. And whatever happens, Everest will remain one of the keys to its development.

So where does this leave us?

If you are thinking of following the dream and climbing Everest, but are concerned about the impact you will have if you do, there are choices you can make.

Firstly, you can climb on the north side, like I did. Some of the issues I have highlighted, particularly those involving the dangers of the Khumbu Icefall, relate only to the Nepalese side of the mountain. Most of your money will be going into the Chinese and Tibetan economy, but most teams operating on the north side also employ Sherpas from Nepal.

You can take your time; there is no hurry. Climb at high altitude as much as you can before attempting Everest. If you can, follow the seven steps that I did, and when the time comes you will be ready and able to make the right choices.

There is a chance many of the issues I have highlighted will be solved.

And if you are just an armchair observer, all I ask is that you be a friend to Everest and those who climb it. And if you are able, go out and climb a different hill, or just enjoy the mountains.

Whoever you are, ask questions about the media hype. A couple of months ago I was contacted by a neurosurgeon who said he was keen to climb Everest but didn't have any experience. He asked me whether I thought it was practical for him to climb Everest first and then get more experience later.

I'm not kidding, a neurosurgeon – in other words, a bright cookie!

If even he had been taken in by the stories and believed that climbing Everest was easy, who else had? I was so taken aback by his question that I thought he must be a troll. I wrote back and said I had always dreamed of carrying out brain surgery. I asked him if he thought I could carry out a brain operation first, then study for my medical qualifications later. He turned out to be real and his question was genuine, but he was also an intelligent man and he took my sarcasm the right way.

Having read this book I do not believe you will make his mistake. You now know that Everest is an inclusive mountain that has enriched the lives of those with the determination to pursue a dream, regardless of their natural talent. It has provided a livelihood to thousands, lifted them out of poverty and given them greater opportunities. And you also know that Everest needs to be given respect.

Personally, I feel incredibly grateful to live in an age when the world is becoming more accessible. I've been to some pretty amazing places in the last few years. Instead of sitting at home or behind a desk and becoming fretful about what happens on a mountain many miles away in a place that is very different from your own, it's much more satisfying to get out there and take advantage of the new opportunities. While I'd love it for those places to remain quiet, it would be churlish of me to deny them to other people.

I will leave the final words to the great Tenzing Norgay. They are the same words I used to begin this book, and they might as well be the last:

What is Everest without the eye that sees it? It is the hearts of men that make it big or small.[73]

ACKNOWLEDGEMENTS

This wouldn't be the book it is without the help of a number of people.

I would like to thank my editor Alex Roddie, who doubles as a gifted writer of mountain literature, for his help throughout.

I was very lucky to have the mentoring support of another indie author, Sophie Schiller, writer of historical adventure fiction, who provided many suggestions to improve the book.

My brother Perran and father Ian have been particularly helpful, annotating the manuscript with many improvements.

I am extremely grateful to my other beta readers Roland Hunter, Ruth Kay, Ozzie Orlowski and Anya Page, who read early versions of the manuscript and provided much constructive feedback.

I would like to thank Andrew Brown of Design for Writers, for producing an amazing cover which I love, and James Fernandes for his invaluable assistance with the design.

Thanks to Robert Anderson and Jon Barton for their assistance obtaining permission for several quotes used in this book, and to Jon's company Vertebrate Publishing for republishing many out-of-print mountaineering classics as digital versions.

I have tried wherever possible to obtain permission for quotes used in this book, and would like to thank all those who have granted it. I would also like to thank Jeremy 'Bunter' Anson, Huw Davies and Grant 'Axe' Rawlinson for delving into their photo collections on my behalf.

My thanks to all my friends on Facebook and readers of my blog who provided enthusiastic feedback about the cover. I have frequently trialled content for this book in blog posts, and I would like to thank the many readers of my blog who have provided feedback in comments.

Most of all I would like to thank the many people I have met and travelled with over the years, who have made all my adventures special. Some of you made it into the finished book, some made it into earlier drafts and were then edited out, while others didn't make it at all. This in no way reflects your importance to my journey, and I would like to thank all of you equally.

Well, almost equally. I would like to single out all the members of my Everest team for a special mention: Ian Cartwright, Phil Crampton, Mark Dickson, Mila Mikhanovskaia, Grant 'Axe' Rawlinson, Margaret Watroba and of course Ang Gelu Sherpa, Chedar Sherpa, Da Pasang Sherpa, Dorje Sherpa, Kami Neru Sherpa, Nima Neru Sherpa, Pasang Nima Sherpa, Pasang Ongchu Sherpa, and Pemba Sherpa. I cannot express enough my gratitude to Chongba Sherpa, for being there when it mattered most.

My gratitude also goes to every individual involved with all the trekking and mountaineering operators I have used over the years, from those in the office, to guides and leaders in the field, and everyone in between.

Thanks to Edita Nichols for being amazing and providing a peaceful environment for me to finish the book.

ACKNOWLEDGEMENTS

I would like to thank my mother Elisabeth, who is no longer with us. She never got to see the end of the journey, but I have her to thank for making me who I am.

I am very grateful to all the readers of my blog and travel diaries. I enjoy the writing nearly as much as the travelling, and you are the people who make it worthwhile.

Last, but by no means least, I would like to thank *you* for reading this book (especially if you have got all the way to the last sentence of the acknowledgements). I hope you have enjoyed it, and I look forward to welcoming you back sometime.

PHOTOGRAPHS

If you're wishing this book contained many more photos from my journey, thanks to the miracles of the internet you can view all my photos from every expedition via the photo-sharing website *Flickr*.

Each trip has its own album, and I have grouped them by the relevant chapter of the book. You can access them all at:
www.flickr.com/markhorrell.

1 Hill walking

Snowdon. Britain, *various dates*:
www.markhorrell.com/Snowdon

2 High-altitude trekking

Annapurna Foothills. Nepal, *February 2002*:
www.markhorrell.com/AnnapurnaFoothills
Khumbu Valleys. Nepal, *February 2002*:
www.markhorrell.com/KhumbuValleys
Huayhuash Circuit. Peru, *July 2002*:
www.markhorrell.com/HuayhuashCircuit

3 A high-altitude summit

Mount Kenya. Kenya, *October 2002*:
    www.markhorrell.com/MountKenya
Kilimanjaro (Shira Route). Tanzania, *October 2002*:
    www.markhorrell.com/KilimanjaroShira

4 Ice axe and crampons

Parque Nacional Los Glaciares. Argentina, *February 2003*:
    www.markhorrell.com/ParqueNacionalLosGlaciares
Chamonix Valley. France, *August 2003*:
    www.markhorrell.com/ChamonixValley
Gran Paradiso. Italy, *August 2003*:
    www.markhorrell.com/GranParadiso
Mera Peak. Nepal, *October/November 2004*:
    www.markhorrell.com/MeraPeak
Mera, Island & the Gokyo Lakes. Nepal, *April/May 2009*:
    www.markhorrell.com/MeraIsland

5 Expedition style

Aconcagua (Normal Route). Argentina, *December 2005*:
    www.markhorrell.com/AconcaguaNormal
Aconcagua (False Polish Glacier Route). Argentina,
December 2010:
    www.markhorrell.com/AconcaguaFalsePolish
Everest North Col. Tibet, *April/May 2007*:
    www.markhorrell.com/EverestNorthCol

6 The first 8,000er

Muztag Ata. China, *August 2007*:
www.markhorrell.com/MuztagAta
Gasherbrum. Pakistan, *June/July/August 2009*:
www.markhorrell.com/Gasherbrum
Cho Oyu. Tibet, *September/October 2010*:
www.markhorrell.com/ChoOyu
Manaslu. Nepal, *September/October 2011*:
www.markhorrell.com/Manaslu

7 The Big One

Everest North Ridge. Tibet, *April/May 2012*:
www.markhorrell.com/EverestNorthRidge

NOTES

1. Jones, *The Complete Guide to Snowdon*, 65.
2. Shipton, *That Untravelled World*, 275.
3. Davis, *Into The Silence*, 168.
4. Holzel and Salkeld, *The Mystery of Mallory & Irvine*, 290.
5. Davis, *Into The Silence*, 169-70.
6. Young et al., *Snowdon Biography*, 36-7.
7. Holzel and Salkeld, *The Mystery of Mallory & Irvine*, 51.
8. Smythe, *The Six Alpine/Himalayan Climbing Books*, 69.
9. Streetly, *Bloody Slab*, http://www.cumc.org.uk/journals/54/BLOODY.html.
10. Young et al., *Snowdon Biography*, 11.
11. Noyce, *Climbing the Fish's Tail*, 119.
12. Tilman, *The Seven Mountain-Travel Books*, 878.
13. Ibid., 767.
14. Harrer, *The White Spider*, 93.
15. Tilman, *The Seven Mountain-Travel Books*, 846.
16. Ibid., 868.
17. Ibid., 879.
18. Isserman and Weaver, *Fallen Giants*, 381.

19. Alpine Mapping Guild, *Cordillera Huayhuash, Peru, 1:65,000*.
20. Stedman, *Kilimanjaro*, 107.
21. Mackinder, *A Journey to the Summit of Mount Kenya, British East Africa*, 456.
22. Ibid., 460.
23. Shipton, *The Six Mountain-Travel Books*, 336-7.
24. Ibid., 340.
25. Ibid., 355.
26. Young and Hastenrath, *Glaciers of Africa*, 55-7.
27. Meyer, *Across East African Glaciers*, 42.
28. Ibid., 134.
29. Ibid., 157.
30. Mote and Kaser, *The Shrinking Glaciers of Kilimanjaro*, 322.
31. Stedman, *Kilimanjaro*, 122.
32. Tilman, *The Seven Mountain-Travel Books*, 103.
33. Shipton, *The Six Mountain-Travel Books*, 347.
34. Ibid., 348-9.
35. Meyer, *Across East African Glaciers*, 195.
36. Nations Online, *Countries by Gross National Income*, http://www.nationsonline.org/oneworld/GNI_PPP_o f_countries.htm.
37. Braham, *When the Alps Cast Their Spell*, 11.
38. Roberts, *South of Everest*, 59.
39. Ibid., 62.
40. Duff, *The Other Side of the Mera*, 90.
41. Ullman, *The Age of Mountaineering*, 139.
42. Fitzgerald, *The Highest Andes*, 79.
43. Ibid., 81-2.
44. Conway, *Aconcagua and Tierra del Fuego*, 32.
45. Norton, *The Fight for Everest 1924*, 82.
46. Shipton, *The Six Mountain-Travel Books*, 426.
47. Isserman and Weaver, *Fallen Giants*, 47-49.

48. Mummery, *My Climbs in the Alps and Caucasus*, 160.

49. Moravec, *Gasherbrum II*, 125.

50. Tichy, *Himalaya*, 92.

51. Imanishi, *The First Assault Party*, 183.

52. Davis, *Into The Silence*, 385.

53. Ibid., 487-8.

54. Unsworth, *Everest*, 97.

55. Hemmleb, Johnson and Simonson, *Ghosts of Everest*, 182.

56. Davis, *Into The Silence*, 544.

57. Odell, *The Mount Everest Dispatches*, 223.

58. Norton, *The Fight for Everest 1924*, 130.

59. Shipton, *That Untravelled World*, 97.

60. Tenzing, *Tiger of the Snows*, 82.

61. Conefrey, *Everest 1953*, 212.

62. Hillary, *View from the Summit*, 34.

63. Ibid., 13.

64. Bruce, *The Assault on Mount Everest, 1922*, 158.

65. Hunt, *The Ascent of Everest*, 204.

66. Footsteps on the Mountain, *The world's most terrifying ridge walk*, http://www.markhorrell.com/blog/2012/the-worlds-most-terrifying-ridge-walk.

67. Outside, *Everest Explained: Why Did So Many People Die Last Weekend?*, http://www.outsideonline.com/1929146/everest-explained-why-did-so-many-people-die-last-weekend.

68. The Guardian, *Everest: from mythical peak to the world's highest garbage dump*, http://www.theguardian.com/commentisfree/2013/jun/04/everest-mythical-peak-garbage-dump.

69. Telegraph, *Dying to get there: the perils of adventure*

travel, a middle-aged obsession,
http://www.telegraph.co.uk/travel/
activityandadventure/9300192/Dying-to-get-there-
the-perils-of-adventure-travel-a-middle-aged-
obsession.html.

70. Footsteps on the Mountain, *5 media myths about Everest busted,*
http://www.markhorrell.com/blog/2012/5-media-
myths-about-everest-busted.

71. The Guardian, *Mount Everest to be declared off-limits to inexperienced climbers, says Nepal.*
http://www.theguardian.com/world/2015/sep/28/mo
unt-everest-to-be-declared-off-limits-to-
inexperienced-climbers.

72. Footsteps on the Mountain, *The cod science of Everest hate,* http://www.markhorrell.com/blog/2014/the-
cod-science-of-everest-hate.

73. Tenzing, *Tiger of the Snows,* 294.

BIBLIOGRAPHY

Personal diaries

Unsurprisingly, I have drawn extensively from my own diaries while writing this book, a selection of which are available as ebooks from the principal online book stores.

Horrell, Mark. *In the Footsteps of Mallory: A journey to the North Col of Everest*. Mountain Footsteps Press, 2007.

Horrell, Mark. *Islands in the Snow: Climbing Nepal's trekking peaks*. Mountain Footsteps Press, 2009.

Horrell, Mark. *Snowshoes and Shipton: Climbing Muztag Ata in the Chinese Pamirs*. Mountain Footsteps Press, 2007.

Horrell, Mark. *The Ascent of Manaslu: Climbing the world's eighth highest mountain*. Mountain Footsteps Press, 2011.

Horrell, Mark. *The Chomolungma Diaries: What a commercial Everest expedition is really like*. Mountain Footsteps Press, 2012.

Horrell, Mark. *The True Peruvian Route: An ascent of Aconcagua, South America's highest mountain*. Mountain Footsteps Press, 2011.

Horrell, Mark. *The Wrath of the Turquoise Goddess: Battling blizzards on Cho Oyu, the world's sixth highest mountain.* Mountain Footsteps Press, 2010.

Horrell, Mark. *Thieves, Liars and Mountaineers: On the 8000m peak circus in Pakistan's Karakoram mountains.* Mountain Footsteps Press, 2009.

Other sources

All of the following books and journal articles served as reference while writing the historical sections of this book.

Armington, Stan. *Trekking in the Nepal Himalaya.* 8th ed., Melbourne: Lonely Planet, 2001.

Arnette, Alan. *Everest 2008: Mountain of Politics.* 2008. Web. 29 October 2013.

Benuzzi, Felice. *No Picnic on Mount Kenya.* New York: Dutton, 1953.

Biggar, John. *The Andes: A Guide for Climbers.* 3rd ed., Castle Douglas: Andes, 2005.

Bonatti, Walter. *The Mountains of My Life.* New York: Random House, 2001.

Bonington, Chris. *The Climbers: A History of Mountaineering.* London: Hodder and Stoughton, 1992.

Bowman, W.E. *The Ascent of Rum Doodle.* Max Parrish, 1956. Arrow ed., London: Arrow Books, 1983.

Braham, Trevor. *When the Alps Cast Their Spell: Mountaineers of the Alpine Golden Age.* Castle Douglas: In Pinn, 2004.

Bruce, Charles. *Himalayan Wanderer.* Gurgaon: Shubhi Publications, 1934.

Bruce, Charles, et al. *The Assault on Mount Everest 1922.* London: Edward Arnold, 1923.

Conefrey, Mick. *Everest 1953: The Epic Story of the First*

Ascent. London: Oneworld Publications, 2012.

Conway, Martin. *Aconcagua and Tierra del Fuego: A Book of Climbing, Travel and Exploration*. London: Cassell, 1902.

Davis, Wade. *Into The Silence: The Great War, Mallory and the Conquest of Everest*. London: Random House, 2011.

Dickinson, Matt. *The Death Zone*. London: Arrow Books, 1997.

Duff, Mal. *The Other Side of the Mera: The First Ascent of the SW Pillar of Mera Peak (6487m), Hinku Valley, Nepal*. Alpine Journal, Vol. 92, Issue 336, 89-91, 1987.

Else, David. *Trekking in East Africa*. 2nd ed., Victoria: Lonely Planet, 1998.

Fitzgerald, Edward. *The Highest Andes: A Record of the First Ascent of Aconcagua and Tupungato in Argentina, and the Exploration of the Surrounding Valleys*. London: Methuen, 1899.

Fleming, Fergus. *Killing Dragons: The Conquest of the Alps*. London: Granta, 2000.

French, Patrick. *Younghusband: The Last Great Imperial Adventurer*. London: Harper Perennial, 1994.

Freshfield, Douglas. *The Conquest of Mount Everest*, Geographical Journal, Vol.63, No.3, 229-237, 1924.

Gillman, Peter, ed. *Everest: Eighty years of triumph and tragedy*. London: Little, Brown and Co, 2001.

Gregson, Jonathan. *Blood Against the Snows: The Tragic Story of Nepal's Royal Dynasty*. New Delhi: HarperCollins, 2002.

Harrer, Heinrich. *The White Spider: The Story of the North Face of the Eiger*. Rupert Hart-Davis, 1959. Flamingo ed., London: Flamingo, 1995.

Hemingway, Ernest. *The Snows of Kilimanjaro*. Jonathan Cape, 1939. Arrow ed., London: Arrow Books, 2004.

Hemmleb, Jochen, Larry Johnson, and Eric Simonson. *Ghosts of Everest: The Authorized Story of the Search for Mallory*

& *Irvine*. London: Pan Books, 2000.

Hemmleb, Jochen, and Eric Simonson. *Detectives on Everest: The 2001 Mallory & Irvine Research Expedition*. Seattle: The Mountaineers, 2002.

Herzog, Maurice. *Annapurna: The First Conquest of an 8000-Metre Peak*. Jonathan Cape, 1952. Pimlico ed., London: Pimlico, 1997.

Hillary, Edmund. *View from the Summit*. London: Corgi, 2000.

Holzel, Tom, and Audrey Salkeld. *The Mystery of Mallory & Irvine*. 2nd revised ed., London: Pimlico, 1999.

Hunt, John. *The Ascent of Everest*. London: Hodder and Stoughton, 1953.

Imanishi, Toshio. *The First Assault Party*. The Mountain World, 1958/59, 180-190, 1958.

Isserman, Maurice, and Stewart Weaver. *Fallen Giants: A History of Himalayan Mountaineering from the Age of Empire to the Age of Extremes*. New Haven: Yale, 2008.

Jones, Robert. *The Complete Guide to Snowdon*. Gwasg Carreg Gwalch, 1992. Poetry Wales ed., Bridgend: Poetry Wales Press, 2007.

Kirkpatrick, Andy. *Psychovertical*. London: Arrow Books, 2009.

Krakauer, Jon. *Into Thin Air: A Personal Account of the Mount Everest Disaster*. London: Pan Books, 1998.

Kolff, Adam, and Jim Bartle. *Cordillera Huayhuash*. Huaraz: The Mountain Institute, 1998.

Madge, Tim. *The Last Hero, Bill Tilman: A Biography of the Explorer*. London: Hodder and Stoughton, 1995.

Mackinder, Sir Halford. *A Journey to the Summit of Mount Kenya, British East Africa*, Geographical Journal, Vol.15, No.5, 453-476, 1900.

Maki, Yuko. *The Ascent of Manaslu, 1952-1956*. The Mountain World, 1958/59, 176-179, 1958.

Mason, Kenneth. *Abode of Snow: A History of Himalayan Exploration and Mountaineering from Earliest Times to the Ascent of Everest*. Rupert Hart-Davis, 1955. Diadem ed., London: Diadem Books, 1987.

McDonald, Bernadette. *Keeper of the Mountains: The Elizabeth Hawley Story*. Toronto: Rocky Mountain Books, 2012.

Messner, Reinhold. *All 14 Eight-Thousanders*. Marlborough: Crowood Press, 1988.

Messner, Reinhold. *The Crystal Horizon: Everest - The First Solo Ascent*. Marlborough: Crowood Press, 1989.

Meyer, Hans. *Across East African Glaciers: An Account of the First Ascent of Kilimanjaro*. London: George Philip, 1891.

Moravec, Fritz. *Gasherbrum II*. The Mountain World, 1958/59, 112-125, 1958.

Morris, Jan. *Coronation Everest*. London: Faber and Faber, 1958. Paperback ed., London: Faber and Faber, 2003.

Mote, Philip W., and Georg Kaser. *The Shrinking Glaciers of Kilimanjaro: Can Global Warming Be Blamed?* American Scientist, Vol.95, No.4, 318-325, 2007.

Mummery, Albert. *My Climbs in the Alps and Caucasus*. London: T. Fisher Unwin, 1895.

Newby, Eric. *Great Ascents: A Narrative History of Mountaineering*. Vancouver: Douglas David & Charles, 1977.

Ngawang Tenzin Zangbu, and Frances Klatzel. *Stories and Customs of the Sherpas*. 4th ed., Kathmandu: Mera Publications, 2000.

Norgay, Tenzing, and James Ramsey Ullman. *Tiger of the Snows: The autobiography of Tenzing of Everest*. New York: G.P. Putnam's Sons, 1955.

Norton, Edward, et al. *The Fight for Everest 1924*. Kathmandu: Pilgrims Publishing, 2002. New edition, 2015, available from Vertebrate Publishing.

Noyce, Wilfrid. *Climbing the Fish's Tail*. London:

Heinemann, 1958. Delhi: Book Faith India, 1998.

Noyce, Wilfrid, et al. *Snowdon Biography*. London: J.M. Dent (The Orion Publishing Group), 1957.

Noyce, Wilfrid. *South Col: One Man's Adventure on the Ascent of Everest, 1953*. London: Heinemann, 1954. Birlinn ed., Edinburgh: Birlinn, 2003.

O'Connor, Bill. *The Trekking Peaks of Nepal*. Marlborough: The Crowood Press, 1989.

Odell, Noel. *The Mount Everest Dispatches*, Alpine Journal, Vol.36, No.229, November 1924.

Patey, Tom. *One Man's Mountains: Essays and Verses*. Victor Gollancz, 1971. Canongate ed., Edinburgh: Canongate Books, 1997.

Peissel, Michel. *Tiger for Breakfast: The Story of Boris of Kathmandu*. London: Hodder and Stoughton, 1966. TBI paperback ed., New Delhi: Time Books International, 1990.

Perrin, Jim. *Snowdon: The Story of a Welsh Mountain*. Llandysul: Gomer Press, 2012.

Reynolds, Kev. *Annapurna: A Trekker's Guide*. 2nd ed., Milnthorpe: Cicerone, 2003.

Roberts, David. *True Summit: What really happened on Maurice Herzog's first legendary ascent of Annapurna*. London: Constable, 2000.

Roberts, J.O.M. *South of Everest*, Himalayan Journal, Vol. 18, 59-64, 1954.

Sale, Richard, and John Cleare. *On Top of the World: Climbing the World's 14 Highest Mountains*. London: HarperCollins, 2000.

Secor, R.J. *Aconcagua: a climbing guide*. 2nd ed., Seattle: The Mountaineers, 1999.

Senior, Michael. *Yr Wyddfa: The story of Snowdon summit*. Pwllheli: Llygad Gwalch, 2010 .

Shipton, Eric. *The Six Mountain-Travel Books*. London: Baton Wicks, 1999.

Shipton, Eric. *That Untravelled World*. London: Hodder and Stoughton, 1969.

Simpson, Joe. *Touching the Void*. Jonathan Cape, 1988. Vintage ed., London: Vintage, 1997.

Smythe, Frank. *The Six Alpine/Himalayan Climbing Books*. London: Baton Wicks, 2000.

Stedman, Henry. *Kilimanjaro: The Trekking Guide to Africa's Highest Mountain*. 3rd ed., Hindhead: Trailblazer, 2010.

Steele, Peter. *Eric Shipton: Everest and Beyond*. London: Constable, 1998.

Stewart, Alexander. *Kilimanjaro: A Complete Trekker's Guide*. Milnthorpe: Cicerone, 2004.

Streetly, John. *Bloody Slab – Clogwyn D'ur Arddu*, Cambridge University Mountaineering Club Journal, 1954.

Tenzing, Tashi, and Judy Tenzing. *Tenzing Norgay and the Sherpas of Everest*. Camden: Ragged Mountain Press, 2001.

Terray, Lionel. *Conquistadors of the Useless: from the Alps to Annapurna*. Gollancz, 1963. London: Baton Wicks, 2001.

Tichy, Herbert. *Cho Oyu: By Favour of the Gods*. London: Methuen, 1957.

Tichy, Herbert. *Himalaya*. London: Robert Hale, 1971.

Tilman, H.W. *The Seven Mountain-Travel Books*. London: Baton Wicks, 2003.

Tuckey, Harriet. *Everest - The First Ascent: The untold story of Griffith Pugh, the man who made it possible*. London: Rider, 2013.

Ullman, James Ramsey. *The Age of Mountaineering*. Philadelphia: J.B. Lippincott, 1954.

Uney, Graham. *Backpacker's Britain, Volume 2: Wales*. Milnthorpe: Cicerone, 2004.

Unsworth, Walt. *Everest*. Oxford Illustrated Press, 1989. Grafton ed., London: Grafton, 1991.

Venables, Stephen, et al. *Everest: Summit of Achievement*.

60th anniversary ed., London: Bloomsbury, 2013.

Viesturs, Ed, and David Roberts. *K2: Life and Death on the World's Most Dangerous Mountain*. New York: Broadway, 2009.

Wyss-Dunant, Edouard. *Acclimatisation,* The Mountain World, 1953, 110-117, 1953.

INDEX

ABOUT THE AUTHOR

For five years Mark Horrell has written what has been described as one of the most credible Everest opinion blogs out there. He writes about trekking and mountaineering from the often silent perspective of the commercial client.

For over a decade he has been exploring the world's greater mountain ranges and keeping a diary of his travels. As a writer he strives to do for mountain history what Bill Bryson did for long-distance hiking.

Several of his expedition diaries are available as quick reads from the major online bookstores. His first full-length book, *Seven Steps from Snowdon to Everest*, about his ten-year journey from hill walker to Everest climber, was published in November 2015.

His favourite mountaineering book is *The Ascent of Rum Doodle* by W.E. Bowman.

CONNECT

You can join Mark's **mailing list** to keep updated:
www.markhorrell.com/mailinglist

Website and blog: www.markhorrell.com
Twitter: @markhorrell
Facebook: www.facebook.com/footstepsonthemountain
Flickr: www.flickr.com/markhorrell
YouTube: www.youtube.com/markhorrell

DID YOU ENJOY THIS BOOK?

Thank you for buying and reading this book. Word-of-mouth is crucial for any author to be successful. If you enjoyed it then please consider leaving a review. Even if it's only a couple of sentences, it would be a great help and will be appreciated enormously.

Links to this book on the main online book stores can be found on Mark's website:

www.markhorrell.com/SnowdonToEverest

CPSIA information can be obtained at www.ICGtesting.com
Printed in the USA
LVOW10s2047040816

499092LV00004BA/189/P